AMERICAN GOVERNANCE: POLITICS,
POLICY, AND PUBLIC LAW

Series Editors:
Richard Valelly, Pamela Brandwein,
Marie Gottschalk, Christopher Howard

A complete list of books in the series
is available from the publisher.

Er

WIT

EMBRACING DISSENT

Political Violence and Party Development
in the United States

Jeffrey S. Selinger

UNIVERSITY OF PENNSYLVANIA PRESS

PHILADELPHIA

Published by
University of Pennsylvania Press
Philadelphia, Pennsylvania 19104-4112
www.upenn.edu/pennpress

Printed in the United States of America
on acid-free paper

1 3 5 7 9 10 8 6 4 2

Library of Congress Cataloging-in-Publication Data
Names: Selinger, Jeffrey S., author.
Title: Embracing dissent : political violence and party
    development in the United States / Jeffrey S. Selinger.
Other titles: American governance.
Description: Philadelphia : University of Pennsylvania Press,
    [2016] | Series: American governance : politics, policy, and
    public law | Includes bibliographical references and index.
Identifiers: LCCN 2015039598 | ISBN 978-0-8122-4797-8
Subjects: LCSH: Political parties—United States—History. |
    United States—Politics and government—History.
Classification: LCC JK2261 .S425 2016 | DDC 324.273—dc23
LC record available at http://lccn.loc.gov/2015039598

For Barbara and Carl Selinger

CONTENTS

CHAPTER 1

Legitimate Party Opposition and the Early American State

Standing before a sympathetic audience adjacent to his home in Auburn, New York, after years of civil war and just weeks before the election of 1864, Republican secretary of state William Henry Seward issued a scathing denunciation of the party in opposition: "It will seem a hard thing when I imply that a party, like the democratic party, can either meditate or inconsiderately adopt measures to overthrow the Republic. All experience, however, shows that it is by the malice or madness of great parties that free states have been brought down to destruction."[1] Seward was mindful that the public had grown accustomed to the rituals and practices of political parties and would find it jarring for a leader of his stature to malign the party in opposition in such stark terms. It was, indeed, a "hard thing." He pressed his audience nonetheless to consider the difficult proposition that a vote for the presidential ticket of the Democratic party was a vote for defeat and the dismemberment of the federal Union. Modern ears are accustomed to discounting apocalyptic pronouncements of this kind, especially when they are offered in an election season. In this instance, however, Seward may have been correct in his assessment. After all, the opposing ticket was committed to a platform that called for a cease-fire followed by negotiations to seek a compromise with the Confederacy. Most politically astute observers understood that once the fighting was stopped, it could not be easily resumed and that the Confederacy would accept no settlement short of full independence from the federal Union. In Seward's view, the Confederacy, with the assistance of their Democratic party allies to the north, would obtain through the Union's peaceful electoral process that which they could not secure through military means.

In this speech, unofficially titled "The Allies of Treason," Seward echoed
some of the most notable American voices from the late eighteenth century
who likewise conceived of parties as political formations that destroy free
states. Like Seward, these Founding figures had reason to look askance at
parties. Writing in 1813 to his old friend and political adversary Thomas
Jefferson, John Adams vividly described the scene in Philadelphia when the
French Revolutionary Wars broke out: "You certainly never felt the Terrorism excited by Genêt, in 1793, when ten thousand People in the Streets of
Philadelphia, day after day threatened to drag Washington out of his House,
and effect a Revolution in the Government, or compel it to declare War in
favour of the French Revolution and against England."[2] Adams and George
Washington had witnessed firsthand this "terrorism" incited by Edmond
Genêt, foreign minister from France, and it powerfully influenced their appraisal of the risks political parties and other extraconstitutional amalgama-
tions posed to the young republic. Just a few years after the Genêt affair
passed, President Washington issued his often-quoted Farewell Address,
where he admonished the American people to avoid foreign entanglements
and beware the "baneful effects of the spirit of party."[3] These two recommen-
dations went hand in hand: political parties, in Washington's view, would
only continue to polarize a polity divided by foreign war.[4] The first president
was particularly suspicious of the Jeffersonian Republican party, which he
believed had encouraged Francophile partisans to take up arms in support
of the French revolutionary struggle against Britain and other powers. With
limited resources at its disposal, his administration would be hard-pressed
to stop such partisans from undermining the federal government's policy of
neutrality and drawing the young republic into a war that it could ill afford
to fight.

Leading figures from the Founding to the Civil War years fully expected
parties to form in a free society; they were far less certain, however, that a
republican form of government would endure if political parties contested
the most fundamental or polarizing questions of the day. The status of
party, nonetheless, has come a long way in American society and politics;
American democracy is today inconceivable without party opposition.[5]
The problem of party, that party formation cannot be prevented in a free
society, but that parties may catalyze civil disorder or lead to the dismemberment of republics, raises a fundamental question: how, and on what terms,
did party opposition become a regular, "normal" feature of the American
political landscape?

This question has not been systematically addressed since the publication of Richard Hofstadter's 1969 classic *The Idea of a Party System: The Rise of Legitimate Party Opposition in the United States, 1780–1840*.[6] Hofstadter raised this question in the context of the polarized opposition between the Jeffersonian Republicans and the Hamiltonian Federalists. The politics of this first party system has taken on a new relevance today as America has returned to a pattern of polarized political discourse not unlike that of the late eighteenth and early nineteenth centuries. Then, as now, partisans debated the value of debate itself when fundamental matters of national well-being were at stake. Then, as now, partisans in the minority bore the burden of having to reassure a sometimes skeptical and impatient public that dissent would in no way compromise American security. Then, as now, bipartisanship or nonpartisanship was taken to be the normative default when the country's vital interests were perceived to be at risk.

Public ambivalence today about the role of partisanship in American democracy, however, is qualitatively different from that advanced by statesmen and thinkers of the late eighteenth century. And it is different for a reason. Political parties in the United States once posed a credible threat to public order and the territorial integrity of the Union. Parties still pose such a threat in many developing countries around the world. In some emerging polities in Africa, Latin America, and the Middle East, "party competition" is more closely associated with civil war than it is with democracy. And so it was in the United States from 1783 (when the United States formally won its independence) to the conclusion of the Civil War. The central government did not possess coercive control within its territory until Union forces achieved victory in 1865. Political leaders quite reasonably feared in the 1780s that parties would trigger class violence led by indebted, backcountry agrarians. As the French Revolutionary and Napoleonic Wars raged in Europe (1793–1815), statesmen worried that party opposition would produce a proxy war between France and Britain on American soil. During the antebellum years, politicians went to great lengths to prevent the parties from taking on a geographical dimension and igniting a sectional conflagration between slaveholding and nonslaveholding states.

In the United States today, by contrast, there is no reason to fear that a partisan debate will trigger a secessionist movement, a violent class struggle, or a civil war. The coarse and adversarial discourse one hears and sees on cable news may be off-putting or unpleasant; it may erode public trust, promote political cynicism, or lead to policy stalemate. It is, nonetheless, unlikely to trigger political violence. Indeed, as disruptive and unreasonable as partisan actors may be or appear, political parties have been shorn of their capacity to instigate political violence that threatens the structural integrity of the republic.[7]

How were political parties, in this limited but important sense, "made safe" for American democracy? This book tells the story of this political transformation in the United States. Parts of this story have been told before, but they've been framed in different terms and offered with contrasting conclusions. Indeed, the emergence of parties as a regular feature of the American political landscape has been narrated through the prism of the burgeoning democratic norms, practices, and institutions of the early to mid-nineteenth century. From this vantage point, parties were not merely accepted but were embraced as salutary and useful as American society grew more democratic. Tracing the lineage of legitimate party opposition by emphasizing the democratization of the polity has much to recommend it. This book, nonetheless, offers a corrective to this outlook by suggesting that the legitimacy of party opposition gained ground as parties were designed to avoid, or better yet, actively subordinate the most divisive and controversial issues of the day. Parties gained acceptance so long as they sidestepped questions that threatened to trigger political violence. I make the case, moreover, that the capacities and limitations of the central state have powerfully influenced the development of party legitimacy in the United States. Legitimate party opposition advanced as the central state secured a near monopoly over the exercise of violence and developed the means to assuage class divisions, thwart separatist movements, and prevent partisan controversies from sparking political unrest.

Legitimate Opposition and Party Pluralism

Legitimate party opposition is a category of both political science and political thought.[8] As a concept, it should be defined to allow for a degree of interpretive flexibility; it must, nonetheless, offer some fairly clear parameters to generate insight into how political actors make sense of the place and propriety of parties in a regime. Surprisingly, Hofstadter never paused to offer a clear definition of party legitimacy. As he explained, "The idea of a legitimate opposition—recognized opposition, organized and free enough in its activities to be able to displace an existing government by peaceful means," encompasses numerous elements: recognition, organization, liberty, and the capacity to govern.[9] His study, moreover, focuses on the antipartisanship of leading statesmen and thinkers and parses, with characteristic nuance and insight, distinct variants of antipartisan thought. In this manner, he tacitly equates antipartisanship with party illegitimacy and proparty sentiment with commitments to party legitimacy.[10] The prominent political communications scholar Diana Mutz treats legitimate opposition as the perception of citizens that the opposition has an "understandable basis" for its views and that "reasonable people may disagree."[11] In a recent study of the development of American judicial politics, Stephen M. Engel identifies the belief of those in power that opposition is natural and unavoidable and does not "destabilize or threaten the Constitution" as a commitment to a loyal opposition.[12] Public intellectuals, for their part, consider legitimate party opposition a matter of civility in political discourse and denounce those who demonize their political competitors.[13]

Together, these usages stake out the position (either explicitly or implicitly) that partisan dissent is a norm that not merely should be tolerated but is worthy of praise, much in the way that dissenting speech is tolerated and often elevated as essential to the proper functioning of a liberal democracy. To capture the close association between the norm to tolerate party opposition and the freedom to dissent, I will define legitimate party opposition with the help of Giovanni Sartori's concept of "party pluralism," a concept developed in his classic *Parties and Party Systems*.[14] Sartori was mindful that the toleration of party opposition was achieved in parallel with the broader "realization that diversity and dissent are not necessarily incompatible with, or disruptive of, political order. In this ideal sense, parties are correlative to, and dependent upon, the *Weltanschauung* of liberalism." As Sartori explains, "parties and pluralism originate from the same belief system and the same act of faith."[15]

There are two ideational metrics one must track when tracing the development of party pluralism or the legitimacy of party opposition.[16] The first holds that there must be more than one effective party in a polity for the governing regime itself to be legitimate. We see the first element of party pluralism at work today when party elites holding offices of high responsibility appear to challenge the legitimacy of their partisan opponents. Publicly expressed doubts of this kind are treated as highly newsworthy and often provoke countercharges of political intimidation or bullying.[17] The code of conduct that regulates the relationship between leaders of governing parties—presidents in particular—and opposition parties permits presidents to defend their policy views against partisan opponents, but rarely permits presidents to challenge their critics for the fact of their opposition. To do so would be tantamount to foreclosing public debate itself.

It is thus taken for granted that if the president and his party are not answerable to an opposing party, then they are answerable to no one; for the governing regime to be legitimate in a modern liberal democracy, it must also grant legitimacy to the shadow government standing in opposition. As Nancy Rosenblum reminds us, one can be partisan (in the sense of being partial) and therefore political without parties; one may participate in politics through individual action or become a member or supporter of an association, group, or movement.[18] Party pluralism implies, however, that *party* opposition is indispensible to the democratic legitimacy of government.[19]

The second metric may be derived from the first: if government must defend the right of at least one major party to oppose, does it follow that the dissent of any and all parties must be equally defended? The emergence of party pluralism, as Sartori explains, entailed a shift in thought from a willingness first to use the instrument of party to advance one's own notion of the common good (while disavowing its use by one's political opponents) to an acceptance of some partisan differences as compatible with—and perhaps even necessary for—the advancement of public purposes.[20]

Sartori's sketch of the trajectory of party pluralism obscures a crucial ambiguity. If some forms of partisan dissent are acknowledged to be compatible with the common good, it would go one very significant step further to avow that all kinds of party opposition comport with the public interest. Does the ideal of legitimate party opposition require that the public should tolerate any and all partisan differences?

For most statesmen and thinkers, in fact, there is an outer limit to the principle that partisan dissent is compatible with the public good. William Seward, a man whose career was spent working through the ranks of parties, believed that any party willing to compromise the Union went too far. As we shall see with Martin Van Buren, Andrew Jackson, and numerous other figures from the antebellum era, parties were desirable so long as they did not politicize the question of slavery. This conditional understanding of party legitimacy is also embedded in Hofstadter's portrait of the political consensus that circumscribes party politics in America. Hofstadter maintains that opposition parties throughout the course of American political history have agreed with their opponents on the fundamental, constitutional rules of the game. An opposition party is "constitutional," according to Hofstadter, if it is "bound by the rules of some kind of constitutional consensus. It is understood . . . that opposition is directed against a certain policy or complex of policies, not against the legitimacy of the constitutional regime itself. Opposition rises above naked contestation; it forswears sedition, treason, conspiracy, *coup d'etat*, riot, and assassination, and makes an open public appeal for the support of a more or less free electorate."[21] As "constitutional" parties, the Jeffersonian Republicans and successive opposition parties operated within definite bounds; their commitment to the Constitution, in Hofstadter's story, was a condition—a prerequisite for the acceptance of party opposition as loyal and serviceable to the commonweal.

We gather from these illustrations that party opposition is worthy of respect, if and only if it is delimited; the boundary condition is essential to the judgment that partisan dissent is acceptable.[22] The outer limit to this notion of pluralism, it turns out, is as important as the insight that opposition comports with the public good. In fact, pluralist ideas and their outer limits are mutually constitutive: a notion of pluralism cannot be fully understood without an account of its limits. What we learn, furthermore, is that objections to the legitimacy of party opposition often concern the *policy substance* of political contestation and not philosophical objections to partisanship alone: since the conditions attached to party legitimacy are based on policy positions (to return to Seward, a party's stance on peace negotiations), support for party pluralism (or lack thereof) usually hinges on what the dissenting party or parties stand for.[23] Statesmen and thinkers rarely (if ever) commit themselves to philosophical views on parties in general without regard to the concrete policy choices available at a given moment in history.

To clarify the point, one might imagine the ideal of legitimate party opposition without conditions attached. Indeed, the ideal, when taken to its logical conclusion, is most fully realized when party opposition is accepted as a necessary feature of a free and democratic society, regardless of what the opposing party or parties represent or the positions they take on the issues of the day. Opposition parties are accepted in a democracy just as dissenting speech—in all its variety—is accepted as essential to the "free market of ideas." The ideal of legitimate party opposition thus entails a kind of content neutrality akin to the content neutrality standard of First Amendment law.[24]

The nature of this definition of party legitimacy raises crucial developmental questions. Party opposition is arguably never without conditions—never without an outer limit, so to speak. The ideal of legitimate party opposition is never fully realized. Yet what is most interesting for our purposes are the patterned ways in which the polity falls short of the ideal. How have the conditions attached to legitimate opposition changed over time? How, moreover, have political and institutional developments shaped the *kinds* of conditions that have bounded the range of legitimate party opposition in the United States? These are the questions that a historical examination of the development of party pluralism must investigate.

Legitimate Party Opposition and the Democratization Narrative

Scholars have traced the emergence of legitimate party opposition with varying degrees of attention to the conditionality of party legitimacy. Yet no matter how scholars treat the subject matter conceptually, they rightly focus their attention on the early national and antebellum periods (1789 to 1815 and 1815 to 1859, respectively), when the status of parties was in the greatest flux. Their chronologies usually begin with the Founders' curiously conflicting views and actions with respect to political parties. Indeed, the nature of the American Founders' antipartisanship has puzzled scholars for some time. It is a familiar irony that some of those who most forcefully inveighed against the dangers of party spirit (such as Thomas Jefferson and Alexander Hamilton) were themselves founders of the first two national parties. According to conventional wisdom, parties in the late eighteenth century were received by some members of the governing elite as necessary evils and by others as harbingers of national disintegration and decline. By the 1820s and 1830s, however, the terms of discourse had changed: many skeptical voices remained, but a new, proparty persuasion gained ground.[25] Parties, as the new thinking went, would connect the common man to his government and make that government more accountable by adding a supplementary set of checks and balances to the existing constitutional framework.

The tendency to equate the development of parties—mass "modern" parties in particular—with the rise of American democracy itself has colored scholars' understanding of the terms on which party systems were founded.[26]

The rise of parties, treated as the advent of democracy, is represented by some as an important step in the progressive enlightenment of American political *thought*. Indeed, the Founders' resistance to parties strikes some modern observers as a quaint relic of the eighteenth century—a naïve sentiment that would inevitably give way with political modernization. As one party scholar notes, "Federalists and Republicans were prisoners of inherited assumptions" that prevented them from accepting the role of political parties, "institutions essential to the survival of free government." Federalists and Republicans were simply "unaware that they were experiencing political modernization."[27] In a similar spirit, Joseph Charles claims that parties are "indispensable" for representative government, and that the failure to recognize their role in the functioning of the government was "the great illusion of this period."[28] Hofstadter makes this point more directly in the preface to *The Idea of a Party System*: "I believe that the gradual acceptance of parties and of the system of a recognized partisan opposition which I record here marked a net gain in the sophistication of political thought and practice over the antiparty thought and unlegitimated or quasi-legitimated opposition that had prevailed in the Anglo-American tradition in the eighteenth century and earlier. The emergence of legitimate party opposition and of a theory of politics that accepted it was something new in the history of the world; it required a bold new act of understanding on the part of its contemporaries."[29] Accordingly, he portrays the first generation of American statesmen as backward, naïve, or otherwise falling short of a more tolerant or realistic standard set by second-generation statesmen such as Martin Van Buren and Andrew Jackson. Hofstadter betrays this modern bias when he characterizes George Washington, Thomas Jefferson, and James Monroe as politically and intellectually naïve. He observes, for example, that Washington's "intellectual confusion about the problem of government and opposition was altogether genuine and that it partook of an intellectual difficulty quite common among his contemporaries."[30]

If, for some scholars, the acceptance of party represents a step in the progressive enlightenment of American statesmen, the rise of parties also registers as a net gain in the political advancement of yeoman farmers, settlers, and working-class men—at the expense of the gentry's control of politics. The second generation of American statesmen were lawyers, professionals, and businessmen who repudiated the patrician norms and practices of the Founders. A new class of men, unwilling to defer to their "betters," made their way into politics—and with them came their chosen organizational form: political parties. Thus, the status of party gained ground as the common man began to assert himself in politics.[31]

With the democratization of the electorate came a corresponding decline of republican norms and values. Indeed, the decline of republican values has been closely associated with the advancement of party. For scholars of early American political thought, republican ideology, drawn in particular from English commonwealthmen, uniquely informed the political, social, and constitutional outlook of the revolutionary generation.[32] With its emphasis on public virtue—understood as the willingness of a frugal and industrious citizenry to forgo the expression of individual self-interest and its portrait of the common good as the good of a homogenous people—republicanism is hostile ideational terrain for the advancement of party. Indeed, the idea of party militates against traditional republican ideas of civic virtue and the common good: party pluralism entails the acceptance of self-interest in the public sphere, assumes a differentiated conception of the "people," and embraces a peaceful, but adversarial, majoritarian process to decide what shall pass as the common good.[33]

These interpretations of the emergence of legitimate party competition—the democratization narrative and its republican decline variant—have much to recommend them. Indeed, parties were embraced by the common man well before they were accepted by social elites. The emergence of the idea of legitimate party opposition also closely coincided with the gradual elimination of property qualifications, culminating in what is often heralded as the great early achievement of American democracy: universal white male suffrage.[34] Social norms, moreover, changed in sync with evolving political and institutional conditions. As Gordon Wood explains, new opportunities for the common man to advance socially, economically, and politically entailed the fraying of vertical bonds of authority that existed between social classes for generations. As authority structures transformed, classical republican understandings of political obligation and citizenship changed in turn.[35]

Despite their considerable merits, these interpretations of the emergence of legitimate party opposition are incomplete. Scholars who emphasize the incorporation of new social classes into the democratic process tend to focus exclusively on the domestic social and political forces that gave rise to the party politics of the Jacksonian era, downplaying or ignoring altogether the role of international political developments.[36] American politics in the early national period was intimately intertwined with the tumultuous events unfolding in Europe, from the French Revolution and the French Revolutionary Wars to the Napoleonic Wars. The democratization narrative, however, focuses our attention primarily on the homegrown social and political forces that gave rise to the idea of legitimate party opposition and turns our attention away from the impact of foreign wars on American electoral politics.

This domestically focused view, moreover, does not provide a complete picture of the terms on which parties were embraced when they were accepted into the mainstream. Those who equate party competition with democracy often fail to account for the conditions that limited the scope of legitimate partisan dispute, set in place as parties came into fashion in the 1820s and 1830s. Thus, we are left with the impression that the second party system was without conditions and constraints—that it reflected the virtues of unfettered political competition.[37]

When scholars treat the second party system as an unfettered system of political competition, they assume that this party system was fundamentally representative—that the issues of greatest consequence to the people were the issues that ultimately defined partisan dispute. This implication is evident in James Sundquist's observation that throughout American history, "the parties lined up naturally on opposite sides of whatever were the great issues of the day—creating a national bank, opening the West with turnpikes and railroads and canals financed by the national government, prohibiting slavery in the western territories, raising or lowering tariffs, mobilizing the national government to help the victims of the Great Depression, and so on."[38] A more compelling case can be made, however, that some of these matters were front and center on the parties' agenda because they were *not* the great issues of the day. As Arthur M. Schlesinger Jr. observes,

> [Slavery] was the most accusing, the most tragic and the most
> dangerous of all questions . . . like a man banishing a dreaded image
> from consciousness, [the nation] turned and twisted desperately to
> suppress and deny and bury the terrible fact. For almost a quarter of
> a century after the Missouri crisis, slavery was blocked from gaining
> full embodiment as a specific political issue. The trauma of 1820
> was too intense. Yet the question could not be exorcised by repres-
> sion. It remained ever just out of sight, occasionally flaring up for a

moment in an exchange on the floors of Congress . . . like a wild
dream, shaking the night with its burst of anxiety; then disclaimed
and forgotten, as the morning came again, and people returned
securely to debating the Bank or the tariff.[39]

As Schlesinger suggests, the Bank and the tariff questions, though consequential in and of themselves, were secondary matters that ascended to the
top of the agenda because they could be securely debated. A full portrait of the
second party system would account for the ways in which party competition
was delimited and contrived by political leaders to be, in effect, unrepresen-
tative: elites did what they could to subordinate some of the most divisive
and consequential policy questions. Scholars who celebrate the democratic
virtues of the second party system either ignore or have forgotten E. E.
Schattschneider's crucial insight that parties prioritize some issues to avoid
or displace others.[40]

The history of party development in the United States is, in no small part,
a story of how political leaders modulated what Schattschneider called the
"scope of conflict" to protect a structurally fragile union.[41] Political elites designed the U.S. Constitution to mute the contentious class divisions that
were deepened by the economic depression of the mid-1780s. In so doing,
they put an end to a rash of violence in the states and prevented the formation of a party cleavage that would only amplify the growing rifts between
debtors and creditors and between taxpayers and the owners of public debt.
In the early national period, political elites hoping to prevent a proxy war
between French and British partisans at home went to great lengths to avoid
policy controversies that would force the country to take sides in the French
Revolutionary and Napoleonic Wars. Statesmen and politicians from the
1790s through the antebellum years did what they could to build coalitions that reached across the geographic sections of the Union, forging compromises on tariff policy and the regulation of slavery to avert a sectional
division of the parties. The underlying vulnerability of the new republic
powerfully constrained the partisan agenda and, in so doing, shaped the kinds
of coalitions that party builders plausibly could and could not construct.

Yet the structural fragility of the Union, as important as it is, is largely
overlooked by scholars who study parties in the United States.[42] Students of
political parties have, to be sure, learned a great deal in the last two decades
about the processes that impact party formation (and collapse) in the
American political setting. The publication of John Aldrich's *Why Parties?*

The Origin and Transformation of Political Parties in America (1995), in particular, advanced the study of American party development more than any other study in recent memory.[43] Aldrich portrays parties as solutions to problems that purposive actors—actors who are not narrowly self-interested, but possess principled policy goals—hope to solve.[44] He shows that parties were constructed to produce stable legislative majorities, to mobilize voters, and to regulate the ambitions of office seekers. Party development more generally is driven by the efforts of policy-minded politicians to achieve these strategic ends. His analysis yields a persuasive account of why parties formed in Congress in the 1790s and why politicians in the 1830s built an organizational apparatus that extended the reach of parties into the electorate. He also demonstrates how ambition theory may be employed to illuminate one of the most complex episodes in American party development: the collapse of the Whig party in the 1850s and the rise of the Republican coalition.[45]

As comprehensive as it is, Aldrich's analysis overlooks several important dynamics that have shaped the course of American party development. His theoretical framework, in particular, does not account for why another set of party coalitions that would have solved the collective action problems he identifies were not assembled. Aldrich maintains in *Why Parties?* that leaders in Congress and in the executive branch prioritized policies that placed rival visions of "how large and active the central government would be" at the center of dispute.[46] Aldrich refers to this dimension as the "great principle."[47] Political leaders since the early 1790s focused their attention on this dimension after the passage of the Bill of Rights because "the remaining and most pressing unsettled issue about the new order was the great principle."[48] Yet there were other latent policy divisions that political leaders could have, if they had so chosen, made manifest. Leaders might have, for example, advanced rival programs highlighting the distinct interests of the geographic sections of the country on subjects ranging from western expansion and relations with Native American nations to trade policy and, most critically, the regulation of slavery.[49] A party that united the southern states would address these matters very differently from a party that consolidated the middle and eastern states. Yet, as all understood, party coalitions forged along a sectional axis were not compatible with the territorial unity of the republic. The parties, to be sure, did not have to maintain a perfect sectional balance.[50] Political leaders nonetheless understood that policy questions that put the fundamental interests of one section or the other in jeopardy should not be politicized.

Aldrich describes the great principle as "the remaining and most pressing unsettled issue about the new order"; yet it would be more precise to say that the great principle was the most pressing issue that could be politicized without triggering political violence or risking the dissolution of the republic.[51] The great principle raised a comparatively "safe" question—and it took on this character in part because political leaders had already constructed institutions (the Constitution) to settle the contentious political economic schisms of the 1780s. The Constitution had shorn the question of central state authority of its most volatile class dimensions and fashioned this subject into a policy arena that could be peaceably debated (see Chapter 2 for a detailed discussion). The amended Constitution, in this manner, narrowed the issue agenda from the outset, constricting the scope of conflict just enough to allow a relatively peaceful competition between rival answers to a question (viz.: how "strong and active [should] the new national government" be?) that was not so threatening to begin with.[52]

The Framers of the Constitution effectively laid to rest one kind of polarizing conflict to make way for a more temperate politics addressing the size and capacities of the federal government. The "origin" of party rivalry in America was, in other words, as much an ending as it was a beginning. To capture this critical step in the process of party formation, scholars must first examine the politics that preceded and gave rise to the framing and ratification of the Constitution. Yet party scholars all too often begin their analysis with the First Congress, just as the curtains on this formative episode are closing.[53]

Aldrich's treatment of the second party system is limited in a different way. His discussion of the development of parties in the antebellum years reflects a keen awareness of the connection between the structural fragility of the Union and the substance of policy contestation. This is evident in his description of the institutions that politicians constructed to prevent the question of slavery from ascending the party's issue agenda. This discussion, however, remains at the level of description: the logic for why parties must contain one question (such as slavery) and not another is not incorporated into his theoretical framework. Aldrich's analysis, moreover, does not consider how the horizon of coalition-building alternatives might change if the risk associated with one of these "dangerous" questions is effectively neutralized by the changing capacities of the central state.

This limitation notwithstanding, Aldrich's analysis of the strategic challenges that ambitious politicians faced makes it clear that the second party system was not designed primarily to contain the question of slavery.[54] Political motivations were more complex. The desire to subordinate the slavery question was, no doubt, an impetus for the development of the Democratic party. Yet as Aldrich demonstrates, the Democratic party was formed, most immediately, to solve the collective action problems confronted by ambitious politicians with diverse policy interests hoping to elect a presidential candidate who stood a good chance of winning (General Jackson).

Whether attention is focused on the incorporation of new social classes into the electorate, the decline of republican notions of virtue, or the coordination problems faced by political leaders, existing narratives fail to come to terms with a historical reality that American statesmen of the early national and antebellum periods understood very well: that parties needed to be contained and carefully regulated if they were to be compatible with civil peace and the union of the states. This sensibility, that the Union was fragile and its institutions vulnerable, was widely shared by diverse leaders of the pre–Civil War polity. It also closely accords with the well-developed literature assessing the limited capacities of the early American national state.

Political Parties and the "Flexible Capacity" of the States to Oppose Federal Authority

The bounds of toleration in the early national and antebellum periods were defined by an underlying political and institutional assessment: the well-justified belief that polarized parties would fracture beyond repair a polity with a weak and fragmented central state. This appraisal of the capacity of the early American state, however, has itself become a subject of considerable scholarly debate. Several of the most important studies conducted in the field of American political development have assumed as a matter of course that the early American state was severely limited in its administrative and regulatory reach.[55] A growing and more recent body of literature, however, has demonstrated the myriad ways in which the early American state capably promoted economic development, removed Native Americans from their ancestral lands, and fostered communications throughout a great territorial expanse.[56] In his critique of the exceptionalist claim that the early American state was weak or even invisible, Brian Balogh insightfully notes that the early American state governed differently, but not less, when compared to contemporary governments in Europe. He argues, moreover, that the state was most influential when its role was most effectively obscured.[57] Thus, as Balogh suggests, descriptors such as "weak" and "strong" are too simple for the task of evaluating the capacities of states: states have numerous functions and achieve their objectives through a variety of means. The early American state, no doubt, operated differently from its contemporaries. It was also more capable in some respects than others.

Yet some functions are more fundamental than others—and none are more fundamental than the control of the territory and the preservation of civil order. These particular state functions require a different sort of analysis. Balogh and others assess the administrative and regulatory reach of the federal *and* state governments together.[58] Of interest to the present study is not so much the capacities of the federal and state governments together but the capacity of the federal government taken alone, and at times *against* the coercive capabilities of the states. Indeed, the balance of coercive capacities between the federal government and the states is more pertinent to the problems of governance presented by political parties: a deep partisan division could prompt a party out of power in the general government to rally resistance in a state or a subset of the states, upsetting the delicate balance of power between the states and the federal government and setting rival sovereigns at odds.[59] The standoff that would then ensue would introduce a potentially grave uncertainty into the operations of government.

As this balance of power stood in the early national and antebellum periods, there was no clear superiority between the federal government and the states. One might even argue that the federal government stood in a position of relative weakness vis-à-vis its constituent parts. The federal government, scholars agree, was no leviathan. It was, as John M. Murrin surmised, a "midget institution in a giant land."[60] Crucially, the "general government," as it was called in these times, lacked the capacity to reliably enforce national policies that were contested by a motivated popular opposition. Federal forces were numerically insignificant—consisting of a few thousand men scattered across a vast territorial expanse, armed only with the rudimentary military and surveillance technology available at the time. And the number of federal forces did not grow appreciably with American territorial expansion.[61] The federal government could not, without the assistance of the states, control America's vast borders or curb the influence of foreign agents operating in American territory; nor could it, without great effort, force the states to obey federal law if they were intent on resistance.

To be sure, the federal government was strong enough to be serviceable to the states. As Ira Katznelson persuasively argues in his essay, "Flexible Capacity: The Military and Early American Statebuilding," the American state, contrary to the conventional story told by scholars of American political development, was quite effective in meeting the military objectives of the young republic. Because the American state was, by and large, a "liberal state based on popular sovereignty, consent, and representation," this state was distinctive insofar as it marshaled power from the bottom up and was able to "harness the pluralism of civil society by hitching 'stateness' to competing political coalitions."[62] Crucial to Katznelson's argument is the insight that the capacities of states—liberal states in particular—are variable: they can be adjusted to meet changing circumstances. Because they draw on popular support, military capacities in a liberal state are capable of rapid mobilization in times of large-scale conflict. They could demobilize during "normal times" but expand as necessary to meet the military needs of the polity. The early American state, in his interpretation, was an illustrative example: unlike its continental European counterparts, it possessed a "flexible capacity," enabling it to secure new territories, expropriate the lands of Native Americans, and promote economic development without adopting the regimentation and permanency that is associated with the Weberian, Prussian model of stateness.[63]

It is important to note, however, that when Katznelson writes of the military capacities of the "American state," he is referring to the efforts of the federal and the state governments together.[64] By looking at instances where both levels of government successfully combined forces, Katznelson sidesteps the chief problem state builders confronted: that state and federal authorities often did not comfortably combine.[65] Indeed, there is little doubt that these governments were capable of achieving significant undertakings when they joined forces. However, when state and local energies were directed against federal authority, the central state has found itself severely limited in what it was able to accomplish. Just as federal and state capacities have been flexible and expandable in response to governing exigencies, state and local capacities have been equally flexible in opposition to federal authority when the people are given a clear purpose that is at odds with federal law.

Madison offered a comparable assessment in 1788 to buttress his claim that the people and the states never had to fear the usurpation of authority by the federal government: even if the federal government was granted the resources to amass a powerful standing army hostile to the rights and interests of the people (though he thought it would be highly improbable that the people's representatives would do such a thing), the states nonetheless possessed the means to thwart the designs of any force that ambitious federal leaders could assemble. He drew a hypothetical scenario to make the point:

> Let a regular army, fully equal to the resources of the country, be formed; and let it be entirely at the devotion of the federal government: still it would not be going too far to say, that the State governments with the people on their side would be able to repel the danger. The highest number to which, according to the best computation, a standing army can be carried into any country does not exceed one hundredth part of the whole number of souls; or one twenty-fifth part of the number able to bear arms. This proportion would not yield, in the United States, an army of more than twenty-five or thirty thousand men. To these would be opposed a militia amounting to near half a million of citizens with arms in their hands, officered by men chosen from among themselves, fighting for their common liberties and united and conducted by governments possessing their affections and confidence. It may well be doubted whether a militia thus circumstanced could ever be conquered by such a proportion of regular troops.[66]

The balance of power between the state and federal governments (or, in Madison's rendering, the imbalance of power favoring the states) was highly consequential. In this institutional setting, national political leaders understandably viewed "party competition" as little more than a euphemism for civil war. Political parties did not amass armies against one another; they did, however, tend to introduce polarizing disagreements between competing state and federal sovereigns—disagreements that could lead to constitutional crises and political violence. Parties were seen as divisive, semiautonomous agents that operated in a delicately balanced institutional landscape. Statesmen and thinkers of the time understood that competing parties did not merely represent political divisions in the electorate, but could actively distort existing disagreements and raise the salience of their preferred disputes onto the national political agenda.[67] Party organizations, in other words, could misrepresent the desires of the people and bring competing sovereigns to blows. The risk that a crisis of this description might unfold hinged on the capacities of the states to effectively resist federal authority. A brief review of the coercive resources available to state and local governments is therefore in order.

Coercive Capacities of the States and in Civil Society

Though there was a good deal of variability from state to state, a number of the states possessed the means to capably resist a federal government that was itself quite limited in its regulatory reach. The coercive resources that states could draw on were quite diverse: state militias, territorial militias, private volunteer militia companies, and slave patrols, as well as an assortment of paramilitary vigilance groups (especially in the South just before the outbreak of the Civil War) all played roles in the defense and security of states and local communities. Each of these entities possessed different rules, resources, and purposes; they were also often closely interrelated. The boundaries between state militias, slave patrols, and paramilitary vigilance groups often blurred, as did the boundary between the state militias and the volunteer militia companies when the latter were sanctioned and subsidized by the states.[68] Their capacities, moreover, varied over time and from place to place.

Much of the historical evidence suggests that the state militias, with some exceptions, were notoriously unreliable. The citizens' militia was widely viewed during the early national period as the republican alternative to the dreaded "standing army"—a professional corps that operated during peacetime, associated with corrupt monarchical regimes.[69] Constituted by the Uniform Militia Act of 1792, the state militia system required that all free and able-bodied white men between the ages of eighteen and forty-five furnish themselves with firearms and necessary accessories and take part in periodic training exercises as prescribed by this law and supplemental state law.[70] Though there was a great deal of state-by-state variation, the state militias were typically ill equipped and poorly trained.[71]

The reputation of the state militias did not improve with time. Though reliable data on participation rates are scarce, participation in the state militias appeared to decline in the antebellum years as interest in its occasional musters and ceremonies waned.[72] The apparent decline in participation rates is attributed to the advance of white male democracy: more and more men saw service as an imposition, and politicians, ever inclined to appease voters, were reluctant to press citizens to do their duty as defined by the Militia Act.[73]

Just as the state militias appeared to decline, two other institutions thrived: slave patrols and volunteer militia companies. The members of slave patrols were, in fact, drawn from the state militias. As historian Sally Hadden suggests, the shift in capacities and resources from the state militias to the slave patrols in the South makes sense from the standpoint of the security threats facing the slaveholding public: in the early national period, militias were necessary not only to stem the threat of slave revolt, but also to contend with threats posed by Native Americans and foreign competitors for territory such as the Spanish in the Floridas and the British during the War of 1812. As the antebellum years wore on, threats from the Native American and Atlantic frontiers subsided, but the domestic enemy, the slave population, remained. A subset of the militia—the slave patrols—was ideally suited to meet this particular threat.[74] Members of slave patrols, however, just like any other servicemen, could always be repurposed to meet other needs.

Privately funded and organized volunteer militia companies also thrived just as the state militias saw their rates of participation decline. Many of these volunteer units were most interested in ceremony, parades, and martial showmanship, but quite a few were also selective, well-trained, and capable forces.[75] They were often incorporated into states' military organizations and subsidized by state governments, blurring the lines between public and private.[76] Many of these volunteer companies served effectively in conflicts with Native Americans on the frontier, in the cities to quell riots, and alongside state and federal forces during the Mexican War and on both sides of the Civil War. When these independent forces were given a guiding principle and the support of their communities, they often proved to be quite capable.

No purpose was clearer or had the potential to galvanize local energies more effectively than resistance to federal authority. Indeed, state militiamen in the slave states, though they remained largely inactive in the antebellum period, could be rallied to reorganize for just such a purpose. This is precisely what happened in the late 1850s and during the secession crisis in the South when so many of the regular members of the slave patrols and state militias were readied in anticipation of slave revolts (sponsored, they feared, by northern abolitionists), federal invasion, or both. The mobilization of security forces in the southern states in the late 1850s was remarkable in its scale: this "do-it-yourself mobilization," as the prominent historian James MacPherson described it, rapidly assembled a force of sixty thousand men through the consolidation of a diverse array of volunteer and state militia companies organized by states and localities.[77] It was a striking demonstration of the states' flexible capacities to marshal their resources and strike a posture of resistance to federal authority.

The threat of state and local resistance was a foundational problem for state builders like James Madison. Statesmen of the early national period clearly understood that the federal government could not easily coerce a state opposed to federal law because the recalcitrant state could, depending on the circumstances, draw on local armed supporters prepared to coalesce in its defense. James Madison spoke directly to this concern when he posed the following question to fellow delegates at the Constitutional Convention: "Could the national resources, if exerted to the utmost enforce a national decree agst. Massts. abetted perhaps by several of her neighbours? It would not be possible. A; [sic] small proportion of the Community in a compact situation, acting on the defensive, and at one of its extremities might at any time bid defiance to the National authority."[78] Should a state "bid defiance to the National authority," the federal government required the assistance of other states willing to dedicate their militia to the cause—a "coalition of the willing" (to use a twenty-first-century expression) that might be marshaled as the circumstances required. The resistance of any of the states to comply with federal law, in other words, could quickly devolve into a war between the states.

This fact of institutional life rendered national sovereignty distinctly vulnerable to the activities and influence of parties. Federal leaders who depended on the states to respect and occasionally enforce federal law were aware that state governments—and the militias they commanded—might well come under the influence of an opposing party. Volunteer militiamen, though not formally under the command of their states, could be expected to rally in defense of their states or in support of the dominant local partisan persuasion.

Foreign affairs only amplified the risk and potential costs of party division. Statesmen of the early national and antebellum periods understood that the balance of power between the states and the federal government was precarious on its own; it was exposed to even greater uncertainty when situated in a broader international political arena with imperial European powers jockeying to divide up control of North America and the Atlantic.[79] These global powers would not hesitate to involve themselves in American domestic affairs should it serve their broader imperial ends. The first generation of American statesmen understood that a schism between a subset of the states and the federal government, if permitted to grow too deep, could turn into an intractable civil conflict if foreign powers threw their weight into the balance. Hamilton addressed this strategic vulnerability when he contemplated a future where the states remained loosely connected under the Articles of Confederation. If they refused to adopt the charter framed in Philadelphia in 1787, then America, "by the destructive contentions of the parts into which she was divided, would be likely to become prey to the artifices and machinations of powers equally the enemies of them all. *Divide et impera* must be the motto of every nation that either hates or fears us."[80]

Building consensus across the geographic sections of the Union was, for these reasons, rightfully perceived to be a governing exigency during the early national and antebellum periods. Statesmen who understood that party rivalries could fracture the republic practiced a politics of evasion to thwart the escalation of party conflict into political violence or civil war. Political leaders attempted (with varying degrees of success) to settle, subordinate, or avoid the most contentious questions of the day. They did what they could to sidestep or contain the most controversial matters confronting the polity and minimize the potential political violence that party divisions could unleash. This they attempted to do using three broad strategies: institutional design, party coalition building, and repression. Whether leaders were framing a constitution, structuring a crucial policy compromise, forging an innovative party coalition, or passing a sedition law or "gag rule" in Congress, political leaders used these tools to subordinate some disfavored partisan persuasion by prioritizing an alternative mode of political expression. The use of these tools was guided by prevailing understandings of what policy questions could and could not be peaceably politicized; these tools, moreover, shaped the horizon of desirable party-building alternatives and thereby helped to reproduce conceptions of legitimate party opposition in the polity at large.

The outcome of the Civil War altered the balance of power between the federal and state governments and, in so doing, fundamentally recast the terms of legitimate party opposition in the United States. With the Confederacy vanquished, the federal government possessed an unmistakable coercive advantage against any state(s) that might contemplate secession or challenge the collection of federal revenue. The central government attained attributes of sovereignty that it had never before possessed. Through the early national and antebellum periods, the force capacities of the federal and state governments were roughly comparable. The federal government could not, without considerable risk, expense, and uncertainty, subdue the resistance of a powerful state like Massachusetts or Virginia, either acting on its own or in conjunction with neighboring states. Yes, the federal government possessed the means to disperse a group of poor and disorganized farmers in western Pennsylvania (the Whiskey Rebellion of 1791), but it could not reliably marshal the resources to discipline a powerful state acting on the defensive.[81]

The Civil War transformed this strategic landscape. It was clear by 1865 that, even if the Union Army should be dismantled (as it, in fact, was), the Union was more than capable of mobilizing anew the men, funding, and arms necessary to defeat any attempt to secede or interfere with the collection of tariff revenue. The federal government had demonstrated its coercive potential, and the demonstration was enough to teach refractory elements of the population that some forms of resistance were, for all intents and purposes, futile.

To be sure, the federal government was not all-powerful after the Civil War, not by any means. It attained the capacity to reliably thwart some, but not all forms of resistance. The national government possessed an unrivaled capacity to guarantee the territorial integrity of the Union and to enforce the collection of tariff revenue in the ports. Yet it did not, as we shall see in Chapter 6, possess the administrative wherewithal or the political support to sustain a lengthy occupation of the South or to prevent the spread of vigilante violence directed at freedmen in postbellum America.

Though significant limitations remained, the augmentation of central state capacity produced a noteworthy change in the status of party in American democracy. Indeed, the stakes of sectionally defined party divisions were lowered when secessionist appeals and threats of armed resistance to the collection of revenue were taken off the table. The horizon of coalition-building strategies was extended in the aftermath of the war: a major political party could, for the first time in American history, forge a coalition that wholly excluded one significant geographic section of the Union. The second Republican party (the party of Lincoln), unlike its major party predecessors, could become a sectional party without risking a rupture in the Union.[82]

Standards of political danger were repatterned after the Civil War. Party opposition, once conceived as one of the principal dangers to the regular rhythms of the republic, could be redefined as a natural and ordinary process (as "party competition") once the potential for party violence had been stemmed. The transformed conditions of sovereignty enabled new ways of thinking about the role of parties in a democracy. With the peaceable transfer of power all but assured and with party leaders free to construct electoral

coalitions, uninhibited by the unionist preoccupations of the past, some social scientists and political leaders sought to redefine the status of parties,
presenting them as innocuous creatures that can and should compete in a
political "marketplace."

To be sure, new limitations emerged in the postbellum period that cir-
cumscribed the scope of party pluralism. Labor violence, agrarian "radicalism," and the spread of European ideas about class conflict introduced new
inhibitions that restructured the parameters of legitimate party opposition.
These governing anxieties shaped policy and institutional design and delimited the horizon of acceptable party coalitions in new ways. The historical
development of legitimate party opposition did not "end" at Appomattox; the
legitimacy of party opposition was not institutionalized once the central government cleared some threshold of coercive capacity. Rather, elite understandings of what kinds of party rivalries the republic could sustain were
shaped by the continued codevelopment of the central state's capacities and
the landscape of security threats that continued to evolve after the Civil War.
The Civil War nonetheless carries a significance unlike any other event in
American political history; no other single development (aside from the
framing of the Constitution itself) has had as pronounced an impact on the
emergence of party pluralism in the United States.

The pages that follow trace the lineage of legitimate party opposition
through the "long nineteenth century," reaching roughly from 1783 to World
War I. They examine successive iterations of a pattern in American history
where political leaders, ever mindful of the fragility of the institutional order, resorted to a practice of political evasion to prevent party rivalries from
escalating into civil conflict. Their efforts reinforced existing understandings
of the limits of party pluralism and ultimately, in the postbellum years, set
the stage for a significant reconceptualization of the role of party in American government.

Though the chapters do not follow a simple formula, they all aim to
achieve three key purposes: to describe the risks contemporaries associated
with partisan divisions; to present the strategies or remedies leaders advanced to contain the violence that parties threatened to unleash; and to
account for the impact of these remedies, both for the subsequent progress
of electoral and institutional politics and for the struggle to normalize party
politics. Existing studies that equate party development with democratic
progress have tended to downplay the risks that party rivalries posed to civil
order and the integrity of the Union. The chapters below emphasize some of

these governing challenges and elaborate on their generative potential: as I show, the potential violence of partisan rivalries motivated leaders to build new institutions and introduce new political practices. They also prompted leaders to police some forms of partisan discourse, prioritize others, and tether their aims to a political mainstream that they themselves contrived.

This book emphasizes the close relationship between governance and party legitimacy; it also places special emphasis on the thought and initiatives of political elites. These actors, whether they were presidents, party leaders, or other power brokers, often held positions of high responsibility and, in this capacity, were most inclined to call attention to the problems of governance (whether real or imagined) produced or exacerbated by party spirit and partisan activism. Elite actors, moreover, also played crucial decision-making roles that shaped institutions, built party coalitions, and advanced repressive measures—all strategies that played an outsized role in molding the contours of party pluralism. The present analysis is nonetheless limited insofar as it accords comparatively little space to the thought of everyday citizens and midlevel political actors or their efforts to negotiate the scope of party legitimacy in America. As important as the role of these actors may have been to the story of party legitimacy in America, considerations of space and the want of reliable survey research in the long nineteenth century makes it particularly difficult to examine their role in a sustained or systematic fashion.

Chapter 2 begins the analysis with a look at the efforts undertaken in the 1780s by the Framers of the U.S. Constitution to thwart the development of agrarian, debtor parties in the states. This chapter considers how the institutional devices built into the U.S. Constitution to frustrate agrarian activists may have limited the horizon of national party coalitions that could plausibly form before national parties (which emerged in the 1790s) even appeared on the American scene. Chapter 3 picks up on this proposition that party formation reflects, in important ways, the structure of the governing regime in which parties operate. It then examines how the first national parties—molded as they were by the new constitutional regime—were recast by the French Revolution and the larger transatlantic ideological struggle that ensued between republicanism and monarchism. The emphasis shifts from the socioeconomic conditions that stoked the contentious politics of the 1780s (the focus of Chapter 2) to the foreign policy dilemmas that defined the elite politics of the 1790s. The first generation of American statesmen, as we shall see, restrained their inclinations to choose sides in a world divided by the

French Revolutionary and Napoleonic Wars to prevent party conflict from escalating into a proxy war between the French and British on American soil.

Chapter 4 turns to the tension between slaveholding and nonslaveholding states that had been latent in American politics during the early national period. This division burst to the forefront of American political attention in 1819 over the extension of slavery into the Missouri Territory. The conventional wisdom among leaders at the time held that if the Missouri controversy did not provoke an immediate dissolution of the republic, then it would beget sectional parties that would surely hasten this result. Chapter 4 explores how party builders of the antebellum era sought to push the slavery question off the national political stage by constructing an alternative basis for partisan dispute. American democracy took its first significant step toward the legitimization of party opposition as political leaders cultivated new partisan attachments that they believed would reinforce the union of the states.

The Missouri Compromise settlement went a long way toward institutionalizing party competition in the United States. This settlement, however, unraveled in the 1850s, and hopes for a peaceful transfer of power in 1860 were dashed as eleven states seceded in protest of Abraham Lincoln's election. Chapter 5 explores how party leaders in the North sought to leverage party coalitions in support of the political and military effort to restore the Union. This chapter examines these efforts to tailor party coalitions to the exigencies of war in order to advance a broader proposition: that the capacities of the central state shape the coalition-building decisions made by political elites.

Chapter 6 and the Epilogue examine the long political and institutional shadow of the Civil War. They reflect on how the defeat of the Confederacy altered the political landscape of the republic and set the stage for a significant reconceptualization of the status and function of political parties. The problem of organized opposition was not solved by the outcome of the Civil War; the problem, instead, was redefined. An academic discipline—political science—emerged in the late nineteenth century, which set two-party competition as a normative default and posited a major party opponent as an institutional requirement. This new analytical persuasion marked alternative means of political dissent—through minor parties and ethnic and labor associations—as foreign and potentially subversive channels of contestation. Following the outbreak of World War I and the Bolshevik Revolution soon thereafter, the inclination to rationalize new limits for legitimate contestation using the language of the social sciences gained ground.

The historical developments described in this book provide some much-needed perspective on the significance and consequences of today's polarized political landscape. Too often, public figures exaggerate the significance of partisan differences and minimize the breadth of political consensus that permeates the politics of postbellum America. We casually use expressions like "party conflict," forgetting, as Sartori explains, that our "consensus on fundamentals provides the self-restraint that make [*sic*] conflict something *less than conflict*, as we endlessly if often too late rediscover whenever we are confronted with the reality of a people shooting at each other."[83] The pages that follow will, I hope, remind readers of the long history of Americans "shooting at each other" and explain the political developments that disarmed them.

CHAPTER 2

Economic Collapse and the Constitutional Construction of Party Politics

Most histories have to begin before the beginning.
—Alfred Chandler Jr., *The Visible Hand: The Managerial Revolution in American Business*

Elbridge Gerry was none too subtle in his diagnosis of the difficulties that brought delegates to Philadelphia in 1787: "The evils we experience flow from the excess of democracy." In Massachusetts, he continued, "it has been fully confirmed by experience that [the people] are daily misled into the most baneful measures and opinions by the false reports circulated by designing men. . . . He had he said been too republican heretofore: he was still however republican, but had been taught by experience the danger of the levilling spirit."[1] The "levilling spirit" was the bête noire of the Constitutional Convention. At this forum, Hamilton professed alarm at "the amazing violence & turbulence of the democratic spirit. When a great object of Govt. is pursued, which seizes the popular passions, they spread like wild fire, and become irresistable."[2] Hamilton, certainly no friend of democracy, was fairly convinced that the difficulties confronting the states grew from an imbalance of political power between the separate orders of society: "In every community where industry is encouraged, there will be a division of it into the few & the many. Hence separate interests will arise There will be debtors & Creditors &c. Give all power to the many, they will oppress the few. Give all power to the few they will oppress the many. Both therefore ought to have power, that each may defend itself agst. the other. To the want of this check we owe our paper money—instalment laws &c."[3] A well-ordered political process, Hamilton suggests, would accord countervailing power to "the few & the many" and prevent the politicization, not only of the terms of lending, but of the medium of exchange itself. The politicization of the money supply and (in Hamilton's view) the subversion of debtor-creditor relations were the immediate byproducts of the democratic energies that had been unleashed in the states.

State politics in the 1780s—where the "problem" of democracy was focused—was dominated by contention over monetary and fiscal policy: the states were rife with proposals to alter the nature and supply of money, modify the terms of private contracts between debtors and creditors, adjust the schedule and manner on which state and federal debt ought to be repaid, and rework the form and distribution of the tax burden. The energies produced by the "democracy" that Gerry deplored were not limited to Massachusetts. The political violence that these issues provoked was widespread, erupting in every region and nearly every state in the Confederation. This outbreak of violence was particularly unsettling for political elites at the time who knew that the states lacked the means to reliably enforce the law against a popular and determined political movement.

Chief among the Framers' tasks, as they saw it, was to create a regular political process, a "normal politics," that minimized popular mischief of this sort. Contention between debtors and creditors, to be sure, was not the only problem confronting the Framers. Indeed, the Constitutional Convention was "about" many things.[4] The political violence emanating from backcountry agrarians, however, was the delegates' most immediate and urgent concern.[5] In this first look at the development of legitimate party opposition in the United States, I examine the political conditions that prompted leading Americans in the 1780s to forge a new institutional order. The Founding charter made interstate, national parties possible, yet it also delimited the kinds of disputes that could be politicized within the realm of national political affairs. Troubled as they were by the violence of debtor factions that stirred in the states, the Framers all but abolished the class warfare they perceived at the state level by constructing a new fiscal regime at the center that would rely on indirect tariff revenues. By building a new fiscal order and constructing a series of institutional safeguards against contentious politics in the states, the Framers successfully thwarted the development of debtor parties and subordinated (for the time being) the class claims of an increasingly restless, democratic polity. Moreover, by altering the horizon of what kinds of parties could plausibly form, the Constitution shaped the future trajectory of party development before national parties even appeared on the American scene. The story of party development in the United States must, in this sense, "begin before the beginning."

Debt and Class in the 1780s

The American states emerged from the War for Independence in deep economic distress. The loss of British imperial subsidies, the interruptions of trade (from British blockades and harassment on the high seas by the Barbary pirates), the loss of population (as a result of casualties from battle, disease, the departure of loyalists, and the flight of slaves), and the sheer destruction wrought by the war itself all took their toll.[6] Onerous trade restrictions imposed by the British following the war as well as Spain's decision in 1784 to close the Mississippi to U.S. trade compounded the difficulties confronting the new republic. Precise figures are not available, but judging from existing evidence, two economic historians conclude that the war and the years thereafter were "truly disastrous."[7] According to one estimate, per capita gross national product dropped from $804 per capita to $437 from 1774 to 1790, a steep decline comparable in proportion to the economic collapse that took place during the Great Depression (from 1929 to 1933).[8] Taking this data in, one historian memorably observed that trying to understand the U.S. Constitution without an account of this "First Great Depression" is akin to writing a history of the New Deal without reference to the Great Depression.[9]

The scarcity of cash and credit was the most salient fact of economic life for those who experienced the postwar economic depression. Scarcity of this kind was a problem that was familiar to most Americans. In the wake of the Currency Act of 1764 (which prohibited the colonies from printing new paper money as legal tender) the money supply constricted dramatically as the existing supply was taxed out of circulation.[10] This act of Parliament made subsequent measures raising taxes on the colonies, such as the infamous Stamp Tax (which had to be paid in specie), particularly onerous. Historian Terry Bouton provides a compelling illustration of the severity of the money crisis in Pennsylvania in the 1780s: on the eve of the War for Independence, when many Americans were already complaining bitterly of the unavailability of cash and credit, there was $5.33 of paper money in circulation per person. Due to state policy and population growth, this figure shrank to $1.88 in 1786. By 1790, there was a meager $0.31 per person in circulation. Interest rates in Pennsylvania skyrocketed accordingly: from the usual 6 percent per year to between 5 and 12 percent *per month* during the first decade after the war.[11] These economic conditions led to an "epidemic of foreclosures" in Pennsylvania, where enough writs of foreclosure were documented in some counties to foreclose on nearly 70 percent of the taxable population; in several counties, the number of such writs exceeded the number of taxpayers.[12]

The available evidence is not altogether certain, but the "hard-money famine of the 1780s"[13] was likely caused by a commercial bubble: grossly overestimating domestic demand, American merchants in 1784 purchased vast quantities of European merchandise on credit. A net outflow of coin followed as merchants depleted their stocks to pay their debts just as exports to the West Indies were disrupted by British maritime restrictions. The hoarding of gold and silver and the decline of British military expenditures on American soil (with the end of the war) may have also contributed to the problem.[14]

Whatever the cause, the contraction of credit raised the stakes of policy addressing the management of the public debt. Much of the public debt, of course, was incurred by Congress and the states to finance the War for Independence. The Continental Congress and the states sold war bonds and other securities to soldiers, civilians, and foreign governments under the assumption that they would be paid back in full once the states were relieved of the burdens of British colonialism. By the conclusion of the war, however, the states found themselves saddled with a debt of extraordinary proportions. By the late 1780s, most of the states dedicated between 75 and 80 percent of their budgets to retire state debts and to pay congressional requisitions to service the federal debt.[15] Most of this debt was purchased by affluent merchants and speculators, often at a small fraction of its face value.[16] The burden of servicing this government debt was passed down to the people in the form of tax increases.

Direct taxes ("taxes on property and persons") rose precipitously, tripling in most states, and in some states more than quadrupling prewar levels.[17] The War of Independence, ostensibly waged to relieve the Americans of their colonial tax burden, led to a dramatic upsurge in tax obligations (owed to a "moneyed, aristocratic elite," no less). These state tax policies, taken together, represent a program of austerity that was truly extraordinary in scale.

Politics in the 1780s, consequently, featured a policy conflict between creditors and debtors *and* a parallel rift between creditors and taxpayers.[18] Many taxpayers deplored the perceived injustice of tax collectors pressing hard on yeoman farmers in order to pay speculators the face value for bonds they obtained at pennies on the dollar. One essayist writing in the *Newport* (Rhode Island) *Mercury* noted that the war debt had "been nearly all transferred to other hands for one quarter of its nominal sum, and the present possessors mean to have it, and will have it by taxing the yeomanry; if you cannot get the money, your [live]stock must go to [the auction] post."[19] Another writer, from western Massachusetts, bewildered by the upward redistribution of wealth, asked, "Must the substance of the people be sold at [auction] to redeem securities which did not cost the possessors one sixth part of the nominal value[?]"[20] The dearth of hard money amplified the burden on taxpayers and the hardship they endured was registered in the anti-bondholder sentiment that spread among yeoman farmers.[21]

Proposals for tax relief proliferated as a result. The four most common state legislative remedies were proposals to redeem bonds at their market price (rather than their face value), proposals to issue paper money, plans to allow taxes to be payable in paper (rather than gold and silver), and stay laws that would temporarily halt the collection of debts and taxes. In his study of legislative voting blocs during the Confederation era, Jackson Turner Main discovered a similar pattern of political alignment in every state: representatives of poorer, rural, inland districts, as a general rule, tended to favor debtors, the printing of paper money, and leniency on tax collection.[22] These legislators were also inclined to oppose congressional requisitions and the interests of the holders of public debt. Delegates representing more affluent commercial centers where professionals, merchants, and large property holders resided tended to take the opposing position on these issues.[23]

These policy differences, one should note, represented more than the opposition between legislative blocs: they mapped onto preexisting social and economic cleavages between yeoman farmers of modest birth and gentlemen, merchants, and lawyers who speculated in government debt, traded in commerce, and held large tracts of land.[24] This fault line reflected a distinctive preindustrial class schism: the division between yeoman farmers, on the one hand, and commercial, professional, and creditor classes, on the other, was qualitatively different from the class categories familiar to industrializing economies. Yeoman farmers were not members of a proletariat: they owned their own means of production. Yet they constituted a distinct social and economic class from the "gentlemen" who traded securities, speculated in land, and invested in commercial enterprises.[25] From the perspective of some of the most notable figures of the 1780s, the management of socioeconomic divisions in the states was the most immediate and urgent task confronting the American Union.[26]

Crowd Violence and Anti-Partisan Thought
in Post-Independence America

For Madison, the future of republicanism in America hinged on the capacity of government to straddle several critical social and economic fault lines. As he explained at the Federal Convention,

> According to Republican Theory, Right and power being both vested in the majority, are held to be synonimous. According to fact and experience, a minority may in an appeal to force, be an overmatch for the majority. 1. if the minority happen to include all such as possess the skill and habits of military life, & such as possess the great pecuniary resources, one third may conquer the remaining two thirds. 2. one third of those who participate in the choice of rulers may be rendered a majority by the accession of those whose poverty excludes them from a right of suffrage, and who for obvious reasons will be more likely to join the standard of sedition than that of the established Government. 3. where slavery exists, the republican Theory becomes still more fallacious.[27]

Let's pause, for a moment, to consider the implications of this statement. Madison makes the case here that respect for majority rule could not be taken for granted in a setting where the minority, if sufficiently motivated and powerful, could plausibly overturn the majority's will by force.[28] If the numerical minority did not possess sufficient resources on its own, it could mobilize the disenfranchised to this end. This problem was most troubling (from the perspective of political elites) for slaveholding states. For these states, authority sanctioned by "republican theory" was particularly vulnerable vis-à-vis embittered social groups (such as poor, indebted whites who resented the rule of planter elites) and nonslaveholding states that may have an axe to grind against slaveholding states. These groups and states could strategically leverage talk of emancipation in the event of a disputed electoral contest or a constitutional crisis.

Threatening foreign powers, as Madison knew all too well, would exercise less restraint. As a Virginian, he witnessed during the Revolutionary War years the unique risks that a deep political rupture between white elites presented in a slave society. When confronted with resistance in Virginia, Lord Dunmore, Virginia's last royal governor, hoped to silence the planter elite by issuing a decree offering freedom to slaves who would fight in the British army.[29] The impact Dunmore's decree had on the slaves in Dorchester County, Maryland, and on some disaffected whites "among the lower classes" alarmed local Maryland elites: "The insolence of the Negroes in this county is come to such a height, that we are under the necessity of disarming them which we affected on Saturday last. We took about eighty guns, some bayonets, swords, etc. The malicious and imprudent speeches of some among the lower classes of whites have induced them to believe that their freedom depended on the success of the King's troops. We cannot therefore be too vigilant nor too rigorous with those who promote and encourage this disposition in our slaves."[30] British general Henry Clinton expanded on Lord Dunmore's proclamation, promising freedom to those who joined the British and threatening to sell those who joined the patriots back into slavery. As historian Douglas Egerton surmised, "The combined proclamations of Dunmore and Clinton told the slaves that the possibility of freedom existed, especially when whites were split."[31] In this circumstance, political divisions between whites (in this case, between American patriots and British rulers) threatened to unleash a deeply subversive form of violence embedded in society's social and economic structure. Mindful that majority rule was most vulnerable where the disenfranchised and enslaved were numerous and the coercive capacities of the states were limited, political and social elites sought additional precautions against violence "from below."

Madison's broader purpose to prevent the tyranny of majority faction may be interpreted in light of this source of instability. According to the textbook interpretation of *Federalist* number 10, the constitutional blueprint masterfully balances republican, majoritarian forms with safeguards for minority rights.[32] Yet when we consider his ideas in light of the social tensions and inequalities that prevailed at the time, Madison's aim to protect minority rights appears in a little different: he hoped to balance majoritarian forms with safeguards for minority rights in no small part for fear of what an injured minority might choose to do should it refuse to accept the majority's decision. Indeed, Madison hoped to prevent legislative majorities from advancing injurious measures that might, in turn, provoke an aggrieved minority to go to extreme lengths (i.e., mobilizing the disenfranchised or threatening to offer freedom to the enslaved) in search of redress. In this way, safeguards designed to defend the interests of numerical minorities would serve as a prophylaxis for political violence and thereby provide long-term security for the republican principle of majority rule.

Social and political elites took the threat of political violence very seriously during the Confederation era, and it was in this institutional milieu that they issued their most urgent pleas for unity and their most dire warnings against faction, party, and other manifestations of organized opposition. The gentry of the 1780s took great precautions against the effects of partisanship and factionalism not only because these sentiments were incompatible with republican notions of political virtue, but also because leading statesmen of the time harbored a well-justified fear of the disorder such sentiments could provoke.

Manifestations of an increasingly restless and democratic spirit were everywhere, prompted in part by the War for Independence itself. The war, as Gordon Wood argues, transformed the status expectations of the people, as ordinary Americans grew ever more reluctant to defer to the leadership of their better-educated, patrician countrymen.[33] Concurring with this assessment, Alan Taylor observes that "the Revolution did not cease in 1783"; rather, the agrarian conflict characteristic of this moment in history "represented a new, internal, and attenuated stage in the continuing American Revolution, as yeomen and gentlemen . . . came to blows over the nature of property, the local diffusion or central consolidation of power, and the legitimacy of extralegal crowd violence in the new Republic."[34]

Just as riots over land disputes defined the contentious politics of the pre-Revolutionary generation, crowd violence highlighting conflict between debtors and creditors, and between taxpayers and tax collectors, defined the political landscape of post-Independence America.[35] To be sure, not all crowd violence was hostile to established authority. Some outbursts of extralegal violence, particularly those that enforced the law when government officials could not, were condoned by social and political elites.[36] Elite support for extralegal mob violence nonetheless underscored the tenuous condition of government authority in eighteenth-century America. In his influential essay comparing eighteenth-century American mobs with crowd violence in France and Britain, Gordon Wood makes the case that political violence posed a credible challenge to the states' coercive capacities: "What particularly seems to set mob violence in the [American] colonies apart from the popular disturbances in England and France is not so much the character of the mob, the purposeful and limited nature of its goals, its consideration for human life, or even the felt intensity of its grievances; rather it is the almost total absence of resistance by the constituted authorities. . . . If the institutions of law and order were weak in eighteenth-century England and France, in America they were unusually ineffectual."[37] State governments either unwilling or unable to resist the extralegal actions of the crowd submitted instead to popular demands. Wood argues that Shays' Rebellion, where an armed mob was forcefully resisted by government authorities, was an anomaly. This leads him to the ironic conclusion that the weakness of local, state, and Confederation governments prevented the incidence of more serious violence in the American states: as he explains, it was "the very weakness of the constituted authorities, their susceptibility to popular intimidation of various kinds, or, in other words, the very democratic character of legislative politics in the 1780s, rather than any particular self-restraint or temperance in the people, that prevented the eruption of more serious violence during the Confederation period."[38]

The contentious political action that did take place targeted state officials responsible for collecting unpaid taxes, courthouses where debt suits were adjudicated, and state legislatures where laws governing bankruptcy, tax collections, and the supply of money, were made. Crowds rushed the courthouse in Charles County, Maryland, in June 1786 demanding a suspension of suits brought against debtors and insisting that the court remain closed until the Maryland Assembly issued paper money; groups of farmers in other counties threatened state officials responsible for seizing the property of citizens who did not or could not pay their taxes in full.[39] Resistance to tax collection and agitation against the courts was particularly widespread in South Carolina. According to Judge Aedanus Burke, if the legislature allowed creditors to sue debtors, not even "5,000 troops the best in America or Europe could enforce obedience to the Common Pleas."[40] South Carolina governor William Moultrie in 1785 made a plea for additional measures to relieve the debt burden faced by farmers and planters throughout the state: "such has become the situation between creditor and debtor that the fate which awaits the latter, if allowed to take place, will fall little short of ruin. It is not particular. It has become general. It is not confined to one or two families, but exists throughout the state, . . . your courts being insulted, your laws set at defiance, and civil processes confined to a small part of the State. These are melancholy truths."[41] The South Carolina Commons House proclaimed that a new installment law was necessary "for the purpose of preserving Peace and Tranquility in the Country and of avoiding confusion and disorder."[42] Similar protests took place in eight other states. As Roger Brown explains in *Redeeming the Republic*, in nine of the thirteen states, efforts to collect taxes in hard money were met with popular resistance.[43] The four states that did not impose onerous hard money taxes or take a hard line on uncollected taxes were, by contrast, more tranquil and relatively free of violence.[44] Crowd violence was, above all, an institutional problem shaped by the willingness and capacities of states to exercise their limited tools of fiscal surveillance and coercion.

This institutional problem triggered cultural anxieties. The social gentry were, in their temperament and outlook, quite fearful of political crowds. If social elites were wary of crowds, it was for a want of an effective system of crowd control. Such apprehensions were not unreasonable. Left to their own devices, many of the states lacked the means to reliably enforce the law against a popular and determined political movement. If numerous contingents of the Massachusetts state militia (widely regarded at the time to be the best organized among the thirteen states) failed to muster in the face of an agrarian insurrection, then political order in any of the states could be overturned.[45] Perhaps reflecting his aristocratic sensibilities, Tocqueville observed nearly a half-century later that "one must not shut one's eyes to the fact that unlimited freedom of association for political ends is, of all forms of liberty, the last that a nation can sustain. While it may not actually lead it into anarchy, it does constantly bring it to the verge thereof. But this form of freedom, howsoever dangerous, does provide guarantees in one direction; in countries where associations are free, secret societies are unknown."[46] Tocqueville's further qualification, that "there are factions in America but no conspirators," would have been cold comfort for the American gentry of the late eighteenth century, who knew well enough that there were both factions *and* conspirators in America.

Factions were commonly portrayed in the late eighteenth century as malicious, conspiratorial collectives, that conceived plans to advance their private ends contrary to the common good. Faction, according to the authors of the *Federalist*, was "violent," a "disease."[47] Political organization "out of doors" was spontaneous, uncontrolled, and subordinated individual reason to the passions of society.[48] Not only was it unbecoming of gentlemen to participate in such unruly forms of political action; participation of this sort was, in most cases, subversive and threatening to civil peace. As one writer noted in the *New Jersey Gazette*, political parties were "the dangerous diseases of civil freedom; they are only the first stage of anarchy, clothed in mild language."[49] Elites often compared partisanship to physical maladies (e.g., "disease," "contagion," "cancer") that would spread if left untreated. The gentry of the late eighteenth century located faction and parties on a continuum with other unlawful, unpredictable, and potentially violent forms of collective political expression, such as riots, insurrections, mobs, vigilante groups, and private militias.[50]

To keep the political elite's disdain for party in perspective, it is important to remember that statesmen at the time lacked a usable model of loyal and republican party opposition. History had provided the Founders with examples of parties that were strident, dogmatic, and unyielding, as well as parties that introduced corruption and monarchical influence into the legislature; yet there was no precedent for parties that were temperate and respectful of constitutional limits. The political parties extant at the time, most notably the Constitutionalists and Republicans of Pennsylvania, only reinforced contemporaries' antipartisan prejudices. As Madison appraised Pennsylvania politics, the most he could say of the councils of government is that they were "violently heated and distracted by the rage of party."[51]

Gordon Wood, for his part, situates the gentry's aversion to group politics in the context of an ongoing transformation of American society. As he catalogues in *The Radicalism of the American Revolution*, the hierarchical ties that structured society in colonial America began to fray in the mid to late eighteenth century. The independence movement prompted a revolution of rising expectations among all classes of society and a corresponding decline of public deference to the gentry. This social revolution, as Wood describes it, raised questions about how to safely lodge political control in "the people."[52] One solution was to confide power in elected legislative assemblies directed by a natural aristocracy of talent and merit.[53] Faction, party, and other vehicles for popular politics, however, posed a challenge to merit and virtue; it was widely assumed that the charismatic and demagogic were more likely to rise in party ranks than the virtuous. The governing elite of the fledgling republic hoped that a society once governed by the vertical bonds of monarchical authority might peaceably transition to one predicated on consent and legal authority. As Wood observes, "American society would have to be tied together in new ways."[54] Gentlemen, in this rendering of the problem, feared that parties and political societies (such as the Democratic-Republican societies) would tie men together through factional or partisan organizational bonds rather than through the more staid and predictable lines of formal legal authority.

The gentry's antipathy for informal political organization was deeply influenced by the social and ideological developments described by Hofstadter, Wood, and others, but it was also symptomatic of an underlying institutional problem: political organizations were threatening to social and political order because they could not be easily controlled by state authorities. Faction and party were suspect categories, not merely because they introduced passion and self-interest into the public sphere, but also, and perhaps more important, because they threatened to subvert the law and disturb the enjoyment of what Federalists would call "public tranquility" and "domestic peace." Indeed, for political elites of the 1780s, party politics *was* contentious politics.

This problem prompted political and economic elites to seek an institutional remedy to defuse the political contention in the states and address the want of coercion in the center. The Federalist effort, aptly called a "revolution in favor of government," resembled in important respects a counter-revolutionary reaction to the fierce brand of democratic politics unleashed by the War.[55] As I explain below, the institutional remedies established by Federalists in the late 1780s shaped the contours of what would become the first national opposition party, the Jeffersonian Republican party—a party that resisted, in the 1790s, the new Constitution's consolidation of authority.[56]

The Constitutional Remedy and the Genesis of Parties in the "American Mold"

Union was a means before it was an end. Federalists (nationalists who wanted to replace the Articles of Confederation with a charter that created a stronger central government) hoped that the Constitution would establish a governing process where faction and parties would be more manageable in their temper and proportions. A stronger bond between the several states would provide the most efficient means of "guard[ing] the internal tranquility of States" from the disturbances of factional and partisan initiatives brought by the lower orders of society.[57] Yet the capacity of the state governments to manage contentious politics within their borders was frustrated by two other species of conflict.

The first was conflict among the states themselves and concerned the terms of the Articles of Confederation. As it stood in 1783, the Union was a collection of sovereign nation-states brought together by a common struggle for independence and held together only through the careful maintenance of a sectional balance between the southern, middle, and eastern states. The Articles' well-known deficiencies were themselves a byproduct of this delicate balance, reflecting the states' deep-seated reluctance to relinquish sovereignty to a distant Congress representing thirteen socially and economically diverse jurisdictions. The Articles were, at best, a template for the coordination of fully sovereign states. Its well-known want of coercion—its "imbecility," as Hamilton would have it—meant that the states could not, under its auspices, service or retire the national debt, provide for the common defense, enforce the terms of the peace treaty with Great Britain or, for that matter, the terms of the Articles itself. The states, as a result, confronted a variation of the prisoners' dilemma where each state stood to gain more for its constituents by pursuing policies adverse to the collective good.[58]

The states' capacity to effectively contain and defuse political and economic tensions in American society was further frustrated by the strategic position of the American states within the wider international arena of nation-states.[59] Independence raised a host of new security challenges which the states, for the first time, had to address on their own. Hostile Native American tribes, eager to defend their ancestral lands against the encroachments of American settlers, bordered the states to the west; Spain controlled territory, including the Mississippi, to the southwest; Great Britain, which remained unrivaled on the eastern frontier—the Atlantic, continued to hold sway to the north and northwest.

There are numerous ways in which tensions between the American states and foreign adversaries complicated the fraught condition of governance within each of the states. The Confederation, for example, was unable to reliably make payments on the war debt in part because the states could not coordinate to establish a uniform schedule of import duties. Rhode Island and New York had, on separate occasions (in 1781 and 1783, respectively), thwarted Congress's efforts to put such a system in place. The debt crisis was all the more confounding as a result. Indeed, a functional tariff system would have mitigated the burden of debt borne by taxpayers in the states and assuaged tensions between agrarians and socio-economic elites.

The interconnectedness of these three orders of conflict (i.e., between the states, between the American states and foreign powers, and within the states) is equally evident in the failure of Congress to enforce the terms of the peace treaty with the British. Debtor relief measures, such as those passed by the South Carolina state legislature, violated article 4 of the Treaty of 1783, which stipulated that British creditors, when collecting private prewar debts, should meet "no lawful impediment to the recovery of the full value in sterling money, of all bona fide debts here to fore contracted."[60] Several of the states also violated the peace treaty by refusing to compensate loyalists for confiscated and destroyed property (agrarians, in particular, strongly opposed compensation for loyalists).

The British responded in kind by refusing to abandon nine posts in the Northwest and severely restricting American trade in the West Indies. Both forms of retaliation had a pronounced impact on the fledgling American economy: some of the states had hoped to reduce their war debt through the sale of western land. This territory, however, was insecure so long as the British maintained an ongoing political and military presence in the region. Restrictions on American trade had an even more immediate effect insofar as they limited access to markets for American foodstuffs and supplies. These restrictions frustrated the efforts of yeoman farmers to scratch out a frontier subsistence, making the increased tax burden of the 1780s harder to bear.

The U.S. Constitution has been rightly heralded as a means to address a constellation of policy problems at once. First and foremost, it authorized the federal government and the states to come to the assistance of fellow states threatened by an agrarian or slave insurrection. As Hamilton noted in *Federalist* number 21, without a mutual guarantee of the states governments, "A successful faction may erect a tyranny on the ruins of order and law, while no succor could constitutionally be afforded by the Union to the friends and supporters of the government. The tempestuous situation from which Massachusetts has scarcely emerged evinces that dangers of this kind are not merely speculative."[61] In a similar vein, Nathaniel Gorham, a delegate to the convention from Massachusetts, raised the prospect that political parties might take up arms in pursuit of their causes and that, without the authority to come to the aid of states in distress, the general government would be forced to "remain an inactive witness of its own destruction. With regard to different parties in a State; as long as they confine their disputes to words they will be harmless to the Genl. Govt. & to each other. If they appeal to the sword it will then be necessary for the Genl. Govt., however difficult it may be to decide on the merits of their contest, to interpose & put an end to it."[62] The Republican guarantee clause, as it came to be known, was included in

Article 4, Section 4, to grant the federal government the authority to "interpose," should the occasion require.

Other mechanisms were designed to prevent the occasion from arising in the first place. As Madison memorably argued in *Federalist* number 10, majority faction might be prevented from coalescing in a republic that encompasses an extended territorial sphere. "Extend the sphere and you take in a greater variety of parties and interests; you make it less probable that a majority of the whole will have a common motive to invade the rights of other citizens; or if such a common motive exists, it will be more difficult for all who feel it to discover their own strength and to act in unison with each other."[63] The ability of popular majorities to coalesce, Madison proposed, may be frustrated by the extent of America's territorial reach.[64]

Though the Constitution limits the capacity of organized groups to wield power in government, it does *not* confine all factional and partisan movements equally. Though Madison's argument is formulated in general terms, it is hard to escape the conclusion that the Framers had a fairly specific kind of majority faction in mind when they crafted the Founding charter. Several provisions of the Constitution explicitly prohibit state legislatures from wielding the policy weapons most preferred by indebted agrarians. Article 1, Section 10 specifies, "No State shall . . . coin money; emit Bills of Credit; make any Thing but gold and silver Coin a Tender in Payment of Debts." This section also prohibits states from passing ex post facto laws and impairing the obligations of contract. Article 1, Section 8 confers on Congress powers to coin money and regulate its value, to adopt uniform standards governing bankruptcies, and to provide for the collection of revenues. These provisions, as historian Terry Bouton reminds us, were not "throw-ins." James Wilson, for one, insisted that if the Constitution consisted of a single line banning state issuance of paper money, "I think it would be worth our adoption." Benjamin Rush averred that if the Constitution "held forth no other Advantages than a future exemption from paper money & tender laws, it would be eno' to recommend it to honest men."[65]

Following the ratification of the new charter, states could no longer print money or interfere, *post facto*, in the terms of private lending. Taken together, these provisions shifted the locus of fiscal and monetary policy to the center, placing these policy arenas out of reach of agrarian insurgents agitating in each of the American states. Though the causes of faction, in Madison's words, are "sown in the nature of man," factional rivalries—particularly those prompted by agrarian resistance to tax and debt collections—would be less likely to form in the first place if authority governing monetary policy and debtor-creditor relations was shifted from the state governments to the federal government. Indeed, the extended territorial sphere of the republic, when coupled with Article 1's centralization of powers governing fiscal and monetary policy, provided a durable safeguard against the political demands of debtor factions.[66] This, at any rate, was the conclusion drawn by Madison: "The influence of factious leaders may kindle a flame within their particular States but will be unable to spread a general conflagration through the other States. . . . A rage for paper money, for an abolition of debts, for an equal division of property, or for any other improper or wicked project, will be less apt to pervade the whole body of the Union than a particular member of it."[67] Oliver Wendell Holmes was famously mistaken when he proclaimed that "a constitution is not intended to embody a particular economic theory, whether of paternalism and the organic relation of the citizen to the State or of *laissez faire*."[68] On the contrary, the Founding charter took exception to a specific kind of partisan and factional conflict; in so doing, it laid the groundwork for the institutionalization of a distinct political-economic vision.

The Constitution's impact on party development was largely indirect: it makes no mention of parties (or factions for that matter); it does not formally recognize them, prohibit them, encourage or discourage them in any way. The Framers did not intend to design a party system for the new republic; theirs was, as Hofstadter aptly put it, a "Constitution against parties."[69] Yet by constructing a new, national electoral and governing framework, the Constitution set in motion a party system in a distinct "American mold."[70]

The Electoral College and the separation of powers are the institutional formations that most directly impacted patterns of party contention in the United States. Indeed, the requirement that a presidential candidate must secure an electoral vote majority to avoid a decision by the House of Representatives encouraged the formation of majority party coalitions and promoted the two-party pattern familiar to American politics.[71] To be sure, the two-party system was an unintended consequence. In fact, the adoption of the Electoral College system was a contrivance embraced to minimize the influence of faction and political parties. The chief alternatives for selecting the president considered at the Constitutional Convention (appointment by Congress and direct election of the people) were both rejected in part because these procedures would give rise to legislative or popular cabals that would exert undue influence in the selection process.[72]

The decision to create a special assembly—an Electoral College—for the sole purpose of selecting a president, was taken as a third way of sorts that might limit the influence of undesirable political combinations. The rule that bound this assembly, requiring a majority rather than a mere plurality of Electoral College votes to select the president, created a strong incentive for presidential candidates to build majority party coalitions. The crisis of legitimacy that occasioned the four-way election of 1824 proved to be the final straw that prompted political leaders to publicly coordinate the nominations process before the election.[73] As we shall see in Chapter 4, the national convention system for the nomination of presidential candidates represents an adjustment to the realities of the Electoral College. Thanks in no small part to the influence of the Electoral College, a multiparty system was not to be.

Unified, "responsible" party government was equally improbable. In their effort to thwart majoritarian rule, the Framers fragmented the electoral and legislative processes.[74] "Responsible" Westminster-style party government is simply untenable in a bicameral presidential system that diffuses legislative power and responsibility. Though the idea of responsible party government would come into fashion in the discipline of American political science, the prospects for such a system of governance were effectively undermined by the Framers' hostility to the alleged corruption of the eighteenth-century British Crown and Parliament.

It is difficult to overstate the impact of the Electoral College, bicameralism, and the separation of powers on the future of party politics in the United States. These innovations, nonetheless, do not tell the whole story of the Constitution's impact on party development. Most important for our purposes, they do not illuminate how the Constitution settled, at least for the time being, the great political economic dispute that gave rise to the convention in the first place. Nor do they illuminate how this settlement, in turn, prefigured the policy divisions that would constitute the first party system.

The Founding Bailout: Remaking the Fiscal Basis of the American Republic

The new constitutional charter reframed the debate over fiscal and monetary policy, granting lawmakers an opportunity to build a new fiscal state that diffused the cost of government and provided much-needed tax relief to yeoman farmers. As I explain below, the fiscal regime forged by Hamilton and

his supporters at once softened class contention over matters of public finance and sharpened divisions over what Aldrich has called the "great principle": "how strong and active the new federal government was to be."[75] With
Madison and Jefferson leading the charge for distributive justice, the great
question of how to distribute powers between the federal and state governments had been shorn of the class significance that made the matter so ex-
plosive in the 1780s.

The implementation of a uniform tariff policy was the prerequisite of the
new fiscal regime and one of the least controversial provisions in the new
Constitution.[76] Twelve of the states had supported an impost on two separate occasions under the Articles of Confederation yet, as mentioned earlier,
its passage was blocked by Rhode Island and New York. The importance of
the tariff cannot be overstated. Hamilton articulated its economic and administrative advantages best. Experience has shown, he argued, that direct
taxes (poll taxes and taxes on land) were both difficult to administer and politically toxic. As Gouverneur Morris argued at the convention, "For a long
time the people of America will not have money to pay direct taxes. Seize
and sell their effects and you push them into Revolts."[77] Hamilton explained
in *Federalist* number 12 that "it is impracticable to raise any very considerable sums by direct taxation"; "the pockets of the farmers . . . will reluctantly
yield but scanty supplies in the unwelcome shape of impositions on their
houses and lands." Given the rudimentary modes of fiscal surveillance that
were available at the time, he concluded that "personal property is too precarious and invisible a fund to be laid hold of."[78] Direct taxes simply were
not a reliable means to fund a free government that spans a great territorial
space.

Indirect taxes, by contrast, could be collected more efficiently—so long
as the states formed a more durable bond. "If . . . there be but one government pervading all the States, there will be, as to the principal part of our
commerce, but ONE SIDE to guard—the Atlantic coast." Only "a few armed
vessels" and an "ordinary degree of vigilance" would be necessary to enforce
the law. What is more, the United States could demand higher duties of its
trading partners. Ports, Hamilton explained, would not have to compete
with one another by lowering tariffs to attract trade. Thus, government could
be both limited and effective if the states together could rely on the collection of indirect taxes as its principal source of revenue. Morris underscored
this point at the convention in Philadelphia: "Let it not be said that direct
taxation is to be proportioned to representation. It is idle to suppose that the

Genl Govt. can stretch its hand directly into the pockets of the people scattered over so vast a Country. They can only do it through the medium of exports imports & excises."[79]

The political advantages of the tariff were no less significant. The tariff was supported so enthusiastically during the Confederation period because it would have allowed Congress (under the Articles of Confederation) to dodge the question of slavery. As Robin Einhorn explains, other kinds of taxes, such as taxes on population or property of various kinds, require some rule of apportionment. Public debate addressing the apportionment of direct taxes across the states required Congress to determine who ought to count under a rule governing the enumeration of population and property. Direct taxes, in other words, could not be apportioned without a prior settlement of another politically intractable question: whether African slaves should be counted as human (and hence, population) or as property, or both. Imposts or tariffs, by contrast, are not apportioned and required no such decision about the meaning of humanity and property.[80]

The development of a uniform tariff policy made the fiscal consolidation of the republic (through the assumption and funding of the war debt) possible. With a reliable source of revenue available through import duties collected in American ports, the federal government could afford to take on the sizable debt incurred by the Continental Congress and the states in the late war. In 1790, $18 million of debt was transferred from the states to the federal government's balance sheet.[81] Once consolidated, Hamilton made plans to turn this debt from an economic liability to an institutional asset. Hamilton's Treasury Department proposed and Congress agreed to fund the debt by making regular interest payments without hastily retiring the principal.[82]

This debt-management strategy achieved two crucial state-building aims: first, the program of making regular payments on a sizeable war debt helped to build the long-term creditworthiness of the federal government. Second, the perpetuation of government debt fostered the birth of a capital market on U.S. soil—a strategic asset that could prove invaluable to the federal government during a fiscal emergency. As it happens, both of these aims were supported by the charter of the Bank of the United States. Designed by Hamilton to help the federal government make timely interest payments on the debt, the bank was, perhaps, the most controversial institution of the new fiscal regime.[83] For Hamilton and other nationalists, however, it was worth the political price. Indeed, it served as a critical lender of last resort to a fledgling federal government desperately in need of improving its credit standing in capital markets at home and abroad.[84]

The treasury secretary's plan to assume the debts owed by the states was politically advantageous for several reasons. First, the plan committed the creditor class to the solvency of the federal government. With the Treasury Department making regular payments on the war debt but leaving the lion's share of the principal intact, creditors possessed an ongoing interest in ensuring that the federal government meet its obligations over the long term. The notion that a national debt might serve an institutional function had informed Hamilton's thinking for some time. As he famously explained to Robert Morris in April 1781, "A national debt if it is not excessive will be to us a national blessing; it will be a powerful cement of our union."[85]

Second, assumption of state debts relieved taxpayers of the onerous burden of direct state taxes, and in so doing might over time assuage backcountry opposition to the new governing regime. As John Rutledge insisted at the convention in Philadelphia, the assumption of the state debts by the general government was just, necessary, and politic: "The assumption would be just as the State debts were contracted in the common defence. It was necessary, as the taxes on imports the only sure source of revenue were to be given up to the Union. It was politic, as by disburdening the people of the State debts it would conciliate them to the plan."[86] No longer obliged to make requisition payments to Congress or to make payments on the debt overhang from the war, the states reduced taxes precipitously. Direct taxes in all the states were cut sharply, almost without exception. When examined in absolute terms, direct taxes levied in the northern and middle states declined markedly in 1789 and 1790 as states anticipated support from the new federal government (Figure 1). When examined on a per capita basis, average annual tax levies in the northern and middle states declined from $0.66 during the period from 1785 to 1788, to $0.09 from 1792 to 1795.[87]

Among the southern states, property tax rates were cut across the board, taxes on slaves were dramatically reduced, and poll taxes were cut in every state except South Carolina (see Table 1). This momentous decline in direct state taxes was made possible by a uniform federal tariff. As Edling and Kaplanoff find, thanks to the federal tariff, these reductions in state taxes were not offset by heavy internal federal taxes. Rather, revenue from the federal tariff made up the difference.[88]

When viewed in conjunction with the new division of powers between the states and the federal government, Hamilton's fiscal regime weakened

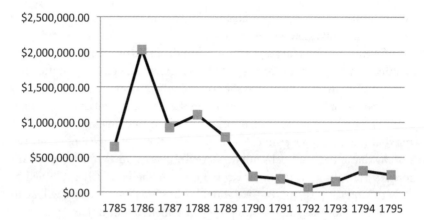

Figure 1. Direct taxes levied in the northern and middle states, 1785–95 (Massachusetts, New Hampshire, Rhode Island, Connecticut, New York, New Jersey, Pennsylvania, and Delaware). From Max Edling and Mark Kaplanoff, "Alexander Hamilton's Fiscal Reform: Transforming the Structure of Taxation in the Early Republic," *William and Mary Quarterly* 61 (2004): 730.

Table 1. Average Annual Tax Rates in the South, 1785–88 and 1792–95

| | 1785–88 | | | 1792–95 | | |
	Property Tax	Slave Tax	Poll Tax	Property Tax	Slave Tax	Poll Tax
Maryland	0.32% of value		$0.50			
Virginia	1.90% of value	$2.36	$1.67	0.25% of value	$0.28	
North Carolina	$0.78/100 acres		$2.30	$0.08/100 acres		$0.25
South Carolina	1.00% of value	$2.00	$2.00	$0.50% of value	$0.75	$2.00
Georgia	1.25% of value	$1.07	$1.07	$0.37% of value	$0.47	$0.47

Source: Max Edling and Mark Kaplanoff, "Alexander Hamilton's Fiscal Reform: Transforming the Structure of Taxation in the Early Republic," *William and Mary Quarterly* 61 (2004): 733.

the will and undermined the capacity of backcountry agrarians to organize in support of redistributive measures in the states. First, his plan provided desperately needed tax relief to yeoman farmers without imposing losses on creditors. The tax relief made possible by the federal assumption of war debts softened what appeared to many to be a zero-sum class conflict between taxpayers and creditors.[89] Second, Article 1, Section 10 shifted the locus of decision-making power over contentious questions of monetary policy, fiscal policy, debtor-creditor contracts, and bankruptcy to the center, where the policy process was better insulated from agrarian resistance. These crucial areas of policy were, for all intents and purposes, placed geographically out of reach of backcountry agrarians. Third, the ability of the most ardent advocates of "levelling" policies to influence federal lawmakers was frustrated by the new system of national representation. Influential debtor and tax "reliefer" factions formed in most of the states during the Confederation period; yet these interests found after 1789 that they could not coalesce at the national level for precisely the reasons spelled out by Madison in *Federalist* number 10.[90] The new system of national representation imposed a logistically onerous burden of interstate coalition building on those who hoped to project power in the national capital.

Consequently, the opposition that emerged to the Washington administration was qualitatively different from the debt and tax relief factions that agitated in the states. The Jeffersonian Republicans represented a coalition of interests that brought debtor interests together with others who were not of the same mind on these important matters. To put it bluntly, the Jeffersonian Republican party was not a debtor party.[91] Rather, it began as a collection of leaders who challenged the Washington administration's economic and foreign policies, not to promote economic justice between the different orders of society, but instead to enforce a textualist fidelity to the Constitution, preserve the prerogatives of state elites, and ensure a measure of distributive fairness between the geographic sections of the Union—the southern, middle, and eastern states. Congressional debates addressing a plan to discriminate between original and secondary holders of debt certificates as well as the Treasury Department's proposal to charter a national bank illustrate the new lines of political division that formed in the early 1790s.

Madison took many contemporaries by surprise when he sponsored a plan in the House that prioritized the interests of those who were original holders of debt certificates. He proposed to offer the present holders of debt the highest market prices attained by their securities at some date to be determined, with the difference between those prices and the face value of the securities to be refunded to the original holders.[92] Justice had not been done to the original holders of American debt: the original holders, he argued, had alienated their certificates for a fraction of their face value because the states and the general government were redeeming these certificates, not in gold and silver, but in depreciated paper.[93] For Madison, the principle was simple: "A debt was fairly contracted; according to justice and good faith, it ought to have been paid in gold or silver; a piece of paper only was substituted. Was this paper equal in value to gold or silver? No. It was worth . . . no more than one-eighth or one-seventh of that value. Was this paper freely accepted? No. The Government offered that or nothing. The relation of the individual to the Government, and the circumstances of the offer, rendered the acceptance a forced, not a free one. The same degree of constraint would vitiate a transaction between man and man before any Court of Equity on the face of the earth."[94]

Instead of giving the windfall of the redeemed value exclusively to present possessors, Madison's proposal would divide the full face value of each debt certificate among original and present holders. In this way, American taxpayers would do justice to those citizens who offered financial support to the patriots without providing undue reward for speculators who purchased debt instruments from the original holders at pennies on the dollar.

Several points are noteworthy about the terms of opposition in this debate. First, the spokesperson for distributive justice in this dispute, James Madison, had been as firm an opponent of paper money and debt relief measures as there was.[95] Second, Madison's proposal to reallocate the full face value of the outstanding debt was not very radical: it was not a plan to repudiate a portion of the debt; nor did he propose to monetize the debt through the adjustment of the money supply (as many agrarians demanded).[96] His proposal favored a more equitable economic balance, not so much between the different orders of society, but between the sections of the Union. It was widely understood after all that the majority of those who speculated in government debt resided in the North.

This proposal in favor of distributive justice, as modest as it was, nonetheless had little hope for success in the new national legislature. Indeed, the legislative deck was stacked against Madison's proposal. His proposed amendment to Hamilton's funding and assumption plan was defeated thirty-six to thirteen.[97] Support for his proposal, as limited as it was, was drawn almost exclusively from the South.[98]

Opposition to the bank bill similarly avoided questions of distributive justice between the several orders of society. As with most other matters of political economy taken up in the 1790s, the case of the bank framed such matters in terms of the constitutional division of powers between the states and the general government and the balance of political power between the southern, middle, and eastern states. Madison led the opposition's critique of the claim that Congress possessed the constitutional authority to charter a national bank.[99] Others, such as James Jackson of Georgia and Michael Jenifer Stone of Maryland, took pains to point out that the benefits of the measure would be distributed unevenly between the geographic sections of the Union: Jackson noted that "the 'general welfare' are the two words that are to involve and justify the assumption of every power. But what is this general welfare? It is the welfare of Philadelphia, New York, and Boston; for as to the States of Georgia and New Hampshire, they may as well be out of the Union for any advantages they will receive from the institution."[100] Stone observed, "It is a fact that the greatest part of the Continental debt has travelled eastward of the Potomac. This law is to raise the value of the Continental paper. Here, then, is the strong impulse of immediate interest in favor of the Bank."[101]

The voices of agrarian insurgents who formerly agitated for debt relief in the states were (to the extent that they were heard at all in Congress) drowned out by a more temperate Jeffersonian Republican outlook. Indeed, one might go so far as to say that the Jeffersonian persuasion was itself a reflection of a new institutional reality.[102] The Jeffersonian, as Alan Taylor explains, was a new political type. Unlike the backcountry yeomanry who greeted tax collectors with "rough music," closed courthouses, and threatened state legislatures, Jeffersonian politicians were less adversarial figures who tended to believe in the natural harmony of interests.[103] Their consensual disposition was a sunny antidote to the hostile oppositions that defined the politics of the 1780s. As Taylor perceptively observes, "Both Federalists and agrarians saw conflict at the center of political life; driven by innate human corruption, rulers and the ruled struggled to encroach on the other's sphere, rulers to enslave the people, the ruled to plunder their betters. Equally suspicious of human nature, agrarians and Federalists believed the worst about the other. Backcountry folk felt they defended republican liberty against encroachment by unscrupulous aristocrats, and Federalists insisted that they protected ordered liberty from the anarchy of licentious mobs."[104] The new fiscal basis of the republic redrew the lines of debate, positioning a new political type in opposition. With Jeffersonian Republicans standing in dissent, political economic questions were reframed as matters of federalism and fidelity to the constitutional settlement.

To be sure, questions of public finance continued to be contentious. Yet it is worth noting that the most significant agrarian protest of the 1790s, the so-called Whiskey Rebellion, was triggered by a directly coercive excise tax on spirits.[105] One cannot say for certain, but backcountry resistance might well have been more pronounced and widespread had direct taxes been higher—as they surely would have been if the United States did not alter the terms of its fiscal union.

Conclusion

The first party system was an unintended consequence of the constitutional settlement. Indeed, the Framers were so consumed with the challenge of balancing different kinds of divisions between the states (small versus large, southern versus eastern, etc.) that they did not contemplate the possibility of *national* partisan allegiances—sympathies that would group Americans first and foremost according to philosophical ideas and policy interests rather than state loyalties. Political leaders in the 1780s were first and foremost partisans of their own states.[106] There simply was no experience with parties or factions that reached across states. A new national government was attractive, in part, because the prospect that national parties would dominate its operations seemed so improbable.

The Constitution, however, achieved the improbable and made national parties a reality. With the advantage of hindsight, the development of national parties should not seem so surprising. The Constitution delegated significant new powers concerning foreign affairs, public finance, and national defense to the federal government. This centralization of powers led to disputes concerning their use. Put simply, parties organized nationally to contest new national and international issues.

The Constitution nonetheless constructed a governing and electoral habitat that was hostile to programmatic, revolutionary, or "great" parties. Though the Framers did not anticipate a national politics governed by parties, the parties that ultimately governed corresponded closely to the preferences expressed by Madison and others for a politics that emphasized consensus building and incremental change. The imprint of the Framers' thought is thus preserved in an institutional formation—a party system—that they did not intend to create.

Given the weakness of constituted authority and the potential violence of agrarian resistance during the Confederation period, political elites were pressed to build new institutions to neutralize (so far as possible) the deep socioeconomic fault lines that roiled the states in the 1780s. In important respects, the Constitution represents a victory for the Federalists and for their conception of the proper ordering of the political landscape. The new charter hemmed in the scope of partisan dispute by shifting the venue of the most divisive questions of the time to the center. Once relocated, new fiscal institutions were built that, for the time being, assuaged existing class divisions by making positive-sum solutions possible.

Yet new institution building raised new questions and sources of contention. The Federalist victory, in other words, was incomplete. Federalists hoped to put to rest several fundamental sources of conflict. Their achievement, as much as it softened the socioeconomic conflict that bedeviled the states in the 1780s, sharpened new sources of dispute and projected them onto a national stage.

CHAPTER 3

The French Revolutionary Wars and the Ordeal of America's First Party System

> Parties seem to have taken a very well defined form in
> this quarter. The old tories, joined by our merchants
> who trade on British capital, paper dealers, and the idle
> rich of the great commercial towns, are with the kings.
> All other descriptions with the French. The [French
> Revolutionary] war has kindled and brought forward the
> two parties with an ardour which our interests merely,
> could never excite.
> —Thomas Jefferson, letter to James Monroe,
> 4 June 1793

The institutions and events that prompted the creation of America's first two national parties—the Jeffersonian Republicans and the Hamiltonian Federalists—differed markedly from the issues that dominated political debate in the 1780s. In the 1780s, debt, taxes, and monetary policy embittered relations between agrarians and socioeconomic elites in the states. During this period "the central issue," as one economic historian explains, "had been whether the heavy specie taxes levied by the states for themselves and Congress could be paid by the rural classes."[1] This political-economic conundrum was settled (at least for the time being) both by constitutional measures to divest the states of power over monetary policy and tax collection, and also by the fiscal and monetary arrangements spearheaded by Hamilton's Treasury Department. Hamilton's policy innovations had the dual advantage of remunerating creditors and commercial interests in the middle and eastern states, and, at the very same time, bringing much-needed relief to taxpayers and Americans of more modest means. The new fiscal regime, featuring a consolidated debt, a uniform tariff, and a Bank of the United States, created positive-sum solutions to what many at the time took to be a zero-sum conflict between taxpayers and creditors. These institutional interventions, taken together with the economic prosperity that began in 1789, made taxation a "non-issue."[2]

With the tax question largely defused for many Americans, political divisions in the 1790s grew on new political turf. The following discussion shifts gears accordingly. The preceding chapter focused our attention on the socioeconomic and institutional conditions that sparked a contentious brand of politics "from below" and the measures taken by elites to contain the threat of political violence. The present chapter also examines elite efforts to contain popular political divisions but directs our attention to the international political developments that roused and divided the American public in the 1790s. From 1793 to 1815, the United States would be almost continuously at war or on the brink of war with two foreign powers (Great Britain and France) that were at war with each other.[3] Foreign war introduced a distinctive partisan cleavage into the American political scene—one based on mutual suspicion of national disloyalty. Jeffersonian Republicans accused Washington and later Adams of supporting a policy of neutrality that favored the British and betrayed the spirit of '76. Federalists maintained that the opposition, intoxicated by their Francophilia, would go to any length to stir anarchy for the advancement of their revolutionary cause, or for their own political aggrandizement. The opposition between Federalists and Republicans constituted a party system that was qualitatively distinct from all others that succeeded it: it was unique in American history because it pitted in opposition two parties that each aspired "to end all parties."[4]

Foreign war polarized Americans in a new way. Fiscal policy was quite contentious in the 1790s, but it was recast by the larger transatlantic ideological struggle between republicanism and monarchism. Constitutional measures, such as those that both moderated socioeconomic divisions in the states and triggered new national oppositions, defined the political agenda of the 1790s. I will discuss below how the political landscape was further defined by a new set of concerns that emerged following the outbreak of war in Europe. Taken together, the divisive question of class as such was at once assuaged by constitutional means and later subsumed by stark recriminations over ideological commitments to republican equality and the French revolutionary cause. Stated in different terms, the contentious divisions of the 1780s were reframed by the cumulative impact of new institutional forms and by the emerging global struggle between republicanism and monarchism.

As many scholars have observed, the 1790s stand out in American history for the intensity of ideological fervor and the rhetorical violence of contending partisans.[5] It is crucial to remember, however, that the rhetorical violence of the early national period took place in an institutional context where the means of coercion remained (despite the consolidation of fiscal and monetary policy) radically decentered. This institutional context raised the stakes of political division and militated against the normalization of party opposition in this period. In this fraught political climate, political leaders—quite understandably—doubted the viability of a "system" of party competition where two national parties might alternate in power and peaceably respect the results of the electoral process.

The high stakes of this period induced, at least in some party leaders, a measure of political restraint.[6] This is most evident in elite efforts to sidestep the most divisive question of the day—the question of war and peace with the European powers. Statesmen grew apprehensive as the French Revolutionary and Napoleonic Wars raged in Europe, fearing that party opposition would produce a proxy war between the old European powers in the new American republic.

Mindful of the fragility of the young republic, political leaders from both parties resorted to a pattern of political evasion to keep polarized party conflict from escalating into a secessionist crisis or civil war. Some key figures, to be sure, wanted to meet the great foreign policy question head-on. This posture, however, was fraught with risk. Hamiltonian "High" Federalists pressed for an open, declared war with France in the late 1790s; Jeffersonian Republicans agitated for war with Britain in the early 1810s. As we shall see, both ran the risk of fracturing the republic beyond repair.

These exceptions notwithstanding, most members of the Founding generation did what they could to settle, neutralize, or minimize matters touching the foreign affairs of the new republic. They struggled, nonetheless, to define an enforceable policy of neutrality and to avoid choosing sides in a world divided by war between the great European powers. Those who hoped to avoid a decisive showdown between Francophile and Anglophile partisans were frustrated at every turn by the limited capacity of the central state to preserve American neutrality when the people themselves were anything but neutral.

The overriding aim to prioritize civil peace is evident in measures leaders took to define a workable policy of neutrality; it is also evident in the steps taken by key officials to peacefully resolve the electoral crisis of 1800. Following a tense standoff between party leaders, power was transferred from the Federalists to the Republicans, largely without incident. This was quite an achievement for a young republic; Hofstadter and others rightfully identify the conclusion of this election as a landmark moment in the development of American democracy. The fortuitous outcome of the election of 1800, however, was not foreordained. Indeed, party leaders prepared for a fight. Federalist leaders did not rely on or expect their political opponents to exercise restraint. That a civil commotion was avoided is a testament to the efforts of a small group of Federalists who had more at stake than their counterparts—they feared for the security of their small states should the Union collapse—and were thus willing to accept the lesser of two evils.

It's important to note, however, that the peaceful resolution to the standoff did not give rise to a more sanguine vision of the role that opposition parties might play in the young republic. With the American Union still caught in the ongoing feud between two superpowers and a federal government that could not control its territory without the assistance of the states, the enforcement of federal law and the integrity of the American Union were vulnerable to the machinations of party opposition. The notion of a party "system" with parties peaceably alternating in power was foreign to statesmen and thinkers in this political and institutional context. A party system might have been possible at this time with more temperate parties or with a more compact and integrated regime, but these were not the cards that the first generation of American statesmen had been dealt.

Neutrality and the First Party System

It is no coincidence that the duration of the French Revolutionary Wars very closely approximated that of America's first party system.[7] Foreign controversies, however, were not the first order of business for the First Congress, convened in 1789. At the head of the agenda instead were matters of public finance (i.e., debating the assumption and funding of the debt), taxation (i.e., arranging a uniform tariff schedule), and the contents of a new Bill of Rights. The first national opposition party in the United States, the Jeffersonian Republican party, began to take shape as opinion in Congress and in Washington's cabinet divided over the new fiscal regime proposed by Treasury Secretary Hamilton. Hamilton's proposal to charter a national bank, as well as his plan for the funding and assumption of state debts mobilized legislators in Congress who saw Hamilton's central state-building objectives as an attempt to replicate British institutions on American soil.[8]

The outbreak of revolution in France introduced a new dimension to these inchoate party formations. News of revolution in France was initially heralded with great fanfare in the United States. The optimism of the moment resonated at the highest levels of government: for President Washington, "The revolution which has been effected in France is of so wonderful a nature that the mind can hardly realise the fact."[9] Some, like Hamilton, were more cautious than others about the prospects for French liberty. As he wrote to the Marquis de Lafayette, "I have seen with a mixture of Pleasure and apprehension the Progress of the events which have lately taken Place in your Country. As a friend to mankind and to liberty I rejoice in the efforts which you are making to establish it while I fear much for the final success of the attempts, for the fate of those I esteem who are engaged in it, and for the danger in case of success of innovations greater than will consist with the real felicity of your Nation."[10] Support for the abstract aims of republican government seemed harmless enough, so long as France's unsteady republican experiment was contained on another continent.[11]

French ideas about government, philosophy, and the rights of man, however, did not stay where they were, and the unanimity of public support in America did not last long. For the Federalists, French ideas spread like a contagion to American soil and infected the minds of Republican sympathizers.[12] Republicans, for their part, were delirious in their enthusiasm for the fall of the old regime and the advance of republicanism in Europe.

The American public began to polarize as revolution gave way to terror and war. The shift in public sentiments against France, particularly within Federalist circles, was spurred by news of the execution of Louis XVI and the French declaration of war on 1 February 1793 against Great Britain, Holland, and Spain. France's declaration of war challenged Americans to choose between the lucrative trade relations with Britain and the ever-spreading republican revolution in France. This cleavage only reinforced the divisions already established by domestic differences over public finance. As Jefferson

observed, the French Revolution "kindled and brought forward the two parties with an ardour which our own interest merely, could never excite."[13]
These partisan divisions, to be sure, were already delimited by the new constitutional regime. The Constitution shaped the horizon of coalitional possibilities for the party that would form in opposition to the Washington
administration. Indeed, the Jeffersonian party in opposition did not advance
a pro-debtor agenda or embrace the monetary prescriptions of agrarian radicals. Partisan disputes instead focused on trade policy, the distribution of
fiscal burdens among the states, and the division of powers between the federal government and the states.

The political division referenced by Jefferson, however, was novel in its
structure: it represented a truly national schism insofar as it assumed new
interstate partisan allegiances. American political differences were organized
in an unprecedented way and this new pattern of division was reflected in
the structure of the first political parties. The Republican and Federalist
parties were not, at first, confederations of like-minded state parties. Rather,
these parties organized in the national legislature first to contest the use of
power by the general government; once organized to shape policies that
were truly national in scope, they spread outward to the state legislatures
and to the electorate at large.[14]

As war broke out in Europe, leading political figures were nearly
unanimous in the view that the United States remain neutral. Preserving
American neutrality, however, was no simple task. As Alexander DeConde
observes, "Americans as individuals were not neutral; American neutrality was a precarious thing."[15]

Fortunately for the Washington administration, there was no dispute
within the cabinet over the basic question of war and peace: all agreed that
the United States must stay out of the war. Debate hinged, instead, on what
terms of neutrality the United States should assume. This was a weighty matter;
indeed, there was little agreement about what would constitute a strictly
neutral trade and maritime policy. A neutrality that appeared too advantageous to one of the feuding powers, moreover, could be construed as a cause
of war for the other.

To a certain extent, however, the United States was already committed.
Two treaties were signed on 6 February 1778, which bound the nation to
"perpetual friendship and alliance" with France. The Treaty of Amity and
Commerce granted the United States formal recognition and most-favored-
nation trading privileges and also permitted the French fleet to enter

American ports with their prizes of war. The Treaty of Alliance included a promise that France would help fight for American independence, a promise that neither nation could forge a peace treaty without the other's consent, and a guarantee that each nation would guard each other's possessions.[16]

Hamilton advised Washington that these treaties would have to be temporarily suspended to forge a neutrality that would not lead to war with Britain. Hamilton was concerned, in particular, with the provision of the Treaty of Amity and Commerce that permitted each country to bring prizes of war into each other's ports and excluded either nation's enemy from the same privileges. Hamilton insisted that this provision, if enforced, would almost certainly provoke war with Britain. Jefferson, who served at the time as secretary of state, maintained that failure to enforce such provisions would violate the French alliance and possibly provoke war with France.[17] The suspension of the alliance and the insult this would deliver was unnecessary in Jefferson's view since decisions about the interpretation of the treaty could be postponed until France asked the United States to implement its guarantees (if France should choose to make such a request at all).[18] Rejecting the alliance outright would not only be a great insult to the French; it could also provoke retaliation. As Jefferson observed, "An injured friend is the bitterest of foes."[19]

Washington agreed with Jefferson that suspending the French alliance would be unnecessary. The president, however, agreed with Hamilton that a formal declaration of America's position should be issued. Diplomatic historian Alexander DeConde observes that Republicans wanted the government to assume a formal status of neutrality while still providing material support for France. A strict neutrality, they maintained, would violate America's existing treaties with France.[20]

The political leadership was clearly divided, but the debate within the cabinet and Congress was nevertheless limited to the terms of neutrality and the constitutional question of whether or not the executive branch possessed the authority to withdraw from a treaty without consulting the national legislature. The contending arguments in this dispute were made most forcefully (and famously) in the spirited exchange between Hamilton and Madison, under the pseudonyms of Pacificus and Helvidius, respectively.[21]

Debate, however, was not so neatly confined within the circles of the political elite. Washington's Proclamation of Neutrality, issued on 22 April 1793, was sharply criticized as a "British neutrality" that abdicated America's obligations to France. According to Hamilton, the partisan presses began "to groan with invective against the Chief Magistrate of the Union."[22] The attacks leveled at the president, the treasury secretary insisted, were carried out by a "party engaged in a dangerous conspiracy against the tranquility and happiness of their country" who are aware that "their hostile aims against the Government can never succeed til they have subverted the confidence of the people in its present Chief Magistrate."[23] The barrage of criticism leveled at Washington's alleged British neutrality was especially distressing for executive officials because they knew that popular action in support of one of the belligerents could in fact undermine the administration's policy of neutrality and destabilize a delicate peace. Issuing instructions to the secretary of state, Washington held that "War having actually commenced between France and Great Britain, it behoves the Government of this Country to use every means in its power to prevent the citizens thereof from embroiling us with either of those powers, by endeavoring to maintain a strict neutrality."[24]

Preserving neutral conduct among the American people proved to be a task that exceeded the capacities of the young, federal government. The crisis of governing authority that emerged with the arrival of Edmond Genêt in the spring of 1793 is an apt illustration of the dangers, both real and imagined, of foreign influence in such an institutional setting. At a time when the Washington administration was trying to maintain a delicate neutrality between Britain and France, the new minister from revolutionary France organized operations to outfit French privateers in American ports and encouraged American citizens to participate in offensive naval actions against the British. Genêt set up prize courts on American soil to condemn captured British goods and drew up an ambitious set of plans to rouse Americans to attack Spanish and British installations in Florida, Louisiana, and Canada.[25]

Genêt's influence also extended to the south and west. Revolutionary War hero George Rodgers Clark accepted a general's commission in the French army from Genêt and led expeditions against the Spanish territories of Florida and Louisiana. Clark was able to assemble a rogue army, recruiting significant support from frontiersmen and French sympathizers in Kentucky, South Carolina, and Georgia.[26] When asked by the Washington administration to help bring Clark's forces under control, the Republican governor of Kentucky Isaac Shelby refused to commit the Kentucky militia outside of the state, claiming that he possessed the authority only to prevent citizens from supporting Clark's army within the state of Kentucky.[27]

The Genêt affair is often remembered for the disrespect and contempt the French minister directed toward Washington and his administration. Yet what is most significant about this familiar story is the way in which Genêt exploited the weaknesses of the federal government and roused political opposition in the process. With a limited navy, the federal government could not, without great effort, hope to effectively regulate armed vessels in American ports. Furthermore, with a federal army of insignificant size and strength, the Washington administration could not enforce other aspects of America's neutrality without the assistance of the states. Genêt was therefore an uncontrolled force inside American borders, popularizing the French cause as well as the opposition Republican party's cause, all while brazenly challenging federal authority.[28] The "Terrorism" felt by the vice president[29] and most likely other administration officials as well was symptomatic of the fragility of the federal government itself.

Washington's aversion to party drew on the operations of political clubs that organized in this period. Indeed, for Washington, the French foreign minister was the father of a mischievous set of offspring: the Democratic-Republican societies.[30] The formation of these political clubs—most of which were Jeffersonian in orientation—appeared throughout the country "as if by magic from one end of the continent to the other."[31] What was magic to Genêt was a scourge to Washington:

> for can any thing be more absurd—more arrogant—or more
> pernicious to the peace of Society, than for self created bodies,
> forming themselves into *permanent* Censors, & under the shade of
> Night in a conclave, resolving that acts of Congress which have
> undergone the most deliberate, & solemn discussion by the Repre-
> sentatives of the people, chosen for the express purpose, & bringing
> with them from the different parts of the Union the sense of their
> Constituents—endeavoring as far as the nature of the thing will
> admit, to form *their will* into Laws for the government of the whole;
> I say, under these circumstances, for a self created, *permanent* body,
> (for no one denies the right of the people to meet occasionally, to
> petition for, to remonstrate against, any Act of the Legislature) to
> declare that *this act* is unconstitutional—and *that act* is pregnant of
> mischief, & that all who vote contrary to their dogmas are actuated

by selfish motives, or under foreign influence; nay are pronounced traitors to their Country—is such a stretch of arrogant presumption as is not to be reconciled with laudable motives.[32]

In Washington's critique of the Democratic-Republican societies, we find his deep suspicion of political organization per se, whether formed as parties or not. For Washington, the Democratic-Republican societies posed a challenge to formally constituted political authority because these clubs were not just meeting "occasionally," but were assuming for themselves an ongoing, permanent existence (indeed, they adopted names for themselves—e.g., the German Republican Society, the Democratic Society of Philadelphia, the Republican Society of South Carolina). Washington pejoratively labeled them "self created bodies" to indicate that they did not spring from the consent of all citizens. They therefore promulgated a will that reflected neither that of an individual citizen nor that of formally constituted authority. Because these groups were constituted without the consent of the polity as a whole, they could form spontaneously—"as if by magic"—anywhere in society. Through their independent actions, they could also tip the balance of American neutrality.

Washington's resistance to parties and other forms of organized opposition was also based on the conviction, whether justified or not, that such organizations could open American government to foreign influence. Washington, for example, referenced the tension between sovereignty and partisanship in his Farewell Address when he observed that the spirit of party "opens the door to foreign influence and corruption, which find a facilitated access to the government itself through the channels of party passions. Thus the policy and the will of one country, are subjected to the policy and will of another."[33] For political elites in this period, partisan division constituted an internal vulnerability that foreign powers could exploit to weaken American political resolve and sway U.S. policy.

Washington crafted his policy of neutrality to insulate American politics from the vicissitudes of European affairs. Yet the domestic conflict that war in Europe provoked could not be so easily curbed. Indeed, American neutrality was becoming increasingly difficult for the administration to maintain as British depredations on American ships continued in the Caribbean and British forces provoked native American tribes to attack U.S. possessions in the Northwest.[34]

Washington endorsed the Jay Treaty, albeit with misgivings, to avert war with America's former colonial masters. The treaty required the repayment of American debts to British creditors (much of it held by southerners). The treaty did not address southern "losses" due to the confiscation of slaves, valued at about $10 million. The United States additionally forfeited the right to impose discriminatory tariffs or tonnage duties on British goods or ships for ten years. Trade discrimination was the centerpiece of the Republican opposition's economic program to rid the United States of the burden of British domination; the Jay Treaty placed this strategy off limits for a decade.[35]

For Republicans, opposition to the treaty was a patriotic imperative. Francophiles understood that the Jay Treaty would shatter their hopes of gaining federal support for the French revolutionary cause. The partisan rage that the treaty elicited was unprecedented in early American history.[36] Effigies of "Sir John Jay" were burned in Philadelphia, New York, and Boston. In Virginia, men toasted to "A speedy death to General Washington."[37]

Relations between the United States and France deteriorated in the wake of the Jay Treaty. The French government viewed the ratification of the treaty as a signal of a decisive departure by the American government—both in letter and in spirit—from the commitments of the French alliance. A naval "Quasi War" ensued as the French retaliated for what they perceived to be a violation of America's treaty commitments. The embittered French government issued a decree on 2 March 1797 abandoning the "free ship, free goods" provision of the Treaty of Amity and Commerce of 1778 and announcing that any American ship not carrying a list of crew and passengers in proper order (*role d'équipage*) would be considered lawful prize.[38]

Aware of the domestic implications of a full-scale war, President John Adams went to great lengths to mend relations with France. Just like Washington before him, the second president doggedly pressed for neutrality to contain the political divisions that war would exacerbate. Adams's first effort to sue for peace with France resulted in the infamous XYZ Affair, where French officials (whose names were replaced in publicized documents with X, Y, and Z for the purpose of confidentiality) demanded bribes and tribute before negotiations could commence. The diplomatic scandal unleashed a torrent of anti-French fury and precipitated a season of nationalist spectacle.

The Alien and Sedition Acts—all passed in June and July 1798—were several of the most significant legislative byproducts of the Francophobic political climate that grew in the wake of this diplomatic scandal. These measures aimed to regulate Republican partisanship by restricting the naturalization of Irish and French immigrants (who disproportionately supported the Republican opposition) and shielding the government (i.e., Federalist elected officials) from criticism.[39]

In addition to these measures to curtail political opposition, Federalists in Congress passed legislation to build a substantial standing army, both to repel a French invasion and to suppress domestic insurrection. In May 1798, Adams signed into law an act that authorized the mobilization of a ten-thousand-man "provisional army." In July 1798, Congress passed and the president signed the New Army Act, which authorized the organization of twelve regiments of infantry and six troops of dragoons, amounting to over twelve thousand regulars.[40]

Referring to a subsequent act that authorized the expansion of existing forces, Federalist Theodore Sedgwick wrote on 18 February 1799, "No act of Congress has ever struck the Jacobins with more horror; and I believe they have at last thought of force against the government as a possible event."[41] As Hamilton calculated,

In times like the present, not a moment ought to have been lost to secure the Government so powerful an auxiliary. Whenever the experiment shall be made to subdue a *refractory* & powerful *State* by Militia, the event will shame the advocates of their suffi-ciency. . . . When a clever force has been collected let them be drawn towards Virginia for which there is an obvious pretext—& then let measures be taken to act upon the laws & put Virginia to the Test of resistance. This plan will give time for the fervour of the moment to subside, for reason to resume the reins, and by dividing its enemies will enable the Government to triumph with ease.[42]

Republicans meanwhile were preoccupied with the creation of the stand-ing army, the tax increases required to fund the army, and the prospect that America's growing military power would be used for domestic purposes. Opposition to these initiatives was widespread. After January 1799, petitions began to arrive in Congress en masse urging the repeal of the Alien and Se-dition Acts, the disbanding of the army, and the repeal of the internal taxes passed to fund Hamilton's statist initiatives. Eighteen thousand signatures came from Pennsylvania alone (only around twenty thousand had voted in Pennsylvania in 1796).[43]

Republican resistance to the Alien and Sedition Acts—most memorably articulated in the Virginia and Kentucky Resolutions—set the stage for a political and constitutional crisis, which, for some Hamiltonian High Federalists, warranted the threat of federal coercion not unlike that which prevailed in western Pennsylvania during the Whiskey Rebellion.[44] But the present circumstance was different. With strong resistance in several states—not several counties—confrontation presented the risk of civil war. The Virginia state legislature, in fact, began to prepare for civil conflict by passing provisions to build an arsenal at Harpers Ferry, organize the militia, stockpile arms, and raise new revenue.[45]

Adams took several measures to short-circuit Hamilton's designs and avert a potentially violent showdown. The schism forming within the Federalist party—most visibly represented by the divide between Adams and Hamilton—was articulated institutionally over the struggle to define the nature, size, and leadership of the new military forces formed during the war crisis. Adams was a firm believer in naval power. As he proclaimed to the Boston Marine Society in 1798, "Floating Batteries and Wooden Walls have been my favorite System of Warfare and Defense . . . for three and twenty years."[46] Congress and the president invested heavily in a significant expansion of U.S. naval power in the spring and summer of 1798: three frigates were finished, harbors were fortified, and the acquisition of twelve sloops and fifteen other ships were authorized.[47] Most notably, a Navy Department was established to manage America's new fleet.[48] Benjamin Stoddert of Maryland was chosen to serve as its first secretary.

Naval defense was the most promising alternative to the expansion of the army. Adams explained to the Massachusetts Republican Elbridge Gerry "that he thought Hamilton and a Party were endeavoring to get an army on foot to give Hamilton the command of it & then to proclaim a Regal Government, place Hamilton at the Head of it & prepare the way for a Province of Great Britain."[49] Seven years after leaving the presidency, Adams would comment: "I have always cried, Ships! Ships! Hamilton's hobby horse was Troops! Troops! With all the vanity and timidity of Cicero, all the debauchery of Marc Anthony and all the ambition of Julius Caesar, his object was the command of fifty thousand men. My object was the defense of my country, and that alone, which I knew could be affected only by a navy."[50] Adams strongly supported the expansion of American naval power, confident that this was the only means to protect commerce from both France and England and to end America's strategic dependence on the British navy. Naval power was particularly desirable, however, because it could not be used against domestic rivals. Reflecting on Federalist hopes to provoke war with

France, Adams wrote in 1809 that such provocations would have set a train of developments in motion:

> Hamilton would have continued as the head of the army—continual provocations and irritations would have taken place between the two nations, till one or the other would have declared war. In the meantime it was my opinion then, and has been ever since, that the two parties in the United States would have broken out into a civil war; a majority of all the States to the southward of Hudson River, united with nearly half New England, would have raised an army under Aaron Burr; a majority of New England might have raised another army under Hamilton—Burr would have beat Hamilton to pieces, and what would have followed next let the prophets foretell.[51]

Adams rightly believed that war with France would mean Hamiltonian military leadership at home; it also might have led to civil war. To avoid these outcomes, Adams betrayed many of his Federalist supporters and undermined his own hopes of reelection by appointing a new commission in February 1799 to negotiate with the French. The Adams Federalists then passed legislation to demobilize the New Army.[52]

Historian Joseph Charles described Adams's pursuit of peace as an "act of political suicide" because it opened a deep schism in the Federalist ranks just before the election of 1800.[53] It was, at a minimum, a testament to the well-justified belief that open conflict with France would provide the most ardent Federalists (led by Hamilton) with a pretext to crush the Republican opposition and embroil the new republic in a domestic conflagration.[54] It was also a demonstration of how some risk-averse statesmen, mindful of the fragile union of the American states, were strongly inclined to shape public debate by avoiding polarizing issues or by neutralizing divisive questions altogether (as Adams did in this case). Indeed, thanks to his decision to send a new mission to France, Adams all but assured that the election of 1800 would not be a referendum on war with France.

The Election of 1800 and the Uncertain Transfer of Power

Margaret Bayard Smith, in attendance at Thomas Jefferson's presidential inauguration, could not help but comment on the example set by the outcome

of the election of 1800: "I have this morning witnessed one of the most interesting scenes, a free people can ever witness. The changes in administration,
which in every government and in every age have most generally been
epochs of confusion, villainy and bloodshed, in this our happy country
take place without any species of distraction, or disorder."[55] Many scholars
have echoed Margaret Bayard Smith's sentiment.[56] The presidential elections of 1792 and 1796 did not produce any noteworthy electoral precedents.
George Washington was reelected in 1792, running unopposed; in 1796, the
presidency stayed within the Federalist fold, elevating Vice President Adams to the highest office while his partisan opponent, Thomas Jefferson, assumed the vice presidency. The election of 1800, however, was different. For
many, it was a landmark event—the first peaceful transfer of power from
one party to another in Western political history. This outcome, however,
was neither foreordained nor expected by contemporaries. Partisan recriminations were too severe and the Union too fragile to expect that a confident
party would passively submit to an unfavorable outcome. Some Federalists
doubted that there would be an election at all, with allegations abounding
that the Republicans would affect a military takeover or a secessionist crisis
before the election could take place; Republicans, for their part, spread ru-
mors that the Federalists would pass legislation making Adams president
for life.[57] The election of 1800, moreover, was the first to take place after
George Washington's death in 1799. Washington's voice, even in retirement,
was a privileged and much-needed source of balance and moderation.[58]

The campaign featured a heated war of words where Jefferson was memorably portrayed as "an *Atheist* in Religion and a *Fanatic* in politics"[59] and
Adams was castigated as a monarchist determined to make the United States
a satellite of Great Britain.[60] For Federalists, the edifice of national strength
they had meticulously constructed would be fatally undermined by a Jefferson victory. Republicans treated the event as one of the few remaining opportunities to restore the republican promise of 1776. The high stakes of this
election reverberated before members of the Electoral College were selected.
The states were rife with proposals to alter the rules for the selection process
in their own states before this process commenced. Most notorious was
Hamilton's appeal to Governor John Jay of New York.[61] The newly elected
New York state legislature would be dominated by Republicans and was expected to select Republican electors; Hamilton implored Jay to call a special
session of the old legislature to change the method of selection to a popular

vote. Jay did not reply. Hamilton was not alone; prominent Republicans also made the case for immediate electoral reform in Virginia, North Carolina, Kentucky, and Tennessee.[62]

The vote of the Electoral College produced a tie between Jefferson and Aaron Burr, the Republican candidates for president and vice president, respectively. Each received seventy-three electoral votes; Adams received sixty-five, and Charles Coatesworth Pinckney of South Carolina received sixty-four. The system of presidential selection, as it was originally designed in the Constitution (and before it was altered by the Twelfth Amendment in 1804), did not permit electors to distinguish between their votes for president and vice president. According to the process set out by the Framers, the candidate who received the greatest number of electoral votes would become president and the runner-up would be designated vice president. In the event that two candidates received an equal number of electoral votes, the decision to select the next president would fall to the House of Representatives, with representatives voting not as individual members, but as state delegations with each state casting one vote. It was assumed that Aaron Burr—the candidate supported by Republicans for vice president—would cede his position to Jefferson, but he did nothing of the sort. The decision was therefore left to the House, where Republicans dominated eight of the sixteen state delegations, Federalists dominated six, and two states were evenly split. The House would vote as states, and a majority of the states (at least nine) was required to select a winner. This meant, in effect, that some Federalist cooperation was required to place Jefferson in the presidency. Federalists in Congress were therefore presented with a unique opportunity to interfere with the Republicans' succession. If a legislative deadlock ensued and a president was not selected by 4 March 1801 (the last day of Adams's administration), the rule of succession would take effect. This scenario would put the presidency in the hands of a president pro tempore selected by the Senate.[63] The Federalists held a majority in the Senate, so the president pro tempore would almost certainly be a Federalist. The election of the Senate president pro-tempore was one option available to the Federalists; they might also pass legislation designating a Federalist officeholder as an interim executive until the House came to a decision.[64]

The most likely scenario that would deny Jefferson the presidency, however, was the prospect that Federalists might strike a deal with Burr and place Burr in the highest office in the land. Federalists seriously considered a plan of this sort. Hamilton sought to feign support for Burr to pressure Jefferson to make a variety of policy commitments.[65] Other Federalists did not pretend, pushing a plan to persuade Republicans to support Burr, even offering a cabinet position to Maryland Republican congressman Samuel Smith if he would switch his support to Burr.[66]

Republicans viewed any outcome that did not place Jefferson in the presidency as a usurpation. Should such a scenario come to pass, Republican representative Joseph Nicholson declared that "Virginia would instantly proclaim herself out of the Union."[67] Jefferson saw it fit "to declare openly & firmly, one & all, that the day such an act passed [to appoint an officer other than Jefferson] the middle states would arm, & that no such usurpation even for a single day should be submitted to."[68] Republican and Federalist leaders appeared to be engaged in a kind of tactical radicalism, signaling that grave consequences would follow if Jefferson was not elevated to the highest office. Republican leaders hoped to shape the decision making of Federalist legislators who were empowered to decide the contest, and Republican leaders did so by seeding doubt in the minds of their opponents about the consequences of an improper outcome (one in which Jefferson was not installed as president). This kind of maneuvering, one must remember, was possible only in an institutional context in which extraordinary consequences—e.g., secession, civil war—were plausible. For some, including the president's eldest son, the question was not so much whether secession was possible, but whether it was possible that the union of the states would survive the party struggle. As he explained to his younger brother Thomas, "the ultimate necessary consequence, if not the ultimate object of both the extreme parties which divide us, will be a dissolution of the Union and a civil war."[69]

The often hyperbolic prognostications of political elites were not all talk: preparations were taken for a confrontation. Pennsylvania's governor Thomas McKean promised to organize as many as twenty-two thousand militia to secure the highest office for Jefferson.[70] After receiving word that a contingent of federal soldiers were camped near the arsenal in New London, Virginia, James Monroe (then serving as Virginia's governor) dispatched militia to prevent federal troops from seizing the muskets, munitions, and artillery stored at this location.[71] Federalists, for their part, did not discount their opponents' will to achieve their ends by force. Indeed, Hamilton insisted in a letter to Rufus King, before the election crisis commenced, "The spirit of faction is abated nowhere. In Virginia it is more violent than ever. It seems demonstrated that the leaders there, who possess completely all the powers of the local Government, are resolved to possess those of the National, by the most dangerous combinations; &, if they cannot affect this, to resort to the employment of physical force."[72]

There was a difference, however, between the public talk of resistance and the more sober plans drawn up by Republican leaders in the event that Burr, or some Federalist officeholder, was elected. Many Republican leaders—most notably, Jefferson, Madison, and Congressman Albert Gallatin of Pennsylvania—were clearly fearful of and opposed to armed resistance.[73] If Congress failed to place Jefferson in the presidency, one of the more probable Republican responses would have been to follow a plan outlined by Gallatin in an undated memorandum. In this memo, Gallatin made the case that Republican states should effectively nullify all new acts that derived from the person who had "usurped" the executive; Gallatin recommended, however, that those federal acts that were not immediately connected with presidential powers should be respected.[74] This would have been a rather restrained response, revealing, as he explained, that "the dangers of civil war, of the dissolution of the Union, or of the stab given to our republican institutions by any assumption of power on [the Republicans'] part not strictly justified by the forms of our Constitution, are the greatest we have to apprehend."[75]

Gallatin's plan would not be necessary. After six days and thirty-five ballots in the House, a group of Federalists from small states brokered an arrangement that would give Jefferson the presidency. According to Jefferson, the "certainty that a legislative usurpation would be resisted by arms" prompted a contingent of Federalists in the House to relent.[76] One of the leaders of this group of Federalists, James Bayard of Delaware, confessed that he broke ranks because he was "perfectly resolved not to risk the constitution or a civil war."[77] Bayard admitted, moreover, that he was particularly fearful for the security of his state. "Representing the smallest State in the Union, without resources which could furnish the means of self protection, I was compelled by the obligation of a sacred duty so to act as not to hazard the constitution upon which the political existence of the State depends."[78]

Historical research has shown that the fear of civil disorder was widespread among political elites and that preparations were taken to resist a usurpation by force. The Republican states, however, may not have been in a position to retake the presidency by force of arms.[79] First, if they chose to do so, the Republican states would have been challenged by better-trained and better-equipped Federalist militias. Of the New England militias, Massachusetts was widely believed to be the best prepared. The militias of the Federalist states would also have been supported by the U.S. Army, whose officer corps was overwhelmingly Federalist.[80]

The other reason Republican states (the southern states in particular) would have, in all likelihood, exercised restraint, pertained to the more basic security challenge inherent in economies based on slave labor. Just months before the election of 1800, a well-organized band of slaves conspired to launch a mass rebellion—what might have been the most extensive in southern history.[81] Gabriel, the chief architect of the plan, was a literate slave who worked as an artisan and came into regular contact with radical Republican artisans in Virginia. He was inspired by the success of black insurgents in the Caribbean and partial to the French regime, which had issued a proclamation in 1794 abolishing slavery in its colonial empire.[82] Gabriel built a network that included potentially hundreds of conspirators and reached across several towns, cities, and counties—a feat of coordination the planter gentry thought impossible for a slave.[83] As Governor Monroe concluded after the plot had been discovered, "It is unquestionably the most serious and formidable conspiracy we have ever known of the kind."[84]

Gabriel's plan was to capture the arms stored in Richmond and to take Virginia governor James Monroe hostage. Gabriel gave explicit instructions that Monroe was not to be harmed; Gabriel saw Monroe as a potentially sympathetic figure—one who was embraced by the French regime when he served as a minister to France under Adams. Gabriel further instructed his troops not to harm Quakers, Methodists, the French, and poor whites. His vision was not to inspire a race war but to enlist radical white Republicans in the cities to rise up against Virginia Federalists (mostly merchants and bankers) and advance the promise of the French revolutionary cause.[85]

Focusing on the schism between Federalist merchants and Republican artisans in Virginia's cities, Gabriel (who spent most of his time in urban settings) did not realize that the key political division in Virginia was between the merchants and the Republican planter gentry. Gabriel, moreover, overlooked the significant influence of Republican planters and agrarian Republicans who were not at all sympathetic with the plight of the slaves.[86] According to historian Douglas Egerton, Gabriel was partial to the Republicans; he was nonetheless disposed to "throw his lot in with whichever side would do the most favor in the coming civil conflict."[87]

Gabriel believed that the overheated partisan passions of the election season would trigger civil disorder; conflict between warring factions of whites, in turn, would open a window of opportunity for slaves to leverage their freedom. As Egerton surmises, "The divisive election of 1800 . . . provided the slaves with an opportunity that had been lacking since Dunmore's decree: a split among white elites."[88] The most significant recent example of such a division—one that shaped Gabriel's strategic outlook—took place in Guadaloupe and Saint Domingue between royalist planters in the French colonies and Republicans in Paris (this was the division that prompted France's landmark proclamation in 1794). Black insurgents were effectively co-opted by metropolitan elites in Paris to subdue the initiative of white elites in the colonies.[89]

In a fortuitous break for Virginia slaveholders, Mother Nature conspired against Gabriel's conspirators. The rebellion he had so meticulously planned, set to unfold on 30 August 1800, was thwarted primarily by heavy rains that made local waterways impassable. Several plantation slaves, moreover, leaked information about the plot to their masters.

Revelation of the details of Gabriel's plan struck Virginia's planter elite with terror. The plot reignited Jefferson's most ominous predictions. As Jefferson wrote in 1793, "I become daily more and more convinced that all the West India islands will remain in the hands of the people of colour, and a total expulsion of the whites sooner or later take place. It is high time we should foresee the bloody scenes which our children certainly, and possibly ourselves (South of Patowmac) have to wade through, and try to avert them."[90] Southern planters learned from Gabriel's conspiracy. The Virginia Assembly passed new provisions to bolster the militia, to restrict the movement of slaves from town to town and at night, and to impose new limits on the personal, familial, and economic autonomy of slaves and free blacks alike.[91]

Gabriel's Conspiracy also influenced the Republicans' strategic outlook during the election crisis of 1800: as Michael Bellesiles astutely surmises, "The fear of slave insurrections precisely delimited Republican actions in the South. There was just no way Republicans were going to enter into a conflict with other whites, leaving themselves open to assault from within their very homes."[92] This limit on offensive military action (i.e., the capacity to march on Philadelphia to retake the presidency) notwithstanding, Virginia and other Republican states were prepared to credibly threaten secession, or, short of that, substantively challenge the constitutional regime either by reviving the Virginia and Kentucky Resolutions or by rallying support for a new constitutional convention.

The incendiary rhetoric that surrounded the election of 1800, whether tactical or sincere, was consequential because it cast the prospects for a peaceful transfer of power in doubt. The rhetorical violence of the rival parties and the institutional context itself, where the states possessed the capacity to resist a usurpation of power by the Federalists, introduced a degree of uncertainty that was palpable. The fortuitous outcome of the election of 1800 came as a relief for political elites, who had every reason to fear the centrifugal effects of party division.

Embargo and the "Civil War of 1812"

President Thomas Jefferson hoped to make the Republicans "the party to end all parties" through a strategy of political absorption.[93] He set this strategy in motion with a conciliatory gesture offered to an embittered Federalist party, in opposition for the first time: "We have called by different names brethren of the same principle. We are all Republicans: we are all Federalists."[94] For Jefferson, the problem of negotiating partisanship and sovereignty could be resolved not so much by transcending parties but by consolidating them into a single party regime. Indeed, as their political thought developed, it became increasingly clear that Jefferson and Madison were not opposed to parties, per se; they were opposed to Federalism. Jefferson averred that "freemen, thinking differently & speaking & acting as they think, will form into classes of sentiment. but it must be under another name. that of federalism is [to] become so scouted that no party can rise under it."[95]

Like his Federalist predecessors, Jefferson had to fashion and enforce a response to British and French violations of America's neutral rights on the high seas. His answer was not a program to build naval strength, but rather a strategy of peaceful, economic coercion: embargo. This was Madison's brainchild, and Jefferson was not immediately converted. However, the disestablishment of the navy under Jefferson's watch left the administration with few alternatives when America's neutral rights were abridged.[96] The choice to avert war through the implementation of an embargo was, in Jefferson's view, not ideal: "What is *good* in this case cannot be effected; we have, therefore, only to find out what will be *least bad*."[97]

Jefferson's embargo was a policy of self-inflicted economic hardship implemented on an unprecedented scale. Federalists claimed that the measure was also a capitulation to Napoleon. The French enjoyed very little trade with the United States since the Royal Navy controlled the Atlantic. Though neutral to the warring powers on its face, the embargo was certain to exact a far greater impact on the British. The American embargo served as a de facto complement to Napoleon's "continental system," which prohibited British trade from ports on the European continent.[98] The only virtue of the embargo from the Federalist point of view was that this measure was certain, according to former secretary of state Timothy Pickering, to "touch their [the American people's] bone and their flesh; when they must curse its authors. If there should be no urgent cause for our coalescing with France, . . . the nation will recover its understanding, and at length see where its true interest lies."[99]

Enforcement of the embargo was an administrative challenge of epic proportions: the temptation for merchants to defy the law was widespread, and opportunities to do so were readily available to any enterprising smuggler. As the embargo law went into effect, added measures were passed to proscribe trade overland on the northern frontier and to ensure that vessels participating in the coastal trade (between ports along the coastline) did not head out to the high seas.[100] This required both manpower for surveillance and a capacity for interdiction both in the ports and near smuggling routes, especially in the Northeast. There was, however, no readily available approach to policing commerce on such a great scale, especially in an institutional context where the allegiances of state militiamen, the enforcement authority of first resort, were often divided.[101] Support from the states, particularly those politically opposed to the embargo, was not forthcoming. Federalist-leaning Connecticut and Rhode Island, for example, refused to assist the federal government in the enforcement of the embargo against Britain and France, signaling to the administration that the federal government could truly rely only on states controlled by fellow Republicans.[102]

The line between criminality and partisanship blurred in New England and on the frontier with Canada—mostly because extensive smuggling burgeoned in regions politically opposed to Jefferson's policy. Treasury Secretary Albert Gallatin, whose department was charged with enforcing the embargo, insisted that the "criminal party-rage of Federalists and Tories" was responsible for the government's crisis of authority.[103] He maintained that the "want of efficiency in the law at first, and of energy in the collectors on Lake Ontario afterwards, have, *together with avarice and the open encouragement by Federalists*, organized opposition in that quarter to a degree which will probably baffle all our endeavors."[104]

The president echoed these sentiments, blaming the "tories of Boston" for inciting violent opposition to the embargo.[105] Republican leaders also alleged that Federalists coordinated with the British to undermine the embargo policy.[106] Jefferson, moreover, insisted that vocal opposition to the embargo signaled to foreign antagonists that American resolve to carry out its own policy could be broken. Many Federalists, he maintained, "disapprove of the republican principles and features of our Constitution, and would, I believe, welcome any public calamity (war with England excepted) which might lessen the confidence of our country in those principles and forms. I have generally considered them rather as subjects for a mad-house. *But they are now playing a game of the most mischievous tendency*, without perhaps being themselves aware of it. They are endeavoring to convince England that we suffer more by the embargo than they do, and that if they will but hold out awhile, we must abandon it."[107] The British, however, did not need to be convinced—the severity of America's self-imposed hardship was well-known within official circles in Britain.[108]

The embargo controversy may help scholars more fully understand Jefferson's vision of single-party government. Indeed, the fate of his embargo policy was a testament to the practical utility (if not necessity) of securing broad-based, popular support for a national regulatory scheme in an institutional climate where the federal government could not guarantee the faithful execution of the laws. The embargo law required a virtual unanimity of opinion, a united front, for the measure to be of consequence. Party opposition was simply anathema to the consolidation of public support that was necessary for the successful implementation of this crucial policy commitment.[109]

One might well argue that the crisis of authority evidenced in this case was provoked not so much by law breakers operating in sections of the country traditionally sympathetic to the Federalists, but rather from the policy itself. Jefferson's embargo policy was both profoundly ambitious in scope and insensitive to the political, economic, and institutional realities on the ground. It was, nevertheless, an extreme case that cast a basic condition of governance in the early nineteenth century in high relief: that enforceable authority across an expansive territorial space was tenuous at best. As with the Genêt affair, federal policy was effectively challenged and, in this case, undermined, by elements of society closely associated (if not actually affiliated) with the party in opposition.

The difficulties of navigating a neutral course continued into Madison's tenure as president. The tensions between the United States and Britain had changed little since 1807. With the option of economic coercion a proven failure, however, war was viewed as the only remedy to the grievances against the British and the French. Indeed, the French were as hostile to America's trade overseas as the British.[110] Yet a confluence of disparate sectional interests galvanized support for war in 1812. Matters in dispute extended beyond the question of spoliations and impressment; the strongest proponents for war, in fact, were westerners who aimed to put an end to Britain's alleged provocation of Native American aggression on the western frontier (most notably at the Battle of Tippecanoe, where tribes attacked William Henry Harrison's armies in the Indiana Territory). A belief that British Orders in Council were responsible for declining tobacco and cotton prices further goaded western war sentiments.[111] The war was also motivated by the temptation to seize Canada. For westerners, Canada was the base from which the British launched their intrigues with Native American tribes in the territories. Southerners hoped to foster support for their claims on Florida by backing war on Canada, and northerners, for their part, believed that seizing Canada would shift the balance of power in the Union toward the free states.[112]

After briefly considering a "triangular war," Madison and his fellow Republicans threw down the gauntlet, choosing sides in the European conflagration by declaring war against Great Britain.[113] Federalist sentiment, particularly in New England, was deeply divided. Opposition to the war within Federalist ranks was commonplace; Federalists differed, however, over the measures they should take to oppose the government. Former secretary of state Timothy Pickering insisted that the New England states "cannot exist, but in poverty and contempt, without foreign commerce. And by a war of any continuance with Great Britain, that commerce will be annihilated."[114] He concluded that "an immediate separation," therefore, "would be a real blessing."[115] Just as Pickering endorsed the idea of a confederation of the New England states, another prominent New England Federalist, John Lowell, called for the arrangement of a separate peace. He proclaimed in the Boston *Centinel* that "throwing off all connection with this wasteful war, making peace with our enemy and opening once more our commerce with the world, would be a wise and manly course. The occasion demands it of us, and the people at large are ready to meet it."[116] Federalist clergyman Elijah Parish of Massachusetts issued a similar sentiment to his parishioners: "proclaim an honourable neutrality; let the southern *Heroes* fight their own battles, and guard . . . against the just vengeance of their lacerated slaves. . . . Break those chains, under which you have sullenly murmured, during the

long, long reign of democracy; . . . and once more breathe that free, commercial air of New England which your fathers always enjoyed. . . . *Forbid this
war to proceed in New-England.*"[117] More moderate Federalists, though sympathetic to the critique offered by the likes of Pickering and Lowell, stopped
short of an appeal for separation. Others were fatalistic: George Cabot, for
one, asked Pickering, "Why can't you and I let the world ruin itself its own
way?"[118]

New England Federalists initially sought redress for their grievances
within the confines of the political system. They supported DeWitt Clinton,
a "peace" Republican, in the presidential election of 1812, to no avail. Facing
defeat for the fourth consecutive presidential election, Federalist politics
thereafter took a radical turn. Indeed, talk of disunion was tempered only
by amusement at the failures of the federal government's prosecution of the
war. There were many to speak of; in addition to being duped by Napoleon
into imposing trade sanctions on the British under the false pretense that the
Berlin and Milan decrees had been revoked, Madison also declared war before adequate measures to build American defenses were taken. Embarrassing defeats in Canada and, later, the burning of the White House and Capitol
would follow. Madison, in fact, acknowledged that the country was unpre-
pared upon his declaration of war. Only declared war, he maintained, would
galvanize political support to build the ranks of the army and navy for the
country to successfully assert itself.[119]

Pickering could barely contain his excitement at the prospect that the
failures of the war would embarrass his political opponents and change the
fortunes for his Federalist comrades: " 'Union' is the talisman of the dominant party; and many Federalists, enchanted by the magic sound, are
alarmed at every appearance of opposition to the measures of the faction, lest
it should endanger the 'Union.' I have never entertained such fears. On the
contrary, in adverting to the ruinous system of our government for many
years past, I have said, 'Let the ship run aground. The shock will throw the
present pilots overboard, and then competent navigators will get her once
more afloat, and conduct her safely into port.' "[120]

Federalist opposition had concrete ramifications for the war effort. Massachusetts and Connecticut, both Federalist strongholds, refused to commit
their militia to the service of the federal government even though the Militia Act of 1792 required them to do so when called on by the president.[121]
Both states instead ordered their militiamen to remain in state in a self-
defense posture. The national war effort quickly devolved into an "every

state for itself" strategy of defense. As Artemas Ward of Massachusetts stated in Congress, "If every State in the Union, with such aid as she can obtain from her neighbors, defends herself, our whole country will be defended. In my mind the resources of the States will be applied with more economy and with greater effect in defence of the country under the State governments than under the government of the United States."[122] Unwilling to rely on federal forces for their defense, the states of Massachusetts, Connecticut, Pennsylvania, Maryland, Virginia, South Carolina, and Kentucky took steps to form their own state armies.[123] Congress, unwilling and perhaps unable to raise forces appropriate to the task at hand, acquiesced to the states' designs to raise their own self-defense forces by agreeing to pay the expense. Such a step might only be explained, to use Henry Adams's uncharacteristically inarticulate words, by "the government's consciousness of helplessness."[124] The federal government could lend whatever support it could to the states, yet, as we've seen with the Genêt affair and Jefferson's embargo, the states, some under the control of contrary parties, could not be relied on to coordinate their efforts through federal institutions when it was needed most.

Provoked by a new federal embargo passed in December 1813,[125] Federalists took their opposition a step further. This embargo appeared to Federalists to be a vengeful, punitive measure directed at the New England states since the British blockade had already effectively shut down commerce throughout the rest of the nation. At this juncture, Massachusetts Federalists mobilized political leadership, mostly from Massachusetts, Connecticut, and Rhode Island, to assemble in Hartford and decide on a course of action to protest the policies of the federal government. The convention was designed by the Federalist elite in part to pacify an increasingly violent popular opposition to the war brewing in the New England states.[126] One may take Harrison Gray Otis at his word when he asserted, "The proceedings of the Convention . . . are adopted rather to appease than produce excitement." The convention "was the consequence, not the source of a popular sentiment; and it was intended, by those who voted for it, as a safety valve by which the steam arising from the fermentation of the time might escape, not as a boiler in which it should be generated."[127]

According to James Banner, the convention report (widely believed to be written by Otis) was "an unmistakable victory for the moderate forces."[128] It urgently recommended that the administration permit the New England states to organize for their own defense and help the states meet the cost of war expenses by directing a portion of what was collected in national taxes to the state treasuries. It also enumerated proposals for seven constitutional amendments: among them was a proposal to apportion representation and taxation according to the free white population and to eliminate the notorious "three-fifths" clause. Two others sought to make federal embargoes more difficult to adopt and to limit their reach if adopted. The convention further took aim at the Virginia dynasty, proposing to limit presidents to one term and to prohibit the election of successive presidents from the same state.[129] The report also included language reminiscent of the Virginia and Kentucky Resolutions, asserting that the states reserved the authority to judge the constitutionality of federal measures: "In cases of deliberate, dangerous, and palpable infractions of the constitution, affecting the sovereignty of a state, and liberties of the people; it is not only the right but the duty of such a state to interpose its authority for their protection."[130] Finally, the report recommended that a second convention should be held in Boston in mid-June if the proposals were rejected, war continued, or the national government continued to neglect the defense of New England.[131] What a second convention would have asserted is a matter for speculation only. Few options, however, would have remained for the Federalists other than to declare neutrality for the New England states, nullify the embargo in their states, or negotiate a separate peace with the British.[132]

Domestic divisions were deeply interwoven with the foreign conflict in this "Civil War of 1812," as Alan Taylor aptly termed it.[133] New England Federalists' flirtation with secession in 1814 and their threat to remain neutral was successfully deployed by Republicans to stigmatize Federalists as traitors and mark them for disrepute; as one prominent historian of the period observes, it was "an opprobrious epithet that was good currency for years."[134] However it was only the *name* of Federalism that was marked with disloyalty; it became, as Jefferson foresaw in 1802, "so scouted that no party can [ever again] rise under it."

The "best effect" of the War of 1812, Jefferson observed, was "the complete suppression of party."[135] By this, he meant the complete suppression of party *opposition*. After all, Republican partisanship was flourishing throughout the country—no doubt a great encouragement to Jefferson and his counterparts who believed that this brand of partisanship was necessary to serve as a caretaker of the Constitution and the liberties of the people. The Republican party was conceived to be a party that would stand alone, not in a party system, but rather as a supplement to a constitutional system, the integrity of which required an extraconstitutional agent that could channel popular action to stand in its defense and ensure its endurance.

The consequences of Federalist opposition, both real and imagined, were amplified in this period both because of the vulnerability of the central state and the Federalists' stance vis-à-vis one of America's chief adversaries, the British. Federalist partisanship was not criminal—despite the protests of some extreme Republicans. The loyalty of an organized opposition, however, was subject to a high degree of scrutiny so long as it was within the means of political dissidents to fundamentally undermine the authority of federal policy and in the interest of a foreign adversary for the domestic opposition to do so.

Conclusion

Federal lawmakers in the early national period were forced to come to terms with an institutional fact of life: that federal policy was vulnerable to the vicissitudes of public opinion. Deep partisan divisions, especially insofar as they spread to the mass public, compromised the capacity of elites to govern. Farsighted leaders accordingly took steps to settle, neutralize, or evade the most polarizing question of the day by forging a policy of neutrality in the ongoing wars between the great European powers. The War of 1812, however, was the exception that proves the rule: the federal government chose sides in the foreign conflict and very narrowly avoided a secessionist crisis led by the New England states. The peace Treaty of Ghent (ending the War of 1812) was signed just days before the Hartford Convention report was written (news of the treaty had not yet arrived in America). The peace that followed rendered the dissent raised in Hartford politically moot, embarrassing New England Federalists who, as Republicans had it, betrayed their country in its time of need.[136]

The political turbulence of the early national period was prompted, in large part, by the wars between Britain and France, which forced both Federalist and Republican leaders to confront the dilemmas of neutrality and war. These dilemmas, however, were effectively resolved after the War of 1812. American leaders, one should note, had no hand in their resolution. The defeat of Napoleon at Waterloo in 1815 and the end of war in Europe settled these questions for the Americans.

Yet the parties were not immediately reinvented when foreign policy controversies abated and threats to national autonomy subsided. As I discuss in the following chapter, the development of a party system required a settlement, however provisional, of the slavery question—a matter that was pressed to the national agenda by America's westward movement and increasingly democratic politics.

CHAPTER 4

The Second Party System and the Politics of Displacing Conflict

Parties under some denominations or other must
always be expected in a Govt. as free as ours. When the
individuals belonging to them are intermingled in every
part of the whole Country, they strengthen the Union of
the Whole, while they divide every part. Should a State
of parties arise, founded on geographical boundaries
and other Physical & permanent distinctions which
happen to coincide with them, what is to controul those
great repulsive Masses from awful shocks agst. each
other?

—James Madison, letter to Robert Walsh,
27 November 1819

Martin Van Buren and Andrew Jackson play a special role in the historiography of party development in the United States. If the first generation of American leaders—those of the early national period—were disparaged for their failure to recognize the advantages of party competition, Van Buren and Jackson are celebrated for their efforts to shatter the stuffy, patrician norms of their predecessors and inaugurate a new era where the role of party in the operations of government was not just acknowledged but actively promoted.[1] The second generation of American leaders, it is said, marked an important advance in favor of toleration by embracing the idea of legitimate party opposition. With their belief that the rivalry between competing groups promotes the common good—a view that echoed and extended the Madisonian realism of *Federalist* numbers 10 and 51—this generation also forged an important advance for democracy itself. Parties, we are given to believe, gained legitimacy in the early to mid-nineteenth century thanks to a progressive enlightenment in American political thought.[2]

Political leaders, however, did not become more tolerant or "realistic"— in a Madisonian or any other sense; indeed, the process of party legitimization was not as linear or progressive as many have imagined. In fact, it is difficult to even think of it as a "process" at all. Rather, parties gained widespread acceptance among political elites thanks to a confluence of developments: political events in Europe, the efforts of domestic leaders to forge a settlement to the slavery question, and the entrepreneurial efforts of Martin Van Buren and others to prevent the reemergence of this question all paved the way for the rise of the modern "mass" party form.[3]

Jackson, Van Buren, and their associates played a pivotal role in the emergence of parties as permanent features of American governing arrangements. They unabashedly projected the virtues of party and endowed the party organization with unprecedented influence in the public sphere. Despite their achievements on behalf of the status of parties in public life, their view of legitimate opposition was conditional. They embraced parties only insofar as the major parties excluded the slavery question from the national political agenda. Whereas Washington's Proclamation of Neutrality and John Adams's declaration of a peace mission to France aimed to tame the party battle by employing the prerogatives of the executive to defuse or render moot deeply divisive controversies touching foreign affairs, Jackson, Van Buren, and fellow party leaders managed the slavery question through a feat of political engineering: they deliberately cultivated a partisan division that allied in each party factions from the both the North and the South. In their vision, a rivalry where both major parties contained a northern and a southern wing would serve as a substitute or an alternative to a sectional division of the parties, which would inevitably push the slavery question to the top of the national agenda. Party institutions were thus reinvented to contain, and preferably erase, the most divisive question of the day from the national political stage. Jackson and Van Buren constituted a system of quasi-legitimate parties that were expected to peaceably alternate in power so long as they realized this basic purpose. As we shall see, their new party system, such as it was, strained under policy tensions (tariff politics and western expansion) that threatened to reopen the very question that Van Buren and others hoped to obscure. In important respects, it was the goad of party competition itself that unleashed sectional tensions over tariff rates and stoked expansionist pressures to secure new western lands for settlement. In both instances (tariff policy and western expansion), elites did what they could to paper over the dispute and preserve a veneer of political regularity. The historic compromises leaders struck in these policy arenas defused constitutional crises and bought the republic sectional comity for a spell; each new accord nonetheless set the terms for subsequent rounds of sectional recrimination and separatist brinksmanship.

European Peace and Partisan Reconciliation in America

The restoration of peace in Europe was a watershed moment in American history because it freed American foreign policy from the controversies of neutrality and neutral rights.[4] The United States was no longer pitted between two superpowers, setting to rest the suspicions of foreign influence and intrigue that had dominated American party politics since 1793. The absence of great foreign policy controversies after the War of 1812 "lowered the temperature" of partisan politics thereafter.[5]

With the restoration of peace between Britain and France, the United States had achieved a measure of political autonomy and was freed from the dangers of a party politics based on a mutual suspicion of national disloyalty. No longer polarized by foreign war, the focus of American politics turned inward. Political leaders increasingly focused debate on the advantages and disadvantages of a system of federally sponsored internal improvements, protective tariffs for the promotion of domestic manufactures, and the establishment of a national bank.[6] The political agenda also turned westward. American settlers moved west in increasing numbers and the state repositioned itself accordingly, emphasizing the management and removal of Native Americans.

The conclusion of the War of 1812 and the collapse of the Federalist party inaugurated a period of single-party hegemony and bitter, intraparty factionalism within the Republican party that lasted until the late 1820s. Martin Van Buren's notion of party government emerged in this setting as a response to the shortcomings of the factional politics of this period.

Van Buren and his associates identified numerous deficiencies with this brand of politics and attributed them to a single cause: President James Monroe's misguided pursuit of party amalgamation.[7]

James Monroe's view of party has been (not unfairly) characterized as a throwback of eighteenth-century antiparty utopianism.[8] In his first inaugural address, he observed, "Discord does not belong to our system. . . . The American people have encountered together great dangers and sustained severe trials with success. They constitute one great family with a common interest."[9] In response to a letter from Andrew Jackson encouraging the new president to bury the party hatchet, Monroe set forth his vision of party amalgamation—a process whereby the Republican party would steadily absorb the moderate elements of its former rival, leading ultimately to the dissolution of party distinctions: "My impression is that the Administration should rest strongly on the republican party, indulging towards the other [party] a spirit of moderation, and evincing a desire to discriminate between its members, and to bring the whole into the republican fold as quick as possible." He then observed,

> Many men very distinguished for their talents are of the opinion
> that the existence of the federal party is necessary to keep union
> and order in the republican ranks, that is that free government
> cannot exist without parties. This is not my opinion. That the
> ancient republics were always divided into parties; that the English
> government is maintained by an opposition, that is by the existence
> of a party in opposition to the Ministry, I well know. But I think
> that the cause of these divisions is to be found in certain defects of
> those governments, rather than in human nature; and that we have
> happily avoided those defects in our system. The first object is to
> save the cause, which can be done by those who are devoted to it
> only, and of course by keeping them together; or, in other words, by
> not disgusting them by too hasty an act of liberality to the other
> party, thereby breaking the generous spirit of the republican party,
> and keeping alive that of the federal. The second is, to prevent the
> reorganization and revival of the federal party, which, if my
> hypothesis is true, that the existence of parties is not necessary to
> free government, and the other opinion which I have advanced is
> well founded, that the great body of the federal party are republi-
> can, will not be found impracticable. To accomplish both objects,

and thereby exterminate all party divisions in our country, and give new strength and stability to our government, is a great undertaking, not easily executed. I am nevertheless decidedly of opinion that it may be done.[10]

The dissolution of party distinctions was therefore both possible and desirable within a republican system of government because parties were symptomatic of the defects of nonrepublican regimes—and not (as Jefferson and Madison maintained) a necessary consequence of human nature.

Martin Van Buren confronted the alleged dangers of Monroe's vision of party amalgamation first in New York state politics and then on the national stage. The "heresy" of amalgamation unfolded in a similar manner in both settings: Republican party fragmentation, amplified by the absence of a clearly identifiable partisan adversary (and, in the case of national politics, the absence of a party nominating caucus), contributed to the ideological drift of the Republican party away from its Jeffersonian tradition of resistance to federal consolidation. In New York state, DeWitt Clinton's leadership of the Republican party represented the elitism and corruption of party principles that, Van Buren believed, inevitably result from the absence of institutions and practices that encourage party discipline and coordination. In national politics, Monroe's aim to dissolve the parties was responsible for the election of the former and unreconstructed Federalist (in Van Buren's view), John Quincy Adams.[11] "Good feelings" were nothing but a trap planted by Federalists unwilling to submit to defeat. "We have indeed heard of the 'era of good feelings,'" wrote the Albany *Argus*, the newspaper of the Van Buren Democrats. "We have been told also, that the federal party was dissolved; and that time and circumstances had destroyed all the old political distinctions. But when have these declarations been obtruded upon the public? Always at the close of a losing election under the influence of renewed convictions of the energies of the Democratic party."[12]

The remedy for party amalgamation was literally to restore the centrality and significance of the party name. Since recognizable family names were electorally advantageous in the absence of party appellations, "no party rule," in the view of Van Buren and his cadre of supporters, would inevitably lead to the rule of great families. No family better typified this pattern than the Clintons of New York. George Clinton served as governor of New York and later as vice president under Jefferson and Madison. His nephew, DeWitt Clinton, inherited a high status in New York state politics with the help of his illustrious name. The nephew was infamous among the Bucktails, Van Buren's partisan club, for his imperious manner and for his willingness to consort with Federalists to preserve his rule.[13] The Bucktails, who formed the party machine known as the Albany Regency, promoted a different breed of politician; Van Buren, for example, came from a humble background and rose to power within the ranks of the Republican party. His program to democratize the organizational structure of the party was a calculated effort to remove Clinton from the leadership of the Republican party and to forge a new regime where the voice of the common man, articulated through party organization and party principle, would replace the electoral aristocracy of great families.[14]

Party amalgamation also militated against Van Buren's egalitarian vision because it did not permit voters to distinguish between candidates who were truly Republican and those who were Republican in name only. Party distinctions were desirable insofar as they segregated political enemies from political allies and added a degree of transparency to the electoral process. Van Buren, in other words, valued clear choices at the polls not so much out of a commitment to a magnanimous party pluralism, but so that Federalists could be identified by the electorate and summarily rejected by the numerical majority. The absence of such transparency provided an electoral advantage to would-be Federalists, as the fateful presidential election of 1824 demonstrated. This election featured a crowded field of four major presidential candidates, all of whom had loyal personal followings, and all called themselves Republicans.[15] The political jockeying was thrown into the House of Representatives because no single candidate achieved a majority of the electoral votes. Once in the House, Andrew Jackson, the recipient of the plurality of electoral votes, was denied the presidency by a "corrupt bargain" between John Quincy Adams and Henry Clay.

Van Buren and members of the Albany Regency encouraged party distinctions because they were conducive to the perpetuation of a more egalitarian electoral order. Party distinctions also served a vital defensive purpose: to thwart the formation of an alternate, sectional scheme of party antagonisms. Van Buren and the members of the Albany Regency maintained that the amalgamation of parties left the polity vulnerable to stratagems advanced by less scrupulous Federalist politicians who hoped to restore the strength of their party by politicizing the latent sectional tensions that threatened to divide the Union. According to the *Albany Argus*, those who sought to amalgamate parties hoped to "ABROGATE THE OLD PARTY DISTINCTIONS—to organize new ones, founded in the territorial prejudices of the people—and in the course of the revolution which they hope to effect, to secure their own elevation."[16] By abolishing the "old party distinctions," Federalists would "array republicans against each other under new and artificial distinctions . . . to enlist prejudices and feelings, drawn from an accidental *geographical location*, such as the *north* and the *south*, the *east* and the *west*."[17]

Below the surface of this talk of "artificial distinctions" was the well-founded fear that the slavery question could be leveraged by activists agitating for social justice and by opportunistic partisans seeking political advantage.[18] As these anxieties illustrate, the parties were not immediately transformed when foreign policy controversies abated and threats to national autonomy subsided. The legitimization of organized party opposition rested on the satisfaction of two crucial conditions: independence from the polarizing divisions in Europe and a settlement (however provisional) of the slavery question, a matter that did not, for the most part, surface as a point of national contention during the early national period.[19] Parties were not tolerated in the early national period because they were certain to set a Francophile Republican party against an Anglophile Federalist party, at odds over the high-stakes question of war and peace. In a similar manner, it is hard to imagine that party competition would have been celebrated in the 1830s if the party system was likely to pit a free-state party against a slave-state party.

The Albany *Argus*'s anxieties evolved in response to the crisis that erupted in 1819 over the extension of slavery to Missouri. The Missouri controversy both exposed the flaws of Monroe's vision and served as a reminder of the potential dangers of party politics in the early nineteenth century. The controversy was precipitated by New York congressman James Tallmadge's amendment to the Missouri Enabling Act to prohibit the introduction of slaves to the state. This proposal prompted a sectional firestorm in Congress. According to Congressman James Cobb of Georgia, those who sought to restrict the spread of slavery were "kindling a fire which all the waters of the ocean could not extinguish. It could be extinguished only in blood!"[20] Tallmadge replied on the floor of the House, "If a dissolution of the Union must take place, let it be so! If civil war, which gentlemen so much threaten, must come, I can only say, let it come! My hold on life is probably as frail as any who now hears me; but while that hold lasts, it shall be devoted to the service of my country—to the freedom of man. If blood is necessary to extinguish any fire which I have assisted to kindle, I can assure gentlemen, while I regret the necessity, I shall not forbear to contribute my mite."[21]

Monroe, like so many others, believed that the controversy could prove fatal to the Union.[22] His response, and that of other Republican party leaders, was tinged with denial: they convinced themselves that the Missouri issue was nothing more than a plot conceived by Federalists to raise new parties that would pit free states against slave states.[23] They maintained that the sectional divide provoked by the crisis was artificial and contrived—the handiwork of opportunistic Federalists who would stop at nothing to revive their party and regain power. Jefferson, for one, observed that, "On the eclipse of federalism with us, although not its extinction, its leaders got up the Missouri question, under the false front of lessening the measure of slavery, but with the real view of producing a geographical division of parties, which might insure them the next President. The people of the North went blindfold into the snare, followed their leaders for awhile with a zeal truly moral and laudable, until they became sensible that they were injuring instead of aiding the real interests of the slaves, that they had been used merely as tools for electioneering purposes."[24]

Van Buren echoed this sentiment, suggesting further that the efficacy of this Federalist strategy was itself a consequence of Monroe's policy of party amalgamation. Indeed, as Forbes explains, southern planters had undoubtedly learned from the Missouri episode that "in the absence of partisan conflict, where northern politicians had need of southern support, the South had no real allies in its defense of slavery."[25] Van Buren famously argued that this strategic predicament would be remedied by reviving old party attachments: "Party attachment in former times furnished a complete antidote for sectional prejudices by producing counteracting feelings. It was not until that defence had been broken down that the clamour agt Southern Influence and African Slavery could be made effectual in the North. . . . Formerly, attacks upon Southern Republicans were regarded by those of the North as assaults upon their political brethren & resented accordingly. This all powerful sympathy has been much weakened, if not, destroyed by the amalgamating policy of Mr. Monroe."[26] This sympathy did not form of its own accord; a new institutional mechanism was necessary to coordinate the efforts of northern and southern "brethren" behind a mutually agreeable presidential candidate. As Van Buren concluded, this sympathy "can and ought to be revived and the proposed [presidential nominating] convention would be eminently serviceable in effecting that object."[27]

Ironically, Monroe may have done more for the development of the second party system than he could have imagined. In his response to the crisis, Monroe proved himself to be a savvy tactician. According to Forbes, Monroe led a group of "anti-slavery pragmatists" who would help to end the standoff by working with antirestrictionists, all while concealing Monroe's aim to settle for a compromise. Monroe's end game was to permit slavery in Missouri in exchange for a more general prohibition of slavery in the rest of the western territories. The Monroe administration orchestrated a "coordinated and centrally directed campaign," working through intermediaries who negotiated with legislators in "backrooms, saloons, boarding houses, and executive department offices." Monroe and his representatives worked behind the scenes to peel off several key northern votes in the House to defeat the Tallmadge Amendment and to narrowly pass a compromise bill. In so doing, Monroe helped to broker an arrangement that ultimately would admit Maine to the Union as a free state, Missouri as a slave state, and would establish a northern limit of 36°30′ for the extension of slavery within the Louisiana Territory.[28]

If Monroe helped to bridge the divide that the extension of slavery had opened, Martin Van Buren's signature achievement was to organize a political party that would prevent this sectional chasm from reopening.[29] Van Buren did not merely resurrect the old party opposition between Republicans and Federalists but imbued the old party divide with an egalitarian ethos to create a fundamentally new party alignment. Van Buren saw himself as resurrecting the old party feelings of the Jeffersonian era (which, in his view, tended to temper sectional antagonisms), confident that the opposition between the Federalist and Republican parties was the surest means to prevent the slavery question from reopening. He explained to Thomas Ritchie, the editor of the Richmond *Enquirer* and a firm opponent of the restriction of slavery in the western territories, "We must always have party distinctions and the old ones are the best of which the nature of the case admits. Political combinations between the inhabitants of the different states are unavoidable & the most natural & beneficial to the country is that between the planters of the South and the plain Republicans of the North. The country has once flourished under a party thus constituted & may again." Proposing to "draw anew the old Party lines," Van Buren insisted that "if the old ones [party attachments] are suppressed, Geographical divisions founded on local interests or, what is worse prejudices between free & slaveholding states will inevitably take their place."[30] A statement issued by party notables appointed to represent the 1835 Democratic-Republican convention in Baltimore elaborated on Van Buren's point that party discipline is an essential bulwark against antislavery agitation. It held that

> it is the power and influence of united Republicanism and patriotism, which ties the hands of the abolitionists and fanatics in the North, and scorns their doctrines. It is this power of united Republicanism which spell binds their deluded followers, and which they feel and dread. Indeed, so sure and safe a guarantee is Republicanism, for the peaceable possession of all the privileges resulting from this confederacy of States, that while there is a Republican in the North, the South will have a friend there. Let then the Republican party every where, stand firm and united, and trusting to her principles, fear not, all will be safe. And why shall not the Democracy of all quarters of our Union, and the several States, implicitly confide in each other? They entered into this Confederacy as independent States, with the express stipulation, that each State reserved to itself the right of managing its domestic concerns and social relations in its own way. The People of no State, therefore, can violate that compromise, on which the Union is based, and call themselves Republicans. It would be subversive of the fundamental principles on which the superstructure of Republicanism itself is based. They could not, as men of honor and truth, violate it, without being guilty of deception, treachery, and falsehood! They could not, as men of sense and true christians, violate it; because they know that, by so doing, the light of a great nation, now brightly shining on a benighted world, would be extinguished forever, and in blood![31]

The commitment to preserve states' autonomy over "domestic concerns and social relations" (read: slavery) was the intellectual and strategic cornerstone of the Democratic-Republican party. Van Buren and fellow partisans did not endorse a free market of party ideas. To the contrary, their system was geared to *resist* the emergence of ideas and sympathies they believed would hasten the dissolution of the Union. The Democratic party, as a result, was highly selective in its commitments. The party line was relatively clear in its opposition to internal improvements, federal debt, and the national bank; the party coalition, however, required compromise on the tariff and silence on the extension of slavery.[32]

"Silence," here, may be taken literally. In a highly influential document printed in the *Charleston Mercury* in 1827, Robert J. Turnbull, anticipating arguments made a decade later against acceptance of antislavery petitions to Congress, made the case that the legislative branch must not even entertain conversation of colonization: "To countenance the American Colonization Society, will be to proceed upon the principle, that slavery is a rank weed in our land. . . . It will be a declaration of WAR, and MUST be treated and resisted as such. It will be the ENTERING WEDGE, with which, at some future day, our VITAL interests are to be SPLIT asunder.—It will be the LANDING of an enemy, and a bitter enemy too, on our soil." He continued, insisting that "there must be no discussion. Discussion will cause DEATH and DESTRUCTION to our negro property."[33] "The Crisis," the title of Turnbull's essay printed in thirty-three installments in the *Mercury*, was a clarion call to repress the question.[34] The commitment to silence, moreover, extended beyond Congress to the postal system, where postmasters, particularly in the South, refused to deliver abolitionist publications, despite their legal commitment to content neutrality codified in the Post Office Act of 1836. Jacksonians in the North also organized antiabolitionist mobs to threaten antislavery agitators and destroy their printing presses.[35]

The doctrine of states' rights permitted the Democrats to be agnostic on questions pertaining to slavery; an alliance between the "planters of the South and the plain Republicans of the North" might be entertained only with the slavery-extension question settled (temporarily, by the Missouri Compromise) and effectively off the table.[36] The common denominators that bound the Democratic coalition—states' rights and strict constructionism—guaranteed the greatest possible latitude for states to act on their own, independent of federal obligations or interference. The disparate elements of the party were united by the promise that their differences would be preserved, shielded from the forces of federal consolidation.

More than anything else, a new party required a charismatic figurehead who could unite the sections under the Democratic banner. Van Buren was confident in 1825 that Adams would be defeated if they added "the General's personal popularity to the strength of the old Republican party."[37] Yet this presumed that General Jackson was, at heart, amenable to the more doctrinaire positions of the Old Jeffersonian Republicans. Prior to his presidency,

Jackson was known as an antipartisan western nationalist, supportive of
federal projects for internal improvements and sympathetic to eastern demands for tariff protection.[38] After becoming a Jackson supporter, Van Buren cautioned Old Hickory not to assume any "opinion on constitutional
questions at war with the doctrines of the Jefferson school."[39] Van Buren
encouraged Jackson to adjust his policy stances to the anticonsolidationist
sentiment that prevailed among Adams's opponents. In this sense, Van Buren helped foster a transformation of Jackson's vision to what would come to
be called "Jacksonianism."

By the time he entered office, Jackson assumed a more partisan cast. He
firmly committed himself to the principle of "rotation" in federal office—
what he termed a "leading principle in the republican creed," aligning him
with the governing practice that defined the Albany Regency, that "to the
victor belong the spoils."[40] Van Buren's early instincts about Jackson were
correct as Jackson's administration followed a programmatic line that would
make the Old Republican purists proud: he supported tariff rate reductions,
took a stand against internal improvements with his veto of funding for the
Maysville Road, assumed a hard line on Indian removal, and led an ideological crusade against the National Bank.

The Jacksonian regime and its embrace of party in government contributed to several enduring institutional changes. The principle of rotation in
office, sanctioned for the first time by a sitting president, was indicative of a
political outlook that was new to the American political scene: this was the
notion that the transfer of political and state power (i.e., the turnover of administrative offices) could be regularized without sacrificing the stability
of the republic. The Democrats' principle was a claim to "clean house" when
they assumed power. But more important, it was an acknowledgment that
they fully expected to be defeated at some point in the future and would then
readily agree to return power to their opponents. This sense of predictability
was operative, of course, only if the parties rotating in power sidestepped the
most contentious issues of the day. The principle of rotation in office was,
nonetheless, an implicit admission that no great harm would come to the
country as a result of a change in the parties' electoral fortunes.[41]

The ascendant, if limited, legitimization of party also contributed to a
notable change in electioneering practices and strategy. Candidates for
higher office during the early national period would make few if any gestures
toward public electioneering at all. Instead, the leading supporters of presidential candidates would substitute for the candidates themselves, making

the rounds among political elites in Congress and in state legislatures to mobilize support for their preferred candidate. This was an exercise that took place exclusively among the political elite. At the level of social etiquette, it was simply unbecoming of a gentleman and statesman to present himself to the mass public in a popular appeal.[42] This etiquette was, at least implicitly, a political argument: the people could not be trusted with weighty electoral choices. Popular appeals would open the door to demagoguery, and demagoguery roused passions in the people that the state could not control.[43] Such popular appeals, nonetheless, gradually became socially acceptable in the Jacksonian era. Parties and elections were popularized, quite literally, in the sense that they became sources of public entertainment and recreation. Party activity, as McCormick notes, had become by the 1830s "a kind of mass folk festival, incorporating . . . the enthusiasms of religious revivalism and the passions of a bloodless internal war."[44]

The contours of the second party system evolved in accord with the formation of two great alliances, neither of which would have been possible without the prior settlement of the Missouri question: the first was engineered by Van Buren, with the crucial assistance of Jackson's charismatic leadership, and the second was a bargain forged by Henry Clay, Daniel Webster, and others, that rallied Jackson's diverse opponents under one banner. National Whig leaders, like their Democratic counterparts, studiously avoided the slavery question. The Whigs, however, managed intraparty divisions over the issue differently: unlike the Democrats, who censured northern politicians for mobilizing antislavery opinion, the Whigs tolerated antislavery among northern politicians and printers.[45] They cobbled together a coalition that could be sustained, in Michael Holt's words, "only by agreeing to disagree, only by allowing northern and southern Whigs to take opposing stands on the issue in their respective sections."[46]

The intraparty alliances forged by Democratic and Whig leaders produced a relatively durable opposition between two nationally competitive parties.[47] The resurgence of national parties was affected through a new institutional formation: the presidential nominating convention. This may have been the most enduring institutional legacy of the second party system. It is especially worthy of note that the stated purpose of Van Buren's famous letter to Thomas Ritchie was to advocate the establishment of a national convention to nominate the next president. With memories of the four-way presidential contest of 1824 fresh in their minds, Van Buren argued that the only hope to revive the old Jeffersonian Republican party depended on the

Republicans' willingness to coordinate their efforts so that they could stand as a united front behind one national ticket. A national convention, he insisted, "is the best and probably the only practicable mode of concentrating the entire vote of the opposition & of effecting what is of still greater importance, the substantial reorganization of the Old Republican Party."[48] And as Van Buren warned Thomas Ritchie, without a revival of the old party schism between Jeffersonian Republicans and Federalists, a more dangerous party schism would invariably rise in its place. Party control of the national nominations procedure was therefore essential to "draw anew the old party lines." Crucially, the convention system forged by the new Democratic party adopted a rule requiring a two-thirds majority to win the party's presidential nomination. This rule effectively ensured that no candidate could be nominated without some support from both the slaveholding and non-slaveholding wings of the party. This mechanism ensured intraparty balance and helped, albeit indirectly, to protect the "balance rule" precedent set in place by the Missouri Compromise.[49]

For Democratic party leaders, restoring party control of national nominations was of first importance. They chose to inaugurate a new nominating system instead of reviving the old Congressional Caucus, in part because the Congressional Caucus system had been discredited as elitist and antidemocratic. The Congressional Caucus (derisively known at the time as "King Caucus") had first formed in the early Jeffersonian years and collapsed in 1824. Unlike the Congressional Caucus, delegates for the party convention could be elected at the state level, perhaps even directly selected by the people. The convention format also presented less of a political risk to party builders because it was perceived to be more democratic. Party leaders may have anticipated that they would encounter less resistance when promoting a convention system, if only because the rhetoric of antielitism and democracy could be used on its behalf. The convention system, moreover, had already achieved a significant measure of acceptance throughout the nation: it had been instituted in several states to ensure party control of nominations for crucial state offices.[50]

This institutional change resulted in a notable reallocation of power in American government. As Theodore J. Lowi has argued, the Congressional Caucus held the president accountable, first and foremost, to party supporters *in Congress*.[51] It thereby accorded congressional leaders a degree of leverage over the president. According to Lowi, the convention system was significant because it made presidents accountable to partisans outside of Congress.

The emergence of the presidential nominating convention represented a shift in power from the supremacy of the first branch, Congress, to the supremacy of party organizations in the states. Presidents had once been the creatures of elite congressional cliques; by the Jacksonian period, they had become the creatures of party.

The legitimization of party in this crucial period, as limited and conditional as it was, possessed an institutional legacy all its own. Yet, in order for these institutional advances to be fully realized, the "Little Magician" (as Van Buren was nicknamed) would have to reconcile the chief coalition partners within the Democratic fold. Keeping latent sectional divisions under wraps proved to be his greatest political challenge.

Staying the Hand of Jacksonian Nationalism

Van Buren's strenuous efforts to manage Democratic silence on the question of slavery was matched only by his efforts to straddle and finesse the question of trade tariffs.[52] Indeed, tariff policy could not simply be "left to the states." According to Robert Remini, the tariff issue, because it risked alienating the planters of the South from the "plain Republicans" of the North, was "one of the most potentially dangerous issues [Van Buren] ever tampered with in his life."[53] Any gains that Van Buren might make on this question could be undone by political agitators stridently opposed to compromise. This was precisely the challenge that South Carolina posed to the Jackson administration in 1832 and 1833 when John C. Calhoun threatened to divide Jackson's coalition by insisting on state authority to nullify the federal tariff.

Tariff policy was potentially polarizing insofar as it was entangled with the slavery question. Nullifiers believed that if northern interests consistently had their way on the tariff—the protective tariff was, in their view, a policy that was not sanctioned by a strict reading of the Constitution—it was only a matter of time before the majority, spurred by northern abolitionists, commenced its assault on the South's "domestic" institutions. North Carolina congressman Nathaniel Macon, writing in 1818, anticipated the nullifiers' reasoning. As Macon wrote in confidence to a close friend, "I must ask you to examine the constitution of the U.S. . . . and then tell me if Congress can establish banks, make roads and canals, whether they cannot free all the Slaves in the U.S. . . . If Congress can make canals," he wrote, "they can with more propriety emancipate."[54] Wielding a loose construction of the Constitution, there was no effective limit to the power northern emancipationists could exert over southern domestic policy. Turnbull echoed Macon's conclusion: with such a powerful weapon at their disposal, "the ultra fanatics and abolitionists of the North contend, that Congress can alter, whenever it pleases, the whole domestic policy of South-Carolina."[55]

Many southern elites saw the South as a permanent minority locked in an enduring struggle against an amassing majority tyranny.[56] Slavery was indirectly defended, according to historian William Freehling, through resistance to the tariff. [57] As Calhoun confessed, "I consider the Tariff act as the occasion, rather than the real cause of the present unhappy state of things. The truth can no longer be disguised, that the peculiar domestick institution of the Southern States, and the consequent direction, which that and her soil and climate have given to her industry, has placed them in regard to taxation and appropriations in opposite relation to the majority of the Union."[58] Calhoun, however, was not a secessionist. He began his political career as a nationalist advocate for a standing army, internal improvements, and a moderate tariff. These measures, he believed at the time, were necessary to preserve an adequate defense during the French Revolutionary Wars. The declining threat of foreign war after the conclusion of the War of 1812, however, permitted southern nationalists like Calhoun to become sectionalists in opposition to internal improvements and tariffs no longer deemed essential to the nation's defense.[59] These policy measures, southern sectionalists maintained, were part and parcel of an effort advanced by powerful northern interests to enrich themselves as the expense of southern planters. Nullification, however, would provide a permanent security against the hegemony of nationalists and protectionists in Washington and thereby ensure the continuity of the Union.[60] Knowing that the South would never accept the abolition of slavery, Calhoun believed that northern abolitionism would eventually force the South to secede; compromises on this question simply would not yield a permanent solution. "If there be no protective power in the reserved rights of the states," Calhoun asserted, "they must in the end be forced to rebel, or submit it to have their paramount interests sacraficed, their domestick institutions exhausted by Colonization and other schemes, and themselves & children reduced to wretchedness. Thus situated, the denial of the right of the State to interpose constitutionally in the last resort, more alarms the thinking, than all other causes."[61] Calhoun therefore conceived of his doctrine of nullification as an institutional safeguard that would preserve the Union.

Bristling at the provocation from South Carolina, Jackson countered with nationalist rhetoric even as he sought to accommodate the South through a reduced schedule of tariff rates. Jackson's annual message of December 1832, widely regarded as a conciliatory address in substance and tone, proposed a return to a revenue standard for import duties.[62] Jackson was more bellicose in his "Proclamation to the People of South Carolina," released only days later, where he espoused a nationalist theory of the Constitutional compact, a position that ran contrary to the "doctrines of the Jefferson school" and threatened to alienate potential allies who were firm states' rights supporters, yet opposed to South Carolina's threats of disunion.[63] Jackson's first maneuver (the annual message) guarded him against the charge of aggression, yet with the second (the Nullification Proclamation), he hoped to send the message that he was not intimidated by the challenge posed by South Carolina. These messages were not intellectually inconsistent; however, they operated at cross-purposes: the benevolence of the message to Congress was undone by the aggressiveness of the proclamation.[64]

Jackson's initial approach to the Nullification Crisis placed the great party builder, Martin Van Buren (the vice president–elect at the time), in an awkward position. Van Buren forged an electoral coalition that successfully bridged sectional differences by embracing the principle of state sovereignty. An impulsive move by the Jackson administration that embarrassed states' rights advocates broadly supportive of the Democratic coalition threatened to undo much of Van Buren's political work.

The standoff with South Carolina, Van Buren estimated, had to be resolved peacefully in order to preserve the Democratic coalition—even the Union itself. It was unclear, for example, whether the governor of Virginia, John Floyd, who was an ardent supporter of South Carolina's cause, would have permitted federal troops to pass through the state.[65] Anticipating the political implications of a Jacksonian drift toward nationalism, Van Buren sought to cultivate in Jackson a more moderate response to Calhoun, one that might both reaffirm the president's commitment to states' rights and nip the nullifiers' appeal to southern sectionalist sympathies in the bud. "You will say I am on my old track—caution—caution," Van Buren acknowledged. However, "the extent to which the hopes of the people rest upon you and the intense anxiety that nothing should be done that can be avoided, which lessens the chances of an amicable adjustment, will ensure, if they do not require, the observance of a greater degree of caution than might otherwise

be deemed necessary."[66] Van Buren correctly surmised that a gentle handling of party affiliates was necessary to preserve the foundations of the new
national party.

Van Buren attempted to finesse the constitutional rift raised by Jackson's
Nullification Proclamation by arguing, in a report written for the New York
legislature, that the people of the individual states—not the people of the
nation as a whole or the state governments—were the ultimate sovereign
authority in the American constitutional system. This conclusion affirmed
a notion of state sovereignty yet denied states the right to nullify or secede.[67]
Furthermore, in response to Jackson's Force Bill Message, Van Buren suggested that Jackson would be wise to refrain from any unnecessary show of
executive and military authority.[68] Jackson heeded Van Buren's warnings, assuming a more reserved role as the crisis progressed.[69] Southern support for
the nullifiers' cause failed to materialize, thanks, in part, to the administration's relative restraint.

Facing significant opposition from unionists within their state, South
Carolina nullifiers sought a means to soften their position. The nullifiers
ended the standoff without having to submit to Jackson by negotiating directly with congressional leaders.[70] Negotiations in Congress presented an occasion for the formation of new alliances. Indeed, extraordinary circumstances
make strange bedfellows. Though the principles of John Calhoun and Henry
Clay were "directly opposed" (as Clay himself admitted), they were both bitterly opposed to Jackson's leadership.[71] Calhoun hoped to save face for himself
and the nullifiers, and Henry Clay aimed to bolster his reputation as the
"Great Compromiser," a nickname that he earned from his role during the
Missouri Compromise negotiations; both sought to deprive Jackson of political credit for managing the controversy with South Carolina. To these ends,
they negotiated a tariff reduction bill that would be amenable to both South
Carolina and northern manufacturers. The result was a proposal to reduce
protective duties to a revenue standard, approximately 20 percent ad valorem,
to be effected gradually over nine and a half years.[72] The nullifiers' hatred for
Jackson helped smooth the negotiation. The Carolinians, Clay observed,
"were extremely unwilling that Jackson should have any credit in the adjustment of the controversy, and to prevent it were disposed to agree to much better terms for the manufacturers, if the measure originated with any other."[73]
Jackson, for his part, was willing to accept Clay's tariff reform bill so long as it
was passed with his Force bill.[74] This was the compromise that ended the
stalemate between South Carolina and the Jackson administration.

According to William Freehling, Jackson ultimately made a compromise possible by occupying the crucial center in this controversy. Clay and Calhoun were largely responsible for tariff reform and opposed in Congress by John Q. Adams and Daniel Webster, while Calhoun, Clay, and Van Buren stood against the Force bill.[75] Jackson alone, among the nation's leaders, stood for both measures.[76]

The alliance of "nationals and nullifiers" that forged the Compromise of 1833 would become the backbone of the "bastard coalition" that constituted the Whig party—a party unified primarily in its opposition to Andrew Jackson.[77] The crisis that threatened to sink the Democratic coalition ultimately presented an opportunity for its diverse opponents to join forces and present themselves together as the antipode to the Jackson party. This new political formation uniting the South and West, Jackson feared, would soon "blow up a storm on the subject of the slave question. Altho they know the east have no such views, still they will try to arouse the southern people on this false tale. This ought to be met, for be assured these men would do any act to destroy the union, and form a southern confederacy bounded, north, by the Patomac river."[78] Such a development would not come to pass. Instead, Webster and the eastern nationalists would be added to the Whig coalition, and the nullifying element subtracted, transforming the Whigs into the nationalist party. The rupture between Calhoun and the Whigs came in 1837 when Calhoun sided with the Van Buren administration in favor of the latter's plan for an independent treasury. "Political parties," Calhoun maintained, "will again be formed on the old and natural division of State Rights and National, which divided them at the commencement of the Government, and which experience has shown is that division of party most congenial to our system, and most favorable to its successful operation."[79] In this manner, Van Buren and Jackson's chief antagonist, John Calhoun, completed the work of drawing anew the old party lines that Van Buren proposed in 1827.

Party-Driven Imperialism and the Unraveling of the Second Party System

As politically delicate as the tariff issue was when it was entangled with the slavery question, the policy matter on its own and in the abstract lends itself to compromise: different goods and commodities can be differentiated and itemized, and rates are scalable. The qualities of goods, moreover, produce a bounty of dimensions for negotiation and adjustment.[80] Territorial expansion was much trickier, since the formation of a territory—a political unit—required that a decision be made about whether or not slaves might be held as property on the premises. This matter of slavery's extension into the territories did not so easily lend itself to an adjustment of differences.

Territorial expansion was pregnant with greater risk because it presented contending factions with what appeared to be a zero-sum contest over the disposition of land: the introduction of slaves, it was believed, depressed wages for whites hoping to settle on the frontier and raise enough funds to purchase their own land.[81] Slave owners, for their part, did not wish to risk bringing their property into territory dominated by free labor. The economic and legal contest was crucial to the ongoing and prospective struggle over political representation, since the economic makeup of the land (whether it was free or slave) powerfully shaped—if it did not determine—the political disposition of its representation. Though new lands promised great bounty for white settlers, the westward progress of speculators, settlers, and slaveholders reopened questions that establishment figures hoped would remain settled and contained under the auspices of past compromises.

Party competition (in conjunction with other forces) goaded America down this path. Territorial aggrandizement had long been a unifying theme for the Democratic party. The impulse to secure lands for white settlers was most clearly articulated during Jackson's years by his uncompromising mission to deny legitimate native American claims to lands in Georgia.[82] The annexation of Texas, for Jackson, was a long-term objective.[83] Van Buren, as president, hesitated at the prospect of annexation. Mired in a depression precipitated by the Panic of 1837 and worried that the Texas question might endanger the prospects for passage of his economic program, Van Buren was inclined to put the matter on the back burner.[84]

A Whig president, John Tyler, put the Texas question on the front burner. Tyler, who was elevated from the vice presidency to the White House after William Henry Harrison's death in 1841, had very little support among leading Whigs once he broke with Clay following his veto of a bill to recharter the Bank of the United States. Tyler had, as historian Michael Morrison explains, been "banished from the Whig Party."[85] His push for annexation received little backing from Whigs and overwhelming support from Democrats in Congress.[86]

Whigs differed (as they did on so many other matters) on the question of expansion. There was, nonetheless, a discernible Whig stance on the matter:

if the republic is to expand, it should do so in a controlled, peaceable manner respectful of existing treaties with native peoples and foreign powers. This position evolved among many high-ranking Whigs to a more categorical opposition to all new territorial acquisitions.[87]

The Whig "go slow" approach, however, had limited appeal. Whig legal and humanitarian hand-wringing was simply not a winning electoral message in diverse parts of the Union. Democrats did not waste the opportunity: they used the issue to brand theirs the party of unrestrained expansion. This was a strategically advantageous course, at least in the short and medium run. The American appetite for new lands was seemingly insatiable, and Whig hesitations, often framed in legal or humanitarian terms and (so it appeared) for the benefit of natives and foreign powers, was easily dismissed by impatient, land-hungry, and racist constituencies. Territorial acquisition, moreover, promised to build a hegemonic electoral alliance by adding the West to the Democrats' bases of support in the mid-Atlantic and southern states.

Yet Manifest Destiny could serve as a source of unity for the Democratic party only so long as party leaders pursued a balanced expansion—catering to the expansionist demands of contending factions of the party. With the Texas question settled by an annexation bill signed by Tyler just as he was leaving office, the test of balanced expansion fell to James K. Polk, who led the Democratic charge for territorial aggrandizement from 1845 to 1849. As the leader of a party and a polity increasingly divided by competing calls for "equal justice," Polk aimed to secure gains that would satisfy northwestern and mid-Atlantic constituents (the Oregon Territory) and their southern counterparts (on the Mexican frontier). Polk, moreover, was driven by the desire not just to extend the accomplishments of the predecessor he so revered (Andrew Jackson), but to leave his own mark on a resilient Democratic regime.[88]

Despite considerable effort, Polk failed to meet the demands of those who pushed for the administration to fight for all of Oregon—up to the 54°40′ parallel. Demands for all of Oregon and expansion in the Southwest stood in an uneasy tension: securing all of Oregon would, in all likelihood, have meant war with Great Britain at a time when war loomed over the territorial dispute with Mexico. Polk, it seems, could commit to war in one section but not both. With a considerably weaker foe to the south and a higher concentration of American settlements in Texas and on the frontier with Mexico (as compared to the sparsely populated Columbia River region),

Polk turned to the Southwest to secure his legacy. Indeed, the border dispute with Mexico presented a more inviting opportunity to solidify his own place in history with new territorial gains and a heroic military confrontation.

Not all Democrats were eager for war with Mexico. Many in the old Northwest (from Ohio, Michigan, and neighboring states) were disgruntled with Polk's willingness to compromise with Britain in negotiations for the Oregon Territory; many in the mid-Atlantic states were frustrated with his support for free trade and alleged that he harbored a sectional (pro-southern) bias. The South, to be sure, was not uniformly supportive of Polk's aims in the Southwest. Some influential southerners—Calhoun, in particular—were wary of war with Mexico, a project that risked a sectional conflict with relatively little payoff for the slaveholding states.[89] Calhoun and like-minded politicians strongly supported the annexation of Texas, but California and New Mexico, unlike Texas, were seen as inhospitable to the extension of slavery. Many Whigs who opposed Polk's war preferred to avoid the whole question of slavery by endorsing a policy of "No Territory"—effectively abstaining from future acquisitions of new land.[90]

To no one's surprise, Mexico's underresourced military was no match for the forces collected by the growing industrial power to the north. As the war drew to a close, Polk submitted a request to Congress for $2 million to serve as a down payment for any land purchased from Mexico through peace negotiations. Polk's appeal for funds presented an opening for discontented Democrats and Whigs to thwart the president's ambitions. A Pennsylvania Democrat, David Wilmot, took advantage of the opportunity, introducing an amendment to exclude slavery from any territory purchased with these funds.

The Wilmot Proviso caused a great stir, first because it cast a shadow on the territorial rewards of the Mexican War—a war most Whigs, including a young Lincoln, vigorously opposed.[91] More important, it was not fully in accord with the Missouri Compromise: the proviso would have prohibited the introduction of slavery into the newly acquired territory south of 36°30′, contrary (in the view of many) to the spirit of the Missouri Compromise.[92]

In his zeal to seize a prize for his party and his presidency, Polk failed to anticipate the sectional schism his achievements would expose. The controversy that erupted took Polk by surprise, in part because he didn't believe that slavery would ever, in fact, take hold in the inhospitable lands of New Mexico and California. There was, he reasoned, no need for Congress to involve itself and legislate on the matter either way.[93] Given the assumptions he was working with, the Wilmot Proviso appeared to him to be a pernicious distraction and a gratuitous provocation of the slaveholding states.

Once the danger that a wider division between the North and the South (and within the Democratic party itself) was evident, Polk aggressively mobilized the resources of his administration to settle the question. In pursuit of a compromise that would permit the territorial organization of the newly acquired lands, Polk resolved to extend the Missouri Compromise line westward,[94] personally intervening in congressional negotiations. As he confessed, this was "an unusual step for the Executive to take, but the emergency demands it. It may be the only means of allaying a fearful sectional excitement & of preserving the Union."[95] Anxious to organize territorial governments for New Mexico and California over the objections of antislavery northern congressmen and uncompromising southern legislators like Calhoun, Polk exclaimed, in evident frustration, "I put my face alike against southern agitators and Northern fanatics, & should do everything in my power to allay excitement by adjusting the question of slavery & preserving the Union."[96]

Polk's failure to balance his expansionist exploits reopened old sectional wounds within the party and the polity more generally. The president's initiatives prompted a revolt by northern Van Buren Democrats (the "Barnburners"), who united with "Conscience" Whigs and members of the Liberty party to form the Free Soil party. By the 1850s, these new alignments would produce a new Republican party, one firmly committed to preventing the extension of slavery into the territories. Henry Clay (among many others) correctly gauged the consequences of Polk's leadership: as he took his stand in 1847 against "the spirit of rapacity" and the "inordinate desire for territorial aggrandizement," he insisted, " We do not want the mines, the mountains, the morasses, and the sterile lands of Mexico. To her the loss of them would be humiliating, and be a perpetual source of regret and mortification. To us they might prove a fatal acquisition, producing distraction, dissension, division, possibly disunion."[97]

These "sterile lands" would put Van Buren's political science to the test. Indeed, Van Buren's promise from the 1820s that party attachments would provide an alternate and more predictable basis for political competition began to ring hollow as the 1840s wore on and the country's westward advance pushed the slavery question onto the national political agenda. Even

Van Buren himself appeared to lose faith in 1848 as he broke with the Democratic party to run for president as candidate of the Free Soil party, though he would return in 1852 to the Democratic party fold to endorse Franklin Pierce.[98]

Despite the sectional cross tensions emergent in the polity at midcentury, party affiliations had, nonetheless, proved to be relatively durable, with voting records in Congress reflecting strong partisan loyalties into the early 1850s.[99] Party affiliations were meaningful to those who carried the denomination "Democrat" and "Whig"; these were not names that were casually discarded when new, sectional questions burst onto the political scene.[100] Party attachments, moreover, served as powerful national adhesives precisely because they carried a deep significance for so many Americans. Strong partisan commitments made it possible for the Democrats and Whigs to achieve the highly improbable feat of binding together a union of states divided by the intractable question of slavery. This is, at least, how Van Buren (writing in 1856) conceived the historical role of the parties:

> That union should so long have been preserved in a confederacy
> which contains an element of discord of such magnitude and of so
> disturbing a nature as that of slavery, is a wonder—more surprising
> than its dissolution would be. This has been owing to the fact, I
> firmly believe, the single fact that there have always been neutral-
> izing considerations of sufficient force to maintain party cohesions
> between men of the free and slave States. Slavery questions have
> from the beginning had more or less to do with our political
> contests, but have never before had the effect of dissolving old party
> connections and sympathies, and the balance-wheel has thus been
> preserved.[101]

Party connections and sympathies were in constant tension with latent sectional identities that rose to the surface as the pressure to settle the West and the crucial matter of territorial governance—slavery—forced itself onto the national agenda. By 1856, it was becoming increasingly clear that the struggle to define the status of slavery in the new territories would upset that organization of countervailing sympathies—that "balance-wheel"—that Van Buren had so diligently calibrated and had maintained the Union in equilibrium for so long.

Conclusion

The contours of the second party system evolved in accord with two great compromises: one engineered by Van Buren, with the crucial assistance of Jackson's charismatic leadership, binding the "planters of the South and the plain Republicans of the North," and the other, a bargain forged by Clay, Webster, and Calhoun, that rallied Jackson's diverse opponents under one banner. The legacy of these strategic machinations was the establishment of a relatively durable opposition between two nationally competitive parties. The second party system originated thanks, not so much to the progressive enlightenment of leading public figures who recognized the democratic advantages of party competition, but to the pragmatic maneuvers of ambitious politicians who took advantage of a moment in political and institutional time when a new kind of party politics became possible.

Van Buren is rightfully known as a party innovator who championed the organizational practices and institutions (such as the nominating convention and the spoils system) most commonly associated with the modern mass party. The Whigs were latecomers to the methods perfected by Van Buren's organization yet grudgingly embraced them thanks to competitive pressure from their better-organized opponents.[102] Van Buren's contribution to the status of party in America was distinctive insofar as he was able, in both thought and practice, to reconcile the egalitarian and integrative potential of party politics. Parties, as Van Buren anticipated, served a positive and a defensive purpose: parties were promoted to meet the representational demands of a rapidly expanding electorate no longer willing to defer to their "betters" and at the same time, to direct the energies of political rivalries in a manner that would not provoke sectional "prejudices." In practice, these purposes worked in tandem as the distribution of patronage jobs (e.g., in post offices, land offices, and customs houses) and distributive resources (e.g., tariff protections, tax exemptions, and public subsidies) promoted party discipline and operated as a surrogate for intraparty ideological unity. The distributive aspect of party organization, in other words, restrained popular inclinations to advance a more programmatic and "principled" mode of party competition between the two major parties.[103]

Entrepreneurial politicians played an important role, but timing and sequence played an equally important part. The restoration of peace in Europe and the settlement of the Missouri question made the emergence of a new brand of quasi-legitimate party politics possible. Yet, the "old" opposition between Federalists and Jeffersonian Republicans, once drawn anew by Democratic party builders, was little more than a glimmer of its earlier form: absent the polarizing suspicion of foreign loyalties, the ideological intensity of opposition between Democrats and Whigs was a faint echo of the bitter battles fought in the 1790s and the early 1800s. The relatively subdued quality of public debate that surrounded questions relating to the bank, internal improvements, and the tariff (when shorn of entanglements with slavery) afforded the space for a regular and manageable competition to emerge between two parties with distinct positions on a delimited range of issues.

American democracy took its first significant step toward the legitimization of party more than a decade after the war in Europe ended and the first party system collapsed. The conditions of American sovereignty had changed, and so had the prospects for a new brand of party politics. America had achieved a measure of political autonomy and so was freed from the threat of a party politics scandalized by foreign intrigue and rival recriminations of national betrayal and disloyalty. Just as the United States achieved a measure of security on the international stage, a great vulnerability was revealed at home. Policy questions concerning the institution of slavery and the passions and prejudices that attended them posed an ever-present, if latent, challenge to the Jacksonian order. Much to the chagrin of Van Buren and like-minded unionists, issues that foreshadowed the unraveling of the new party system resurfaced not long after Jackson assumed office in 1828. Periodic flare-ups of violent sectional antagonisms served as reminders of the unsettled nature of party organizational arrangements in the electorate and in Congress. The ascent in the 1850s of what appeared to many to be a truly sectional party, the Republican party, triggered the final collapse of the détente that had preserved the Union for so long. As we shall see in Chapter 5, this development exposed what contemporaries understood about the second party system: that it was a conditional arrangement designed at once to accommodate the representative demands of a diverse and democratic polity and to prevent, so far as possible, the emergence of the slavery question as a focus of national political debate.

CHAPTER 5

Union, Emancipation, and Party Building as Military Strategy

> It is now for [our people] to demonstrate to the world,
> that those who can fairly carry an election, can also
> suppress a rebellion—that ballots are the rightful, and
> peaceful, successors of bullets; and that when ballots
> have fairly, and constitutionally, decided, there can be
> no successful appeal, back to bullets; that there can
> be no successful appeal, except to ballots themselves, at
> succeeding elections. Such will be a great lesson of
> peace; teaching men that what they cannot take by an
> election, neither can they take it by a war—teaching all,
> the folly of being the beginners of a war.
> —Abraham Lincoln, Message to Congress
> in Special Session, 4 July 1861

In the 1850s, Abraham Lincoln watched in alarm as the Democratic party altered its position on the slavery question and moved public debate onto unsettled ground. The question of slavery might be held at bay, Lincoln believed, only if the country returned to the familiar standards of the Missouri Compromise. His politics, until the outbreak of the war, was oriented toward reestablishing this compromise and thereby reviving the old opposition between Whigs and Democrats. Once war was under way, he remained committed to restoring the order of the past: together with like-minded, pragmatic Republicans, he aimed to secure the reunion of the states, not by military means alone, but also by molding the Republican party into a consensus party, a National Union party, that would win vital support among the border slave states. The Lincoln administration demonstrated a great degree of liberality toward slaveholders in the border states, made a show of appointing War Democrats and border-state politicians to high-ranking executive and military stations, and pushed for frequent opportunities for those who had seceded to vote themselves back into the Union. Lincoln and fellow Unionists hoped, in other words, to subdue the secessionists politically, by transforming the Republican party into an organization with a more inclusive purpose and a national following, thereby seizing the political center and isolating the disunionists.

Lincoln's strategy was a partial success: it helped to keep the border states within the Union fold during the early stages of the war—no modest achievement; it was, nonetheless, abandoned by Lincoln himself when, he claimed, more forceful measures had become necessary. Lincoln's strategic vision is revealing for our purposes because it highlights the lengths political leaders go to tailor party-building strategies to the structural limitations of the polity they are called on to govern. With eleven states in open rebellion, the war emergency brought the foundational vulnerabilities that had shaped American politics since the ratification of the Constitution to the fore. Lincoln's worries mirrored those of James Madison from nearly a century earlier. To return to a discussion commenced in Chapter 1, Madison wondered aloud at the Constitutional Convention how the new republic could manage just the sort of crisis the new Lincoln administration confronted: "Could the national resources, if exerted to the utmost enforce a national decree agst. Massts. abetted perhaps by several of her neighbours? It wd. not be possible. A; [sic] small proportion of the Community in a compact situation, acting on the defensive, and at one of its extremities might at any time bid defiance to the National authority."[1] Substitute Virginia and the rest of the Confederate states for Massachusetts in this passage and one must wonder, with Lincoln, how indeed, these states could be made answerable to the national authority when they were arrayed "in a compact situation, acting on the defensive, and at one of its extremities." Lincoln and his associates were clearly skeptical they could be made to do so without considerable effort and uncertainty. The administration's political and military posture, consequently, demonstrated liberality toward border-state unionists and restraint toward the rebels. As Lincoln counseled, "The severest justice may not always be the best policy."[2]

The war emergency brought the underlying relationship between the structural makeup of the polity and party legitimacy into full view: the major parties could not be relied on to support the preservation of the Union or, for that matter, the restoration of the Union (if a separation had already been effected) if they politicized the most unsettling and polarizing questions of their time. The range of legitimate party opposition was, accordingly, delimited. Lincoln and other national political leaders, mindful of the limited reach of federal authority, did what they could to avoid the most divisive policy questions—emancipation was the most important among them—that might alienate border constituents. Hoping to avoid the great question that might have been raised but wasn't (emancipation), Lincoln, like so many national figures before him, pursued instead a party coalition-building effort tailored to placate border-state unionists and northern "War Democrats." Given the rebel's "compact" and "defensive" posture, this strategy, Lincoln and fellow unionists reasoned, presented the best prospect of hastening a political solution to the civil crisis and averting total war.

Yet the Lincoln administration's grand plans did not yield a new political settlement or an end to the fighting. Unable to win the war by more consensual means, the administration, in January 1863, gave up on the old order—the Missouri Compromise—and committed the Republican "party-state" (the Union government) to emancipation, directing its considerable war machine to destroy the socioeconomic system that itself generated the great matter of contention between the states.[3] The revolutionary character of the Emancipation Proclamation has been much discussed in the historical literature.[4] For present purposes, however, the Proclamation represented a decisive departure from the pattern of unionist party-coalition building most forthrightly defended by Martin Van Buren. It had been the hallmark of political leaders, presidents in particular, to build party coalitions with the aim, not merely to maximize their electoral advantage, but also to silence questions that might trigger political violence or separatist movements. Lincoln staked out a radically different course when he issued his Proclamation; for the first time in American history, a party leader in a position of high responsibility embraced a sectionalist mandate for a major political party on the most divisive question of the day. The Emancipation Proclamation has been rightly heralded as revolutionary on moral and legal grounds; yet it was also revolutionary because it entailed a sectionalist approach to party building, an approach that, tactically speaking, came at a considerable risk.

The backlash produced by the Emancipation Proclamation itself exposed a critical vulnerability in the Union war effort, availing to the South a political means to win the war. Indeed, the Proclamation alienated a significant portion of the Union war effort's political base of support. As the conflict progressed, it became clear to Confederate military and political leaders that a northern Democrat committed to ending the bloodshed could defeat Lincoln in 1864. Northern Democratic voters, in essence, could "win" the war for the South if Confederate forces could continue the fight long enough to see a Democrat in the White House. Thus, the Lincoln administration was in the unusual position of having to win both at the polls and on the battlefield—where defeat in one setting could spell total defeat and a breakup of the Union.

This chapter begins with a description of Lincoln's and like-minded Whig-turned-Republicans' hopes in the 1850s to return to the terms of the Missouri Compromise and restore a crumbling second party system to health. In the section that follows, I examine the Lincoln administration's leadership posture after the onset of the secession crisis, paying special attention to Lincoln's strategy of electoral reconciliation and what this strategy reveals about the relationship between the capacities of government and the coalitional patterns of major parties. The concluding section then examines the implications of Lincoln's decision to jettison the terms of the Missouri Compromise and pursue a path that would destroy the existing socioeconomic structure of the South. Lincoln, in other words, placed his unionist party-building strategy on hold and committed his administration to a sectionalist political and military strategy. As we shall see, a sectionalist party-building strategy is a high risk–high reward undertaking when the federal government does not possess control throughout the territory.

Restoring the Second Party System

Politicians of the antebellum years went to great lengths to sidestep the most intractable dilemma confronting the polity: the problem of two socioeconomic systems, one based on free labor, another based on slave labor, operating under one political roof. The Republican party coalesced behind a narrative that at once repudiated existing alternatives (popular sovereignty for the territories on the one hand, abolition on the other), but was also conservative insofar as it promised a return to an earlier order, represented most concretely by the Missouri Compromise and the Compromise of 1850. In the view of Lincoln and others, these compromises were sanctioned by the original understandings of the Founders themselves. The work of restoration was necessary because the old order had been, in the Republican version of events, gratuitously dismantled.

The Compromise of 1850 had put to rest the controversy over the disposition of the territory ceded by Mexico: this agreement, which supplemented (i.e., did not contradict) the Missouri Compromise, provided for the admission of California as a free state, organized the territories of Utah and New Mexico without restrictions on slavery, prohibited the domestic slave trade in the District of Columbia, and set in place a draconian fugitive slave law.[5] This last provision was crucial to slaveholders because it afforded those slaveholders living in states that bordered free states greater security in their human property. Repealing or significantly weakening the fugitive slave law could have fairly dramatic long-term effects on the balance of political power within the Union. As Richard Bensel explains, repealing the fugitive slave law would force "slaveholders to emigrate into more secure regions of the deep South, thereby eroding support for slavery in the border states."[6]

The regime that governed slavery in the territories (the Missouri Compromise and the Compromise of 1850) came undone in 1854 with the passage of the Kansas-Nebraska Act. Stephen Douglas introduced this proposal, though he received crucial support from the Democratic president, Franklin Pierce. It institutionalized a principle of "popular sovereignty" to allow territorial governments (in this case, Kansas and Nebraska, territories north of 36°30′ latitude) to decide whether to permit the institution of slavery. This was consistent with Democrats' states' rights ideology, but it also represented a critical shift in the Democrats' stance on the issue. The act undermined the long-standing Democratic commitment to bind northern and southern constituencies in an inclusive party coalition; this earlier vision was set aside in favor of the more sectional program favored by the southern-rights wing of the Democrats.

The Kansas-Nebraska Act polarized the country over the slavery question and galvanized anti-Democratic (party) forces across the country.[7] The Whig party, however, failed to capitalize on this opportunity: Free-Soilers moved first, successfully framing the issue in divisive anti-southern terms. Newspapers published a vitriolic protest written by the Free-Soil

senators Salmon Chase and Charles Sumner, who insisted that the legislation would force the nation to submit to "the yoke of a slaveholding despo-
tism."[8] The actions of the Free-Soilers, however, only strengthened support
for the Kansas-Nebraska bill among southern Whigs in the Senate, who
might have otherwise opposed it; once opponents were assailed by the Free-
Soilers, the question became a matter of southern honor.[9] William Seward
had hoped to unite the Whig party in opposition to the bill, but the Free-
Soilers had stolen his thunder. John Bell, a southern Whig who opposed the
measure, correctly surmised that "the tendency of this bill is to stimulate
the formation of a sectional party organization . . . the last and most fatal
evil which can befall this country."[10]

Meanwhile, northern Whigs were increasingly challenged by the rapid
progress of anti-Catholic, nativist sentiment spreading across the country.
Indeed, while Nebraska divided the northern from the southern Whigs, a
resurgent nativism divided the party in the North. The Whig party did not
fall apart, Michael Holt maintains, but instead "bled to death," losing supporters to newer party formations like the Free-Soilers and the Know-
Nothings.[11] Cross-sectional party coalitions became increasingly untenable
after the passage of the Kansas-Nebraska legislation. After 1854, the only
plausible hope for the revival of cross-sectional party competition was
through the organization of a party that would ally Know-Nothings with
southern Whigs.[12] The newly formed Republican party, however, took pre-
cedence as the Democrats' primary opponents.[13]

Together, the divergent components of the Republican party, which included northern "Conscience" Whigs, abolitionists, Free-Soilers, and Barn-
burner Democrats (Van Buren's wing of the party), managed to accomplish
precisely what the northern Whig leadership aimed, but failed, to achieve:
that is, to make a national appeal to restore the old regime of the Missouri
Compromise and the Compromise of 1850. Their message, at least as it was
articulated by leading party spokesmen, was not couched in vitriolic anti-
southern rhetoric but was rather framed as a return to the national compromises that sustained the country for decades.

The new Republican party quickly assumed the conservative high
ground: Stephen Douglas, Franklin Pierce, and the Democrats were typecast
in Republican rhetoric as radicals responsible for undermining the existing
settlement on the slavery question and provoking the agitation that polarized the country. In a speech given in Peoria, Illinois, in 1854, Lincoln described the Kansas-Nebraska Act as

an aggravation, . . . of the only one thing which ever endangers the Union. When it came upon us, all was peace and quiet. . . . In the whole range of possibility, there scarcely appears to me to have been any thing, out of which the slavery agitation could have been revived, except the very project of repealing the Missouri compromise. Every inch of territory we owned, already had a definite settlement of the slavery question, and by which, all parties were pledged to abide. . . . In this state of case, the genius of Discord himself, could scarcely have invented a way of getting us by the ears, but by turning back and destroying the peace measures of the past.[14]

Senator Douglas's shifting position on the Missouri Compromise became a special object of scrutiny after he shepherded the Kansas-Nebraska bill through Congress. Lincoln assailed Douglas's hypocrisy using the senator's own words: "precisely four years and a quarter after [Douglas] declared that compromise to be a sacred thing, which 'no ruthless hand would ever dare to touch,' he, himself, brought forward the measure, ruthlessly to destroy it."[15]

The Kansas-Nebraska Act undermined the political détente between free and slave states not only by unsettling the existing regime governing the territories, but also by undercutting the working assumption that made compromise itself possible: that the free states should be compensated for any advantage secured by the slave states (and vice-versa).[16] The Kansas-Nebraska Act was, in this sense, a landgrab secured by the slave states in bad faith. What is more, many in both the North and the South who believed that a slave economy could not be profitable in a northern climate viewed the act as little more than a symbolic and unnecessary provocation perpetrated by the southern-rights wing of the Democratic party.

The *Dred Scott* decision, handed down in 1857, compounded the political injury inflicted by the Kansas-Nebraska Act. This decision, which held that neither the territorial governments nor Congress possessed the authority to bar slavery from the American territories, contradicted the notion of territorial "popular sovereignty" institutionalized by the Kansas-Nebraska Act. In doing so, it took the proextensionist spirit of this act one step further by affirming that only states possessed the authority to regulate slavery. This decision set in motion a rush to populate the new territories by proslavery and antiextensionist factions to build their respective constituencies in anticipation of a struggle to define the disposition of slavery in the West.[17]

For Lincoln, the *Dred Scott* decision completed a disturbing picture of a legal machinery that he feared would raze all barriers to slavery throughout the Union.[18] The "*working* points of that machinery" were threefold: (1) that no black man or woman may ever be a citizen and thereby attain standing in a federal court of law, (2) that neither Congress nor a territorial legislature had the authority to prohibit slavery in any U.S. territory, and (3) that the question of whether a black man or woman held as a slave in a free state becomes free is to be decided by the courts of the slave state from which the master originates. "This [last] point," Lincoln maintained, "is made, not to be pressed *immediately*; but, if acquiesced in for a while, and apparently *indorsed* by the people at an election, *then* to sustain the logical conclusion that what Dred Scott's master might lawfully do with Dred Scott, in the free State of Illinois, every other master may lawfully do with any other *one*, or one *thousand* slaves, in Illinois, or in any other free State."[19] The free states would not only be bound to enforce the fugitive slave act (the bitter pill they swallowed to secure the Compromise of 1850), but would soon be overrun by slave masters who could transport their human property, unfettered, throughout the North.[20]

Opposition to this "machinery" constituted the center of gravity for the newly formed Republican party organization. Ideologically, the new party was united by an encompassing embrace of free labor and a common bond of resistance to the "Slave Power."[21] Yet their aim to restore the Missouri Compromise was, above all, a conservative objective insofar as it promised a return to the party politics of the pre-Nebraska period. Moreover, their stance was warranted, both by its claims to centrism and originalism. The centrism of Lincoln's brand was defined while he was still a Whig. Lincoln encouraged fellow Whigs to resist partisan extremes by standing with the Missouri Compromise and the terms of the Compromise of 1850, even if doing so required the formation of uncomfortable alliances with abolitionists (to restore the Missouri Compromise), or with southern disunionists (to preserve the fugitive slave law): "In both cases you oppose the dangerous extremes. In both you stand on middle ground and hold the ship level and steady. In both you are national and nothing less than national. This is good old whig ground. To desert such ground, because of any company, is to be less than a whig—less than a man—less than an American."[22] Lincoln's middle ground was especially advantageous because it could boast of a lineage dating to the Founders' sponsorship of the Northwest Ordinance of 1787, which banned slavery from the Northwest Territory.[23] "The spirit of seventy-six and the spirit of Nebraska, are utter antagonisms; and the former is being rapidly displaced by the latter."[24] He leveraged the originalism of his position to scold those who favored the extension of slavery and threatened to break up the Union if their demands were not met: "Do you [extensionists] really think you are justified to break up the government rather than have it administered by [George] Washington, and other good and great men who made it, and first administered it?"[25]

This "old whig" stance on the slavery question, which Lincoln believed the Founders themselves embraced, was taken up by the Republican party. Lincoln was not nostalgic, but he did wish to return to the status quo ante Nebraska when the country was on a course that promised economic, political, and even moral, progress. In his early career, Lincoln was a self-described "old Henry Clay tariff whig."[26] He did not change course on the tariff question or on the advantages of federally sponsored internal improvements. His political thinking, instead, fixated on a problem that Clay and the old Whigs averted through negotiation and compromise. By the mid- to late 1850s his speeches and correspondence reflected a single-minded focus on the slavery question: there was very little talk of tariffs, internal improvements, or any of the other public issues that preoccupied the preceding generation. Slavery, Lincoln maintained, was "*the* question"; "so much more important has it become that no other national question can even get a hearing."[27] A return to the Missouri settlement and to the relative calm of the pre-Nebraska years would reestablish these other, more modest questions in the national political arena. In all likelihood, such a return to the status quo ante would draw anew the old party lines, returning the Union to a more familiar pattern of opposition between Whigs and Democrats.

The Missouri Compromise was the touchstone for Lincoln's political posture in the 1850s, not only because it established a political détente, but also because he believed that it would likely lead to the eventual extinction of slavery. His vision was quasi-utopian: this stopgap measure, secured in 1820 to resolve the status of the Missouri Territory, also offered the ultimate remedy for the great question that divided the nation. The linchpin of this thinking was the soil exhaustion theory, the political economic supposition that slavery required new, fertile soil to persist. This theory held that without new territory, the slave economy would be trapped on land that would increasingly lose productivity, and in the long term, lead to the decline in the value of slave labor. If it was confined to the lands where it already exists, it would eventually wither away. Thus, "Slavery has within itself the seeds of its own destruction."[28] Ultimately, the Missouri Compromise would, in fact, make itself obsolete.[29]

It is unclear whether or not Lincoln believed civil war to be inevitable. He may have agreed with Seward that conflict between the free-labor and slave-labor economies was "irrepressible," but he maintained, at least in public, that there was a political remedy available.[30] Perhaps his most dramatic public statement on this question came on 16 June 1858, in his "House Divided" speech. There he insisted that he did not "expect the Union to be *dissolved*"; he did, however, "expect it will cease to be divided. . . . It will become *all* one thing, or *all* the other. . . . Either the *opponents* of slavery, will arrest the further spread of it, and place it where the public mind shall rest in the belief that it is in course of ultimate extinction; or its *advocates* will push it forward, till it shall become alike lawful in *all* the States, *old* as well as *new*— *North* as well as *South*."[31]

There was no reason, in his view, why the South could not tolerate limitations on the extension of slavery, as it had for over eighty years. If moderate voices in the Democratic party prevailed, Democrats could and would willingly retrench and accept the old compromises that sustained the Union. Disunionist sentiment nonetheless grew within the ranks of the Democratic party as the election of 1860 approached. John Brown's raid on Harpers Ferry was leveraged by southern Democrats to tar "Black Republicans" as radical (if not murderous) abolitionists, ready and willing to invade their states to provoke slave insurrections. The matter of the territories also began to take a backseat to claims that the federal government threatened invasion of the South and its domestic institutions. "The Territories," Lincoln observed, "are scarcely mentioned [by Democrats]. Invasions and insurrections are the rage now."[32]

Many of the presidents who preceded Lincoln (e.g., Washington, Adams, and Monroe) were inclined to disavow polarizing partisan claims or to seek consensual adjustments to the great political controversies of their time. Like his predecessors in office, Lincoln assumed a conservative position vis-à-vis the great issue of his time—he proposed a return to the principles of a preexisting standard. Moreover, he did not change his position on the extension of slavery in response to the secession crisis of 1860. Nor did he attempt to evade the question altogether (though his secretary of state, William Seward, presented him with an opportunity to do just that).[33] He instead confronted the secession crisis with a firm passivity: he inflexibly held his position on the slavery question yet insisted in his Inaugural Address that "the government will not assail *you*. You can have no conflict, without being yourselves the aggressors."[34] This stance characterized his management of the looming crisis surrounding the resupply of the besieged Fort Sumter in South Carolina. Lincoln forced the rebels to take the initiative, which provided his administration with political cover to energetically suppress the insurrection. Once Fort Sumter was attacked, Lincoln obtained a mandate, not to push forth his position on the slavery question, but to preserve the Union.

Once it became clear that the Confederacy would not go easily, he utilized his political mandate to reassert the sovereignty of the Union on Republican terms. Of course, an easier alternative was available: Lincoln might have simply accepted the departure of the eleven slave states that seceded. But he never treated the preservation of the Union as a point of negotiation. Separation, after all, presented the Union with a number of intractable governing challenges. For example, how would the two nation-states settle on a lengthy terrestrial border? How would such a border be enforced in the future? The two countries, moreover, would still have to engage one another as foreign powers, and separation would not solve the political problem that divided them: "Physically speaking, we cannot separate. We cannot remove our respective sections from each other, nor build an impassable wall between them. A husband and wife may be divorced, and go out of the presence, and beyond the reach of each other; but the different parts of our country cannot do this. They cannot but remain face to face; and intercourse, either amicable or hostile, must continue between them."[35] The "decision" to put down the rebellion, in some respects, was not a decision at all. The *Illinois State Journal*, Lincoln's unofficial spokesman during the secession period, proclaimed that the executive possessed "no discretionary power on the subject—his duty is emphatically pronounced in the Constitution."[36] In this effort, the executive would not stand alone: Republican partisans and unionists of all stripes stood steadfastly behind Lincoln's commitment to put down the incipient rebellion.

The National Union Party and the Strategy of Electoral Reconciliation

The outbreak of war brought with it a great mismatch between competing visions of what was necessary to restore the Missouri Compromise accord and the existing party alternatives: many northern Democrats wished to restore the Union on terms that were unacceptable for Lincoln and fellow moderate Republicans.[37] Radical Republicans, on the other hand, sought to prosecute the war with a vengeance that would discourage rebels from laying down their arms and reentering the Union. Such vengeance, Lincoln believed, would prolong the war and exacerbate the awesome burden of reconstruction looming on the horizon. Neither of these alternatives would ease the reentry of rebels back into the Union on terms acceptable to Lincoln and his supporters.

Lincoln's strategy to end the war and achieve reconciliation prioritized the role of persuasion: he hoped to convince wavering secessionists to abandon the rebellion and to provide states in rebellion with the opportunity to vote themselves back into the Union. A crucial corollary to this approach was to strengthen the unionist elements in the slave states that had not seceded (namely, Missouri, Kentucky, Maryland, and Delaware). This strategy, which I refer to as "electoral reconciliation," presented Lincoln with two challenges: on the one hand, his administration had to prosecute the war with enough energy to win on the battlefield and to maintain support within his own party. At the same time, his war plan had to demonstrate a measure of restraint, refraining from unnecessary confiscation of southern "property" (read: slaves), or from gratuitous acts of violence against the South. These objectives were crucial to keep the hope for electoral reconciliation alive and to retain the border states within the Union fold. Lincoln treaded a fine line between the northern Democrats and the Radicals in his own party with an eye for the ultimate reconciliation of the Union, an objective he believed would be achieved through the agency of a new party formation, the Union party. Seward succinctly captured the spirit of this strategy when he made the case to the president that "every thought that we think ought to be conciliatory forbearing and patient, and so open the way for the rising of a Union Party in the seceding states which will bring them back into the Union."[38]

Party leadership in a time of civil war, Lincoln believed, required an inclusive approach that embraced a diversity of unionist elements. His appointments to the cabinet and other positions of leadership reflected this commitment: George McClellan, a Democrat, was selected in 1861 to be the leader of the Army of the Potomac, and later the commander of all the Union forces; Simon Cameron, a former Democrat from the crucial state of Pennsylvania, was selected to be the secretary of war. Cameron was later replaced by Edwin Stanton, a Democrat and former attorney general for the Buchanan administration. To assuage sentiments in the border states, Lincoln selected a moderate Republican from Maryland, Montgomery Blair, to fill the office of the postmaster general.

Once the fighting was under way, Lincoln's war policy strayed from Republican orthodoxy: Lincoln exercised a good deal of restraint toward the opposition, overturning a number of decisions made by officers in the field who made arrests for purely political reasons.[39] He assumed a more permissive stance toward dissenters, not so much out of a liberal respect for public debate, but because he knew that dissenters could not be made into criminals and that any attempt by his subordinates to do so would be counterproductive and probably unconstitutional.[40]

Perhaps even more troubling for Republicans in Congress, he overrode a directive issued in the field by General John Frémont (the Republicans' presidential candidate in 1856) liberating all the slaves of slave owners who supported the rebellion.[41] Lincoln's reasoning reflected the fear that border state loyalists (and army volunteers) from Kentucky, Missouri, and Maryland willing to support the cause of restoring the Union but unwilling to fight for emancipation might declare their neutrality in the conflict, offer their political support for secession, or join the rebellion outright, if Union forces took it on themselves to manumit the slaves. "I think to lose Kentucky is nearly the same as to lose the whole game. Kentucky gone, we can not hold Missouri, nor, as I think, Maryland. These all against us, and the job on our hands is too large for us. We would as well consent to separation at once, including the surrender of this capitol."[42]

Republicans in Congress were not persuaded. Lincoln's rebuke of Frémont and Hunter and his alleged unwillingness to aggressively enforce the Confiscation Acts (authorizing the military to seize rebel property) was, in the view of more orthodox Republicans, symptomatic of the president's misguided inclination to cater to the whims of constituents of questionable loyalty. Lincoln, Horace Greeley maintained, was "unduly influenced by the counsels . . . of certain fossil politicians hailing from the Border Slave States"; "the Union cause," as a result, "suffered . . . from mistaken deference to Rebel Slavery."[43] Lincoln replied to Greeley's essay with a memorable clarification of administration purposes: "My paramount object in this struggle *is* to save the Union, and is *not* either to save or destroy slavery. If I could save the Union without freeing *any* slave I would do it, and if I could save it by freeing *all* the slaves I would do it; and if I could save it by freeing some and leaving others alone I would also do that. What I do about slavery, and the colored race, I do because I believe it helps to save the Union; and what I forbear, I forbear because I do *not* believe it would help to save the Union."[44]

Lincoln's aim was straightforward. His strategy to achieve it, however, was quite nuanced: the restoration of the Union could be hastened, not by a vengeful campaign to punish the South for its sins, but through a political campaign to entice wavering rebels and fence-sitters back into the fold. The war, in other words, might be ended by *political* means.

Emancipation had taken a backseat when the struggle first began. As the crisis wore on, however, Lincoln's views on the strategic merits of emancipation evolved. Emancipation, he thought, would remove the bone of contention between the two sections and, if achieved first in the border states, would crush Confederate hopes that these decisive states would join the rebellion.[45] Consistent with his strategy of electoral reconciliation, the best plan for emancipation, in his view, should have three features: it must include a mode of compensation, it should be gradual rather than immediate, and it should be endorsed by a vote of the people.[46]

The consent of the people was perhaps the crucial element of this scheme. His first proposal for compensated emancipation was offered to Congress on 6 March 1862, nearly a year after the fall of Fort Sumter.[47] This was a voluntary program, so persuasion, not coercion, was of paramount importance to the success of the policy. Lincoln earnestly appealed to the citizens of the slaveholding states—particularly those of the border states—to sign on to his proposal: "The change it contemplates would come gently as the dews of heaven, not rending or wrecking anything." His tone was both conciliatory and sincere: "To the people of those states I now earnestly appeal. I do not argue. I beseech you to make the arguments for yourselves. You can not if you would, be blind to the signs of the times."[48]

After six months, none of the slave states in rebellion or the slave states in the Union, for that matter, had taken advantage of Lincoln's proposal. On 22 September 1862, he renewed his offer, but this time coupled it with a firm threat and a timetable. The Preliminary Emancipation Proclamation, as it was called, offered both a carrot and a stick: it advanced the same compensation scheme but also indicated that in one hundred days (on 1 January 1863), another proclamation would be issued liberating the slaves of all the states and counties still in rebellion.[49] Freedom, he insisted, would be ordered as a matter of military necessity. Slave states were therefore faced with a choice: if they chose to return to the Union, they could keep their human property, or adopt Lincoln's scheme of compensated emancipation. This was the carrot integrated into his scheme. The decision, however, had to receive the blessing of a popular vote.[50]

On the other hand, if they chose to continue in their rebellion, they risked uncompensated emancipation by federal forces—a daunting threat, since slave labor had been crucial to the Confederate cause. If Lincoln's strategy was successful, the "punishment" of emancipation would never have to be implemented: success in one of the seceded states, he hoped, might, according to historian James McPherson, "set in motion a snowballing defection from the Confederacy and a state-by-state reconstruction of the Union."[51]

The notion that the emancipation and enlistment of former slaves would provide a military advantage had been advanced by abolitionists since the beginning of the war; Lincoln was not immediately persuaded that the advantages would outweigh the palpable risks such a strategy entailed. Yet once he publicly committed himself to the idea, he encouraged leaders in the border states to push for emancipation, not as a measure of justice, but as a means to support the war effort. As he explained to the governor of Tennessee, Andrew Johnson, "The colored population is the great *available* and yet *unavailed* of, force for restoring the Union. The bare sight of fifty thousand armed, and drilled black soldiers on the banks of the Mississippi, would end the rebellion at once."[52]

Lincoln hoped to provide an opportunity for the border states to vote on the question of compensated emancipation and to afford the seceded states an opportunity to vote themselves back into the Union. As he explained to Governor Johnson, "If we could, somehow, get a vote of the people of Tennessee and *have it result properly* it would be worth more to us than a battle gained."[53] Compensated emancipation ratified by the vote, Lincoln believed, would hasten the settlement of the matter that divided the polity. Yet the vote of the people was of value only if unionists or supporters of emancipation won.

If southern states were to vote themselves back into the Union, they would need a party to vote for.[54] The available alternatives, in Lincoln's view, would simply not suffice: southern Democrats were committed to secession and a slave economy, and the Republican party was almost universally despised by southerners as the agent of "Northern aggression." Lincoln's aim, consequently, was to transform the Republican party into a party that would unite loyalists from the North and South on an anti*slavery*, but not an anti-*southern*, program. As the election of 1864 approached, Lincoln stood atop of a Republican party ticket renamed the "National Union" party. To make the unionist appeal more persuasive, Lincoln removed Vice President Hannibal Hamlin, a Maine Republican, from the ticket, and replaced him with Tennessee governor and Democrat Andrew Johnson.[55]

Lincoln's strategy of electoral reconciliation was a partial success: though none of the seceded states were enticed by his time line of sticks and carrots to vote themselves back into the Union, the four loyal slave states, Maryland, Kentucky, Missouri, and Delaware, did remain within the Union fold. Yet it appears, in retrospect, that Lincoln may have overestimated the political strength of unionists in the seceded states.[56] He may also have overestimated the malleability of his own image: during the first several years of the war, he staked out a centrist position vis-à-vis the Radical Republicans in Congress, hoping to draw support from unionists of all stripes. Yet a message of inclusion and conciliation, coming from the man who led the "Black Republican" party into power in 1860, was probably not credible to wavering Confederates. Lincoln may have been the wrong man to implement his own plan.

This strategy was succeeded by a more punitive approach that embraced coercive emancipation. The administration's time line for emancipation was originally set in place to encourage states to vote themselves back into the Union—it was the linchpin of his plan for electoral reconciliation. This policy, however, once it was put into effect on 1 January 1863, was a coercive measure at odds with the inclusive strategy that shaped his leadership during the first several years of the war. Emancipation, once implemented by the Union army, was a punitive measure that substantially weakened the political position of unionists in the South and erased all hopes for electoral reconciliation.

The Republican party-state possessed, at least for an American government, an unprecedented capacity to commit men and materiel to the fight. Yet the premise of the Lincoln administration's strategy of electoral reconciliation was that the Union forces, no matter their riches in men and arms, were at a strategic disadvantage, limited by the burden of enforcing federal authority in a republic of continental proportions, against the armed and capable resistance of subnational units (the states) that commanded the allegiance of their people. The federal government in 1861 was called on to restore federal authority in eleven states situated on the defensive and arrayed in a "compact situation"—a tall order, no matter how capable the new industrial power in the North may have been. By the winter of 1862, the federal government had indeed failed. More extraordinary measures were, in the administration's judgment, necessary.

Destroying Slavery and Parrying the Repercussions

The administration's emancipation policy came at a significant political cost: it strengthened the position of conservative Peace Democrats (also known as Copperheads) and polarized northern politics.[57] Indeed, it confirmed for both War and Peace Democrats alike what they had long suspected: that Lincoln's motive to go to war was to abolish slavery. Many Democrats cast the Union as the aggressor in the conflict—now under the leadership of the "abolition [Republican] party"—responsible for pushing the South to rebel and dragging the country into a destructive war of unprecedented proportions. Emancipation contributed to a shift in the balance of power within the Democratic party: War Democrats dominated the party for the first couple of years, but their position vis-à-vis the Peace Democrats weakened as casualties mounted and as the justification for the war shifted. As one scholar observes, "The strength of the Peace Democrats generally ran in inverse relation to the successes (or failures) of the armies."[58]

Northern Democrats occupied a quasi-legitimate position in Union politics during the war. The rule that "every Democrat may not be a traitor, but every traitor is a Democrat," made the opposition an easy target for Republican attacks.[59] Accusing Democrats of disloyalty became a kind of sport during the election season: Republicans, as one observer notes, made a practice of implying that Democrats were treasonous, stopping just short of the accusation, then dismissing Democrats' outrage at having their loyalty impugned.[60]

Though the public rituals and organizational practices of political parties were widely accepted as a regular part of public life by the mid-nineteenth century, the outbreak of war brought into full view the latent conditionality of party legitimacy in antebellum America. Once war commenced, public figures dispensed with social conventions acknowledging the legitimacy of party opposition. Stephen Douglas spoke for many northern Democrats when he said, "There can be but two parties, the party of patriots and the party of traitors. We [Democrats] belong to the former."[61] Yet divisions among the "party of patriots" continued in the North, despite the high-minded, consensual rhetoric of Douglas and others: northern Democrats did not comfortably fall in line behind the Lincoln administration and the Republican party. They were, moreover, well positioned to take advantage of discontent with the war's management.

There was plenty of discontent to exploit. By 1864, Lincoln was deeply unpopular in the North. The Emancipation Proclamation and the Conscription Act, as well as the administration's incursions on basic civil liberties, had all taken a toll on popular support for the Union effort. The Conscription Act passed in 1863 was especially damaging to the administration's political standing. Before the Conscription Act, recruitment was handled primarily by the state governments that enlisted volunteers to meet quotas set by the federal government. The Conscription Act, however, authorized the federal government to reach directly into communities across the polity to draft men when the states could not fill their quotas. The act permitted draftees to hire substitutes or to pay a fee of $300 to commute their enlistments.[62] These provisions deeply antagonized class differences in the North and roused widespread resistance. Some dodged the draft by fleeing to Canada; others organized in their communities to carry out acts of violence against recruitment officers, and in several instances, mob violence broke out, most notably in New York City.[63]

The administration's war measures might have been tolerated by the public had the Union made significant gains on the battlefield. But the war effort was a consistent source of disappointment. Even when Union armies were successful, civilians at home were aghast by the gruesome and unprecedented carnage of the fighting. Union losses on the battlefield damaged Lincoln's political standing just as they strengthened the position of the Copperheads within the Democratic party.

Peace Democrats, however, were not at all satisfied with the selection of former general George McClellan, a War Democrat, to head the ticket for president. Copperheads were asked to rest content with George Pendleton, a Peace Democrat who would serve as McClellan's running mate. McClellan, the former commander of the Union forces, was a bitter critic of Lincoln's management of the war (including his decision to emancipate and arm blacks); though he was known as a War Democrat, his commitment to the war was open to question. In a conversation with a prominent businessman from St. Louis, McClellan reportedly asserted, "If I am elected, I will recommend an immediate armistice and a call for a convention of all the states and insist upon exhausting all and every means to secure peace without further bloodshed, and shall not wait for the call to come first from the other side, but we should make the call first."[64] Such talk was comforting to the Copperheads, who were further reassured by Horatio Seymour, the Democratic governor of New York and the president of the national convention, who ensured the peace faction that "our safety, lies in success and . . . with McClellan, peace is certain."[65]

Though the peace faction did not control the head of the ticket, they did control the platform committee at the Democratic National Convention in Chicago. The platform pulled no punches: it referred to the war as a "failure" and called for "immediate efforts" to commence a cease-fire, followed by a convention that would negotiate a treaty of peace "on the basis of the Federal Union of the States."[66] Few Democrats openly favored peace without Union. Peace Democrats tended to support a cessation of hostilities, followed by negotiations to revive the Crittenden Plan. McClellan and many other Democrats, however, refused to acknowledge what was known by all: that the Confederates were not willing to negotiate without a promise of Confederate independence.[67]

Union reaction to the developments at the convention in Chicago was predictably alarmed: Union general Benjamin Butler wrote the editor of the *New York Times* (and the head of the Republican National Committee) Henry Raymond that anyone who voted in support of this Democratic platform "is more detrimental to the country and more beneficial to the rebellion than if they placed themselves actively in arms side by side with the rebels in the field."[68] Secretary of State William Seward was equally uncharitable. He delivered a speech during the presidential campaign (Lincoln himself did not campaign) entitled "The Allies of Treason," where he insisted that "All experience . . . shows that it is by the malice or the madness of great parties that free states have been brought down to destruction. You often hear alarms that a party in power is subverting the state, and it sometimes happens so. But nine times out of ten it is a party out of power, that in its impatience or its ambition overthrows a republic."[69] Lincoln was more fatalistic as he prepared for what he believed to be an almost certain McClellan victory. Should McClellan win, Lincoln wrote that it would then "be my duty to so co-operate with the President elect, as to save the Union between the election and the inauguration; as he will have secured his election on such ground that he can not possibly save it afterwards."[70] He could not possibly save it afterward, in Lincoln's view, for two reasons: first, McClellan would not be able to keep up the fight for long if he renounced the Union commitment to emancipation: "no human power can subdue this rebellion without using the Emancipation lever as I have done. Freedom has given us the control of 200 000 able bodied men, born & raised on southern soil."[71] Seeing little prospect for enlisting new white recruits in large numbers, the Union simply would not have the physical force to put down the rebellion without the service of black soldiers.

There was also reason to believe that if hostilities were ceased for negotiations (as McClellan had promised), they could not begin again. An armistice would create its own political inertia, making it exceedingly difficult to restart war if negotiations failed to reunite the states. Seward spoke directly to this point in an address on the eve of the election:

> Suppose we seek peace under the counsel of Chicago [where the Democratic Convention took place]—whether according to the naked and detestable text of the resolutions, or as evasively interpreted and glossed by the candidate who stands on that platform. It is to seek peace by conciliating the rebels, and substituting diplomacy, or the arts of statesmanship, for the vigor of war. Adopt that policy, and distraction instantly seizes the North; courage and new resolution inspire the South; your soldiers, betrayed at home, either fall in despair in their trenches, or, what would be worse, recoil before the enemy advancing upon Washington and Cincinnati. . . . When negotiation and all the arts of statesmanship are exhausted, the navy would be scattered, withdrawn from the blockade, and the armies dispersed in their homes, the treasury empty, the national credit sunk, France and Great Britain will have recognized the rebels.[72]

It is not easy to say if these prognostications were well founded. It is equally difficult to gauge if the Lincoln administration, or any other, could rally the public to take up the fight again—and win—once given a taste of peace. Lincoln, for one, did not believe that it was possible: "An armistice—a cessation of hostilities—is the end of the struggle, and the insurgents would be in peaceable possession of all that has been struggled for."[73]

Given that the Confederacy's military objective was to battle the Union to a draw (and not to conquer northern territory), it needed only to hold its ground on the battlefield until it broke the Union's will to persist in the fight. Victory for the South, in other words, could be achieved not only on the battlefield, but could be achieved also by proxy through the electoral success of a peace party in the North. The Confederates were fully aware of this possibility. Noting the growing superiority of the enemy in numbers and resources, Robert E. Lee counseled Confederate president Jefferson Davis, "Under these circumstances we should neglect no honorable means of dividing and weakening our enemies that they may feel some of the difficulties experienced by ourselves. It seems to me that the most effectual mode of accomplishing this object, now within our reach, is to give all the encouragement we can, consistently with truth, to the rising peace party of the North."[74] Lee understood that with prospects on the battlefield deteriorating, the best hope to defeat the Union was through its own political process. He understood, moreover, that there were two "games" simultaneously unfolding and that though the lion's share of the fighting may have taken place on Confederate territory, the electoral battle took place exclusively within the hearts and minds of northern voters.

This strategic dynamic has puzzled political historians for some time. In a message to Congress on 4 July 1861, Lincoln insisted that the rebellion staged by the South had to be put down to send a message to all disgruntled partisans that there can be no recourse from the ballot to the bullet following a defeat at the polls; the only legitimate recourse was back to the ballot, at the subsequent election.[75] The position Lincoln staked out in this address assumed, however, that the ballot was consistent with Union. The possibility of a Democratic victory in the election of 1864, however, suggests a crucial caveat to this general principle: a McClellan victory raised the prospect that the ballot would achieve for the rebels what the bullet could not.

This conclusion is at odds with the argument advanced by some historians, who make the counterintuitive case that the persistence of party politics in the North proved to be a decisive advantage for the Union war effort, fighting against a Confederate regime whose politics was not organized by parties.[76] Eric McKitrick, the leading purveyor of the "two-party system theory," makes three key claims in support of the proposition that party opposition strengthened the northern war effort. First, he argues that organized party opposition in the North made the administration's opponents more accountable and therefore more manageable because it forced opposition out into the open: while Lincoln faced a clearly identifiable adversary, Davis's opponents were "an undifferentiated bickering resistance, an unspecified something that seeped in from everywhere to soften the very will of the Confederacy. Davis could not move against this; he had no real way of getting at it."[77] Northern Democrats could be kept in line, by contrast, because they could be aggregated under one identity and one name, and be roundly dismissed as a whole (e.g., using the principle that "every Democrat may not be a traitor, but every traitor is a Democrat").[78] Democrats could be kept in a subordinate position because all could be rendered guilty by association for the words and actions of an extreme few.

McKitrick makes the case moreover that this suspicion forced Democrats in opposition to moderate their criticism. As he maintains, "There is certainly no need here to discuss the beneficial functions of a 'loyal opposition.' But something might be said about the functions of an opposition which is under constant suspicion of being only partly loyal." This position, in McKitrick's view, prompted the Democratic party to keep "its antiwar wing within some sort of bounds."[79]

Finally, McKitrick argues that Democratic opposition improved federal-state cooperation because it encouraged cohesion between Republican governors and the administration. In his terms, the "binding agency" of the Republican party was made possible "through the continued existence of the Democrats."[80] This conclusion is disputed by historian Mark Neely, who points out that McKitrick overlooks the difficulties the Lincoln administration had in its dealings with Democratic governors—such as the governor of New York, Horatio Seymour—and simultaneously overstates the challenges Jefferson Davis confronted in his dealings with southern governors.[81]

McKitrick may have been correct to call attention to the ways in which party competition forced opposition out into the open and goaded at least a degree of cohesion in the majority party. But such opposition was valuable to the northern war effort, only so long as Democrats of suspect loyalty did not win elections to offices of high responsibility. One cannot say if Republican governors in Illinois and Indiana were justified in dissolving their state legislatures when they came under Democratic control.[82] Lincoln, for his part, did not wish to leave elections in recaptured states to chance, reserving for himself the authority to refuse recognition of the new state governments in Louisiana and Tennessee if state elections did not result "properly."[83] One, however, is hard-pressed to defend party competition during a time of war when the presidential ticket of the opposition might have fatally undermined the war effort simply by achieving the most basic aim that all political parties hope to achieve: winning at the polls. This problem of party opposition—that an antiwar party might undermine ongoing efforts on the battlefield by winning elections was not especially salient during the early years of the war: Copperhead candidacies did not pose a credible challenge to the war effort during the midterm elections because war policy was controlled almost exclusively by the president.[84] According to one prominent Civil War historian, American presidentialism proved to be advantageous to the Union cause: given the early failures of the Union army, Lincoln most likely would have lost a no-confidence vote within the first two years of the war if he had been a prime minister instead of a president.[85] Thanks to the American president's four-year term, the rebellion, in 1860, faced an uphill battle. The Confederacy, for its part, had an even more advantageous arrangement: a presidency with a single six-year term. A presidential election would not take place in the Confederate States until 1866, and, if the Confederacy had lasted this long, the election would not have been a referendum on Davis's performance in office because Davis would've been ineligible to stand for reelection. Of course, as events unfolded, the Confederacy would not last long enough to endure a wartime presidential election.

The North did, however, have to endure a wartime presidential election in 1864, and for the republic to remain as one, Lincoln would have to defeat McClellan. The outcome, one must remember, was not foreordained. Lincoln, in fact, faced steep odds as the election approached and overcame them thanks, not so much to savvy political strategy, but to the changing fortunes of the Union army. General Sherman seized control of Atlanta only days after the Democratic National Convention convened. News of the fall of Atlanta, coupled with Admiral Farragut's seizure of Mobile Bay several weeks prior to Sherman's victory, boosted northern morale and dramatically altered the electoral playing field: McClellan, suddenly thrown on the defensive, struggled to distance himself from his party platform. Pendleton, for his part, came under pressure to explain his record of opposition to the war.[86] The Peace Democrats were ultimately undercut by events on the battlefield in a manner reminiscent of the Federalists' political collapse following Jackson's victory in New Orleans. The war would soon be won, and the Copperheads were on the wrong side of history.

Perhaps what is most surprising about the election of 1864, however, is that it took place at all. It was, arguably, a risk that had to be undertaken, if only because the suspension of elections would endanger Union victory by depriving the ruling party of legitimacy. As Lincoln reflected on the election that had passed, he observed, "We can not have free government without elections; and if the rebellion could force us to forego, or postpone a national election, it might fairly claim to have already conquered and ruined us." The election, Lincoln surmised, was "a necessity."[87]

Conclusion

Since national parties emerged on the American scene, political leaders had avoided defining their parties in sectional terms and gone to great lengths to build political infrastructure in multiple sections of the polity—all for the sake of girding the Union against the threat of dismemberment. At the outset of the Civil War, Lincoln continued in this tradition, defining the struggle exclusively in terms of Union rather than emancipation. Yet he broke with this tradition midstream, initiating a radical departure in the war by redefining its mission and, as a result, undercutting the partisan project he hoped might hasten a political solution to the war crisis. The decision to redefine the mission of the war through emancipation entailed great opportunities and risks. The two most notable advantages of this redefinition (from a strictly strategic point of view) are familiar: first, it made available a vast pool of men of African descent, slave and free, some who may have been fighting formerly in support of the Confederate cause. Second, the Emancipation Proclamation ensured that foreign powers would not rush to the Confederacy's assistance. The British in particular contemplated intervening on the Confederacy's behalf in a struggle over "states rights" or "northern (Union) aggression"; foreign powers, however, were far less likely to intervene in defense of the slave power in a struggle over human freedom.

One of the chief consequences of the Emancipation Proclamation, of particular concern for our purposes, was a consolidation of elite Republican opinion behind a sectional vision for the Republican party. The shift in the Lincoln administration's position marked a significant departure from the central tendencies of more than seventy years of American governance. Political leaders since the early national period avoided defining their parties in sectional terms, and they did so for a reason. To be sure, the risks of a sectional definition of a governing party's mission in the context of an ongoing civil war were comparable, but not identical, to the risks that leaders of the early national and antebellum periods associated with sectionalism. In the early national and antebellum years, party leaders took it as an article of faith that their ultimate purpose was to preserve the Union, that is, to keep all parts in the Union fold. During the Civil War years, by contrast, the overriding aim of the Lincoln administration was to restore the Union, that is, to return parts that were, for the time being, outside the republic, back into the Union. The governing party (the Republican party) was in the unusual position of having to win both at the polls and on the battlefield. The Confederacy, operating outside of American electoral politics, made every effort to take advantage of the Republicans' strategic challenge. The Confederacy designed its battlefield strategy to contend for the hearts and minds of border state constituents and northern voters, all for the purpose of effecting—whether through military or electoral means—a permanent separation of the Union. The Confederate strategy of separation mirrored in this way the Lincoln administration's unionist approach to reconciliation.

Several attributes of the party politics during the Civil War years set the strategic dynamics of this period apart from the "normal" party politics of the early national and antebellum years. Three features are especially salient: the impact of a well-armed and well-commanded force operating inside of American territory but outside of electoral politics; the governing party's unique burden of having to win both at the polls and on the battlefield to perpetuate the union of the states; the governing regime's burden to restore jurisdictions that were, for the time being, outside the polity. These distinctive features of the Civil War years notwithstanding, an underlying structural fact of life remained as true of the early national and antebellum years as it was of this period of civil turmoil: that a sectional party-building strategy was a high-risk undertaking so long as the coercive capacities of government were decentered and the central state lacked a monopoly over the legitimate means of coercion. Indeed, it was not until 1865 that the federal government possessed the minimal attributes of national sovereignty; until then, it could not act with confidence or efficacy to enforce its authority under the Constitution or to guarantee the territorial integrity of the Union.[88]

The wreckage of war and the initiatives of the Lincoln administration and the Republicans in Congress left an institutional legacy that altered the trajectory of party development. The war, of course, ended with the Thirteenth Amendment and the permanent settlement of the slavery question. Controversies surrounding Reconstruction policy and the future of the freedmen framed a new set of divisive questions that shaped party politics for decades. Most important for our purposes, the successful conclusion of the war permanently removed the threat of secession from the political lexicon of mainstream organized opposition. The political and institutional climate was transformed by the defeat of the Confederacy, simply because this secessionist movement was the last of its kind. Thanks to the military success of the Union army, the ballot became the only means available to reconcile or adjust political differences. Even if the coercive institutions of the federal government should be scaled back or otherwise retrenched in the aftermath of the war (as they in fact were), the federal government had demonstrated its coercive potential, and the demonstration was enough to teach future generations of partisans the "great lesson of peace," that "what they cannot take by an election, neither can they take it by a war."[89]

CHAPTER 6

═══════════

Redrawing the Limits of Legitimate Party Opposition: Party Politics and Its Discontents at the Turn of the Twentieth Century

We are ready to study new uses for our parties and to
adapt them to new standards and principles.

—Woodrow Wilson, *Constitutional Government
in the United States*, 1908

The Civil War is rightfully represented as a "second founding" that substantively reconstituted the American political system.[1] The war, for example, bore an unmistakable imprint on subsequent state-building commitments: legislation passed by Republican Congresses during the Civil War and Reconstruction years committed the federal government to a political economic regime that protected the manufacturing interests of the North, promoted western settlement, and fostered the nationalization of the economy.[2] The Reconstruction Amendments (the Thirteenth, Fourteenth, and Fifteenth Amendments), furthermore, set a new foundation for African Americans' long struggle for full and equal citizenship.

The defeat of the Confederacy also altered the nature of the compact between the states: the decisive constitutional question, whether or not the states possessed the right to secede from the Union without the consent of the other states, was settled, not by the force of legal argument, but by the force of arms. Disgruntled partisans could no longer hope to exit the Union and organize a separate republic for themselves. Nor could they interfere with the collection of federal revenue through nullification or some other extraconstitutional means of resistance. The Civil War foreclosed these options.

The central state thus emerged from the wreckage of the war in possession of the minimal attributes of sovereignty: it possessed the capacity to preserve the territorial integrity of the republic and to extract revenue from the population. One must be careful, however, not to overstate the significance of this institutional reconstitution. There are, in fact, two important ways in which this watershed development might be overdrawn: one might, for example, cast a blind eye to the dynamics that limited the coercive reach of the postbellum state. Though the most fundamental forms of partisan mischief were effectively curtailed, the central state was unable to follow through on its commitments to reconstruct southern society when confronted with sustained resistance from Democrats and affiliated paramilitary groups. Indeed, political violence spread across the former Confederate states as Reconstruction faltered. The violence that terrorized freedmen and intimidated white Republican partisans in the South both contributed to, and was an effect of, the failure of Reconstruction policy.

Though this violence exacted an extraordinary human cost, it was, nonetheless, largely localized in one section of the country and was targeted at a politically and socially marginal population (the community of freedmen, freedwomen, and their children). New paramilitary groups terrorized the African American community and challenged the new and untested federal authority created by the Civil War and Reconstruction Congresses. Paramilitary groups, however, did not present a plausible threat to the integrity of the Union. Nor did such groups hope to contest the collection of federal revenue in the ports (tariffs represented the primary source of federal revenue in the United States at this time). Tariff law, to be sure, would remain controversial, but this policy area was settled through the political process in Washington, D.C.

There was another way in which the changes wrought by America's "second founding" might be overdrawn. One might discount the apprehensions of sectional violence that surfaced in the aftermath of the war and overstate the public's perceptions of stability.[3] Yet the fear that the United States might again lapse into civil war did not vanish overnight. Nerves were simply too raw, and the war was too fresh in the minds of so many Americans. The outcome of the war would, in the long run, lower the stakes of party competition, but elites did not immediately alter their perceptions of political danger. Indeed, perceptions of political danger peaked during the tense and uncertain political standoff triggered by the contested presidential election of 1876.

These anxieties were very real; however, the want of a viable military force to challenge Republican claims to the presidency meant that a redux of the Civil War was highly improbable. The threat of a new secessionist movement was, for all intents and purposes, off the table.

And as the threat of exit faded, the major parties came to enjoy a new measure of coalitional flexibility: Republicans were no longer burdened by the unionist party-building inhibitions that, since the 1790s, goaded the major parties to compete in both the North and the South. The Republican party by the turn of the twentieth century effectively gave up on hopes to build a durable multiracial, cross-sectional coalition. The decision to "let the South go" was, no doubt, the result of electoral considerations—Republican leaders opted to expand westward instead. This electoral strategy, however, was predicated on foundational changes in the structure of the polity. The electoral option to forego competition in the South and emphasize competition in the West was made possible by the prevailing confidence that the South, even if not fully integrated by both major parties, would remain in the Union.

In this chapter, I argue that this institutional setting—where the federal government established its authority to guarantee the Union and secure federal revenue—made a significant reformulation of the problem of parties possible. With the minimal attributes of sovereignty secured, statesmen and thinkers of various stripes reconceived the status of party opposition in America. Leaders of the major parties were free to consider a wider range of coalitional possibilities than they could have contemplated before the war. Party coalitions that divided the polity along sectional lines, once considered anathema to the survival of the republic, were no longer treated as harbingers of national disintegration. The postwar guarantee that parties could no longer present a fundamental challenge to national unity also enabled a shift toward a more moderate critique of party offered by a new and diverse generation of "progressive" critics. Progressive observers focused on the myriad ways in which the parties, as they were organized in the late nineteenth century, distorted the judgment of American citizens and resisted public accountability. Unlike past generations of critics who took parties to be a necessary evil—where "evil" meant that party politics raised the risk of a fracture in the Union—progressives treated parties as organizational inevitabilities that could be rationalized with properly designed reforms.

The problem of parties was thus fundamentally redefined: party rivalry, once conceived as a pernicious force that would rend the fabric of the republic if not held in check, was reconceived by leading statesmen and thinkers at the turn of the twentieth century to be a rather ordinary, competitive process. The process of party competition, to be sure, had to be regulated to effectively promote the public good. The new persuasion, nonetheless, assumed that party opposition must serve as an important outlet for political expression—even if the parties extant at the time failed (as so many critics alleged) to provide a meaningful choice at the polls.

As we shall see, a new generation of public intellectuals and self-styled "political scientists" emerged in postwar and post-Reconstruction America that conceived of party politics as a necessary supplement to the formal, constitutional structure of American government and identified party opposition as a fundamental prerequisite for a "modern" system of party competition. Yet just as the outcome of the Civil War made new party formations permissible, new rigidities began to emerge in sync with the rising challenges of a rapidly industrializing polity. Anxieties grew that parties would widen existing class divisions and give voice to foreign and subversive (read: anarchist and Marxist) ideological doctrines. The limits of legitimate opposition were repatterned as the structural foundations of the state changed and a new set of contentious policy questions arose relating, first, to monetary policy and the regulation of monopoly capitalism, and later, following the outbreak of World War I and the Bolshevik Revolution, to citizens' commitments to "Americanism" and their relationships with international collectivist movements. President Woodrow Wilson and other power brokers went to great lengths to minimize the salience of the revolutionary division between collectivists and capitalists in American politics first by taking steps to ensure that the two major parties did not mirror this global divide and then by adopting repressive measures to silence those who sympathized with (or who were themselves) anarchists and Marxists.

Party pluralism was thus transformed thanks to a concatenation of domestic and international factors: the structural transformation of the polity wrought by the Civil War, the formation of new class and party schisms caused by rapidly advancing industrialization, and the domestic impact of two exogenous shocks—World War I and the Bolshevik Revolution. A proposition advanced by Madison in 1819 (and discussed in Chapter 4) may help to describe the new patterning of the limits of legitimate opposition in post-Reconstruction America. Prompted by the excitement of the Missouri Crisis, Madison wrote, "Parties under some denominations or other must always be expected in a Govt. as free as ours. When the individuals belonging to them are intermingled in every part of the whole Country, they strengthen the Union of the Whole, while they divide every part. Should a State of parties arise, founded on geographical boundaries and other Physical & permanent distinctions which happen to coincide with them, what is to controul those great repulsive Masses from awful shocks agst. each other?"[4] In the postbellum years, parties "founded on geographical boundaries" no longer presented the threat they once posed; the problem of party was not a problem of sectional parties as it was during the early national and antebellum eras. Indeed, the hegemonic party of the time, the Republican party, had become a sectional party by the late nineteenth and early twentieth centuries. By the conclusion of the World War I, however, new lines demarcating the permissible from the impermissible were fully in view: partisans that "intermingled in every part"—particularly those of foreign birth or who espoused foreign ideologies and lived in the rapidly growing urban industrial centers—presented a new and, for many, a credible threat to civil peace and constitutional government.

Reconstruction and the Reconstitution of Party Politics

The American polity emerged from the Civil War riven by sectional discord. Southern hostility to the Union did not meaningfully subside with the destruction of the Confederacy; resentment toward the authority of the Union remained as entrenched as ever. Fighting had decimated the political and economic infrastructure of the former Confederate states and had taken the lives of over 250,000 in the South. The defeated rebel states were occupied territories governed by federal military officials until new, loyal state governments could be formed.

The effort to restore social and political order was unprecedented, and the process was untested and often improvised. Constitutional conventions dominated by Republicans assembled to reestablish civil government in each of the former Confederate states between 1863 and 1866. Republican delegates, hoping to build a self-sustaining constituency for their party in the region, adopted a wide range of reforms to empower freedmen in the states

and weaken the political grip of former Confederates.[5] For the party's southern strategy to succeed, newly emancipated freedmen would have to secure
a measure of economic independence and security from white supremacist
intimidation. Party building of this kind is no small undertaking; limited
central state capacity, wavering and uneven support from the judiciary, and
a lack of commitment from northern allies all combined to undermine the
formation of a self-sustaining southern wing of the Republican party.[6]

Land reform was one crucial avenue for reform. A redistribution of land
from the plantation elite to the freedmen would have released freedmen from
dependence on their former owners and enabled them to openly and actively
participate in politics. It also would have impoverished some of their former
masters in the process. In January 1865, General Sherman ordered the distribution of confiscated lands on the coast of Georgia and South Carolina to
about forty thousand freedmen. Sherman's order was followed by an act of
Congress, the Freedman's Bureau Act, which allotted up to forty acres of
abandoned lands to individual freedmen.[7] These measures raised hopes that
former slaves might benefit from a federally sponsored plan to redistribute
lands owned by former slave masters. Hopes for land reform, however, were
dashed when Andrew Johnson, installed as president after Lincoln's assassination, ordered the return of federally confiscated lands to their previous
owners.[8]

Without the freedom to work their own land, freedmen were again placed
at the mercy of former masters for their economic livelihoods. Freedmen
were effectively reenslaved by punitive Black Codes, passed by southern state
legislatures, which severely restricted the economic autonomy of blacks vis-
à-vis their plantation-owning employers.[9] With large numbers of freedmen
economically subservient to their former masters, southern blacks were
uniquely vulnerable to economic and political intimidation by white supremacist elites.

The strength of the Republican party in the South was also deeply dependent on the continued presence of federal forces in the region to protect
freedmen and other Republicans from the terrorism of the Ku Klux Klan,
the White League, and other paramilitary and vigilante groups.[10] The violence directed at freedmen and Republicans of all stripes was widespread and
well organized.[11] The resurgence of white supremacist violence, however,
might have been checked had the federal government committed adequate
resources to the region and projected a clear will to enforce Reconstruction
measures. Coercive support of this kind, however, was not forthcoming.

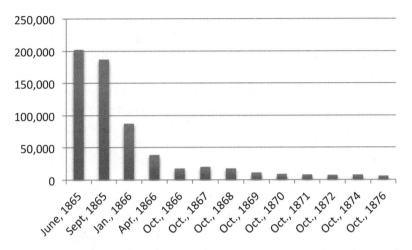

Figure 2. Troop levels during Reconstruction. From James E. Sefton, *The United States Army and Reconstruction, 1865–1877* (Baton Rouge: Louisiana State University Press, 1967), appendix B.

Union forces in general were rapidly demobilized after the war: over two hundred thousand soldiers were stationed in the South in June 1865. They were continuously withdrawn through the Reconstruction years (Figure 2). Many of the enlisted troops that remained were redeployed to the frontier to remove Native Americans from their lands and to protect western settlements.[12] State militias and federal marshals, often asked to step in to guarantee public order, were either politically unreliable (in the case of the state militias) or limited in numbers and regulatory reach (in the case of federal marshals).[13]

The enforcement of blacks' civil and political rights also confronted a number of confounding administrative difficulties. Congress did not establish a long-term federal task force to implement enforcement measures. The Department of Justice, as a result, was pressed to take on the task of enforcement as additional business to their existing workload. Command in the region was also decentralized, and communications were primitive, so effective enforcement depended on the discretion and professionalism of officers in the field. Finally, requesting federal troops when they were needed was slow and complicated because the fulfillment of such requests required the coordination of the Department of Justice and the Department of War.[14]

Making matters worse, the federal government did not signal a clear and unwavering commitment to enforce Reconstruction measures. The Grant administration, deeply reluctant to reignite the past conflict, was largely unwilling to commit significant numbers of troops to the region.[15] The growing reluctance in the North to follow through on Reconstruction measures, compounded by the Panic of 1873 and the recession that followed, contributed to a dramatic electoral swing in 1874 in favor of the Democrats.[16] Democrats, who were deeply hostile to Reconstruction, took control of the House of Representatives and undermined future initiatives to build on and enforce existing Reconstruction laws.

Republican party-building efforts also faltered because federal judicial support for Reconstruction measures was uneven. Indeed, as Richard Valelly shows, the dynamic interplay between party-building efforts and "jurisprudence-building" (i.e., the construction of legal precedents and the institutional capacity to enforce them) powerfully shaped the prospects for a full incorporation of African Americans into the electorate.[17] The case of *United States v. Cruikshank* (1873) offers an illustrative example of this relationship.[18] *United States v. Cruikshank* concerned the federal government's authority to prosecute the leaders of a white militia that executed nearly every member of a black militia company in Louisiana. Justice Joseph Bradley, a member of the Supreme Court who rode on the Fifth Circuit and was widely perceived by southern conservatives to represent the stance of leading Republicans in Washington, supported the conservative majority that exonerated the white supremacist leaders who murdered black militiamen.[19] In *U.S. v. Reese* (1876), the companion case to *Cruikshank*, the Supreme Court went even further and invalidated parts of the Enforcement Acts.[20] Southern conservatives, who took Bradley's position in *Cruikshank* as a signal that the federal government was unwilling to effectively execute its enforcement authority, advanced their efforts to intimidate freedmen with impunity. As Valelly observes, political violence grew noticeably after this circuit court ruling was handed down.[21] The Supreme Court later sustained key aspects of this ruling, in effect requiring Congress to rewrite crucial parts of the enforcement legislation. Such revisions, however, faced an uphill battle after 1875 when Democrats took control of the House.[22]

The electoral considerations of Republican party leaders in both the North and the South ultimately played a decisive role in the collapse of Reconstruction. The will of Northern allies to support Reconstruction efforts is best reflected in the changing electoral landscape in the North and the response of party leaders, reading the popular "tea leaves," to continue efforts to transform southern society. Republican electoral losses, beginning in the late 1860s, shook many party leaders and prompted them to rethink their support for measures that were losing popularity in northern districts. A division between Radical Republicans (those most committed to an aggressive, nationalist vision of Reconstruction) and conservative Republicans (those who favored a "pragmatic" easing and rollback of Reconstruction measures) formed in the wake of electoral developments from the late 1860s. As Paul Frymer notes, party leaders in the North, eager for electoral success in northern districts, pushed Republican party candidates to distance themselves from the cause of freedom in the South. He also describes the strong electoral incentives white southern Republicans faced to maintain an arm's length from civil and political rights.[23] The party in the South split between white and black Republicans—the so-called Lily-White and Black-and-Tan factions. Absent a plausible partisan alternative to the Republican party, blacks had little (if any) choice at the polls. They were, as Frymer describes them, "captured" by the Republican party. Instead of building Republican party strength in the South, Reconstruction managed only to delay the political resurgence of former Confederate nationalists, who, unsurprisingly, returned to state and national politics as Democrats.[24]

Without adequate resources and a clear will to enforce Reconstruction measures, the federal government could not durably secure control in the states of the former Confederacy. Nor could northern Republicans hope to build and maintain a biracial Republican wing in the South. This effort was increasingly untenable. Some leading members of the Republican party hoped to pursue an alternative course in the South by wooing white southern unionists with distributive benefits for their constituencies—patronage appointments and material aid for internal improvements in particular. Rutherford B. Hayes and James A. Garfield (as a congressman) hoped to build a neo-Whig coalition that included white southern unionists, but their efforts were thwarted both by competing northern and western demands for distributive benefits and by the deep resentment toward the national party most closely associated with northern aggression.[25] In light of these obstacles, the Republican party, unencumbered by unionist restraints, ultimately abandoned this course.

Reconstruction sharpened the differences between Democrats and Republicans in national affairs and produced a polarized politics not seen since the 1790s.[26] The nominations of Ulysses S. Grant and Horatio Seymour by the Republicans and Democrats, respectively, to stand in the 1868 presidential election clearly articulated the terms of party politics in the immediate postbellum period. Grant was the war hero of the nationalist cause; Seymour, by contrast, the former governor of New York, was a staunch opponent of Reconstruction and other measures that expanded federal authority. As one leading scholar of American political development observes, "In no other presidential contest in American history were the contrasts with respect to central state power more starkly drawn between the two major parties."[27]

Electoral strategy changed in response to the deteriorating conditions in the South. The Republican party in the late 1870s and the 1880s gradually turned away from its role as the champion of political equality and civil rights and focused instead on expanding its constituency into the West. Republican party leaders built a new "*white-white* North-West coalition." [28] This shift in priorities did not occur overnight: as Valelly shows, Republican efforts to build a southern constituency persisted into the 1880s.[29] Despite continued efforts to maintain political ground in the South, Republicans' willingness to commit political capital to the expansion of industrial capitalism came to outweigh its dedication to political equality.[30]

The Republican party's hopes in the South, however, were not determined by the failure of Reconstruction: the failure of Reconstruction was itself a political choice—and the choice to fail in this endeavor (and to commit resources elsewhere) was made possible by the structural changes wrought by the war. The Republican program of subsidizing western development by underwriting internal improvements and clearing Native Americans from the territories not only required an unchallenged stream of tariff revenue;[31] it was also a program that was only plausible in the absence of a credible secessionist threat. Renewed sectional violence would have prompted a reallocation of resources toward suppression and tilted the balance of power within the Republican party back in favor of the Radical Republicans and away from conservative Republicans' policy aims.

The fate of Reconstruction was effectively sealed in 1877 as leaders in both parties struck an accord to settle the disputed presidential election of 1876—one of the most contentious and closely divided elections in American history. Democrat Samuel J. Tilden of New York won the popular vote in a contest where deceptive electoral tactics and voter intimidation (particularly of black southern Republicans) were widespread. Tilden, however, had only a nineteen-vote advantage in the Electoral College over his Republican opponent, Rutherford B. Hayes, and twenty electoral votes, those of Florida, Louisiana, South Carolina, and Oregon, were in dispute.[32] Uncertainty prevailed for several months as lawmakers negotiated and partisan publicists issued allegations of fraud and misconduct at the opposing campaigns. Some belligerent partisans went further, promising bloodshed if their candidate was denied his seat in the White House.[33]

Much of this talk was hyperbolic posturing, but there were ominous signs that the standoff might take a violent turn. Former general and Democratic presidential candidate George McClellan prepared to build a paramilitary organization that would demand Tilden's accession to the presidency, though no evidence of detailed plans have been found.[34] President Grant, for his part, quietly directed troops to secure vulnerable positions in Washington and to ready Civil War forts for use, should the occasion require.[35]

Contemporaries' most dire fears did not come to pass. The electoral commission appointed to allocate the disputed electoral votes ultimately allotted all twenty to Hayes. To ease Democratic acquiescence to the commission's decision, leading Republicans promised (in a deal called the Compromise of 1877) to withdraw the few troops remaining in the South. The failure of Radical Reconstruction had been evident for some time; this arrangement, however, brought the occupation to an end.[36]

Though this episode concluded without bloodshed, many contemporaries nonetheless feared that the country stood again at the brink of another great war. These fears are understandable: memories of political violence were fresh in the minds of all Americans. These anxieties, nonetheless, appear to have been largely unwarranted. Indeed, those who most adamantly opposed a Hayes presidency were in no position to mount a meaningful resistance. Democrats did have a powerful rallying cry at their disposal (they could protest a "stolen" election); they may also have had a general willing to lead the fight (McClellan). Yet their general had neither an army nor a reliable source of funding.[37] During this moment of crisis, a vastly disproportionate share of the Union's coercive resources were under the command of Republican officers and, ultimately, President Grant. Democrats appreciated the weakness of their position: as historian Michael Les Benedict explains, "A large majority of Democrats, northern as well as southern, recognized both the futility and danger of . . . resistance."[38] A redux of the Civil War was simply not in the cards.

Party Pluralism in the Post-Reconstruction Years

Postbellum politics was deeply sectional in its orientation, but as the Civil War years faded into memory, it grew more and more apparent that separatist hopes to secede from the Union or nullify tax laws were no longer tenable. New ways of thinking about party politics came to the fore as the threat of exit receded. In particular, the view that party rivalries did not foreshadow disunionist violence, but instead constituted a normal attribute of politics in a representative democracy, steadily gained ground in postbellum America.

New policy issues began to force themselves onto the national stage, no doubt contributing to the sense of closure that followed the electoral resolution of 1877. Declining commodity prices prodded discontented agrarian interests in the West to mobilize; worker unrest in the North, typified most pointedly by the violence of the Pullman strike of 1894, focused public attention on the stark class divisions that grew as industrial capitalism expanded; economic stresses stoked nativist opposition to Chinese workers in the West and immigrant workers in urban centers of the Northeast.[39] Prohibition activists agitating for reform added a moral and ethno-cultural dimension to the political economic disputes of the postwar years.

A new intellectual class also emerged in the late nineteenth and early twentieth centuries, one that was politically associated with the causes of civil service and party reform.[40] Journalists, public intellectuals, and self-styled "political scientists" documented a spectrum of public ills associated with party organizations and proposed reforms designed to rid these organizations of corruption and to limit the reach of party influence on government operations. The voices of this new generation of critics were diverse, but taken together, they contributed to a fundamental redefinition of the partisan mainstream and of existing standards of political toleration.

The terms of antipartisan critique were qualitatively different in the late nineteenth century. The "dread of divisiveness," a theme of antipartisan discourse commonplace in the eighteenth and early to mid-nineteenth centuries,[41] gave way to claims that the postwar parties undermined democratic accountability and all too effectively avoided the country's most pressing problems. James Sundquist described the basis for this discontent:

> For twenty years [from the mid-1870s to the mid-1890s], the
> contests between Democrats and Republicans had been little more
> than sham battles that decided no consequential issues (except

the tariff) but ordained mainly who would gain and allocate the spoils of office. The major parties had waged essentially empty campaigns. They appealed to wartime loyalties, they exposed each other's corruption and claimed moral superiority, and they magnified out of proportion the few real issues, like the tariff, that divided them. But on the fundamental question of the time—the role of government in a modern industrial society—the two national parties had no quarrel. Both saw an identity of interest between the government and the great banking, manufacturing, and railroad corporations that had come into being, or whose assets had skyrocketed, in the postwar decades.[42]

These parties, which appeared to elevate the tariff and the spoils above all else, were scrutinized by observers across the political spectrum. Critics on the Left decried the failure of either of the major parties to advance a consistent program to protect vulnerable Americans from the risks associated with monopoly capitalism and industrial consolidation.[43] Instead of pressing reforms that would ameliorate the living and working conditions of the immigrant poor and the laboring class, social reformers like Jane Addams directed their ire at the petty patronage that trapped partisan conscripts in a cycle of poverty and dependence.[44] Conservative business elites, for their part, were obsessed with the system of public corruption perpetuated by the partisan political traders who these quasi-aristocratic "Mugwumps" took to be their social inferiors.[45] Feeding the fire of public indignation, investigative journalists like Ray Stannard Baker, Upton Sinclair, Ida Tarbell, and Lincoln Steffens dug deeply into the depths of underhanded and crooked party dealings. These "muckraking" journalists operated in a changing media landscape where reporters began to identify journalism as a vocation committed to objectivity, demonstrating their independence with attention-grabbing accounts of partisan and public corruption.[46] For reformers like Robert La Follette of Wisconsin and Theodore Roosevelt of New York, the problem was not party rivalry per se, but the way in which the existing parties were organized.[47] La Follette, in fact, raised the status of political parties by drawing a sharp distinction between parties that "[appeal] to every voter" and political machines: "There is no likeness or similitude between a political organization that appeals to every voter in the party and a machine that appeals only to the most skilled and unscrupulous workers of the party. . . . This is the political machine. It is impersonal, irresponsible, extra legal. . . .

It has come to be enthroned in America. It rules caucuses, names delegates, appoints committees, dominates the councils of the party, dictates nominations, makes platforms, dispenses patronage, directs state administrations, controls legislatures, stifles opposition, punishes independence and elects United States senators."[48] Legitimate political parties, by contrast, are organizations dedicated to electing men who are duty bound to carry out the policies and principles articulated in their platforms. Party platforms and elected officials' commitments to follow them, in his view, constitute the vital connection that enables citizens to control their government.[49] Machine bosses have no regard for such pledges to the voters; they disregard the will of the people as they pursue their own political advantage and that of their machine and its dependents. La Follette warned that parties, when organized as political machines, represent the most serious threat to the republic: *"Grave danger lies not in waiting for this republic to destroy its life or change its character by force of arms.* . . . It is insidious, creeping, progressive encroachment that presents the greatest peril. . . . There is no explosion, no clash of arms, no open rebellion, but a sly covert nullification of the highest law of the land [the will of the people]."[50]

La Follette's call to action reveals an important change in the standards applied to parties as they were appraised in the late nineteenth century. The peril, in La Follette's view, was the debasement of the American citizen's ballot, which the machine reduced to currency in support of the spoils and plunder of government.[51] This "danger," however, is not, in a literal sense, dangerous: it did not entail a risk of political violence or a challenge to the integrity of the republic. La Follette issued his indictment of the political machine in the most strenuous terms; his critique, nonetheless, admitted that the "peril" of party organization was qualitatively different than it once was.

Though the prevailing system of parties did not endanger the Union, the parties were widely perceived to aggravate pervasive social and political problems.[52] A raft of reform proposals were advanced at the local, state, and national levels to remedy the alleged ills of party influence. Reforms were designed, for the most part, not to destroy the parties, but to dismantle the institutional channels of partisan excess: these included civil service reform, ballot reform, initiative and referendum, women's suffrage, the direct primary, and the direct election of senators.[53] These measures, as Martin Shefter observed, undid institutions introduced and designed by the Jacksonians.[54] These reforms helped politicize a new generation of policy questions that had long been neglected by the parties—questions concerning public health, corruption in government, the regulation of railroads, and working conditions in the factories, to name but a few.[55] The parties would be pressed to respond to these popular demands, but if they could not, then reforms found alternative channels—either through third parties or "direct democracy"—to place these questions before the voting public.

Progressive ideas were weighed by a new generation of political scientists, some of whom were supportive of party reform and others who were skeptical of their alleged advantages.[56] Reformers and their skeptics in political science nonetheless agreed that the parties had served a vital function in the American polity, acting to assuage deep political differences and to bind a diverse nation together. Parties in America were noteworthy not for their radicalism but for their capacity to politically integrate a heterogeneous people, an expansive territorial space, and a federal governing structure that divides power between the several branches of government.

According to the prevailing narrative of the time, parties had served as the political glue that bound together a nation dangerously fragmented both by sectional and socioeconomic divisions on the one hand, and by the formal divisions institutionalized in the Constitution, on the other. As Woodrow Wilson explained, "For a hundred years or more we have been a nation in the making, and it would be hard to exaggerate the importance of the nationalizing influence of our great parties. Without them, in a country so various as ours, with communities at every stage of development, separated into parts by the sharpest economic contrasts and social differences, . . . full of keen rivalries and here and there cut athwart by deep-rooted prejudices, national opinions, national judgments, could never have been formulated or enforced without the instrumentality of well-disciplined parties which extended their organization in a close network over the whole country."[57] Famed British observer James Bryce echoed this sentiment. "Party organization," he suggested, "has done much to unify the people of the United States and make them homogenous, for it has brought city and country, rich and poor, native American and Old World immigrant into a common allegiance, which has helped them to know, and taught them to cooperate with, one another."[58]

The integrative effects of party, according to leading political scientist Henry Jones Ford, was a clear result of the national reach and influence of party organizations. The party organizations' "nationalizing influence" united the people "into one mass of citizenship, pervaded by a common order of ideas and sentiments, and actuated by the same class of motives."[59]

Their tendency to build bridges and advance common purposes extended, moreover, to the operations of government. "Party organization," Ford argued, "acts as a connective tissue, enfolding the separate organs of government, and tending to establish a unity of control which shall adapt the government to the uses of popular sovereignty."[60] Parties served as the builders of political bridges, the brokers of compromise, and the architects of national unity. A consensus emerged, in other words, that parties were the agents of consensus itself.

Like Wilson and Bryce, Ford read the moderation of late nineteenth-century parties back into history. He dismissed claims made by the "horrified statesmen of the old school" who feared the destabilizing influence of party divisions. Statesmen such as John Quincy Adams and John C. Calhoun had, in Ford's view, erroneously contended that the "manifest tendency [of political parties] is to civil war" (Adams) or that "the appeal to force will be made whenever the violence of the struggle and the corruption of parties will no longer submit to the decision of the ballot-box" (Calhoun).[61] Ford insisted that history did not bear out such bleak assessments: "history plainly shows that party spirit has not had any such tendency. On the contrary, party organization long repressed the operation of the forces which did indeed eventually produce civil war. Before the slavery question could be brought to the front as the decisive issue of national politics, an entirely new and purely sectional party had to be formed. National party organization held the Union together long after the South had become at heart a separate nation, from the distinct interests and purposes developed by slavery."[62] Though sectional parties might be divisive, such parties, in Ford's view, were atypical and contrary to the general pattern of American party politics. American parties, he held, were fundamentally national and benign in orientation. The violence of party, in fact, was something of a ruse:

> The truth is that a remarkable nonchalance underlies the sound and
> fury of partisan politics. The passionate recrimination that goes on
> is like the disputes of counsel over the trial table. Back of it all is a
> substantial community of interest. The violence of politicians does
> not usually go higher than their lips. The antagonists of the stump
> often have a really friendly feeling for one another. It is not an
> uncommon thing for professional politicians of opposing parties to
> display a spirit of mutual good will and helpfulness in promoting

the personal political interests of one another. The extraordinary thing about American party politics is really their amenity.[63]

Party organizations, as the argument went, were a "conservative force" in the polity;[64] they exercised a "moderating influence" that was "of immense importance."[65] Herbert Croly, one of the most prominent progressive critics of parties, shared a comparable appreciation for their role in the polity. He wrote in 1914, "Through these [party] organizations thoroughgoing political democracy obtained its first wilful and masterful expression—an expression which had to be as masterful as it was wilful, largely because sectional feeling, individual and class interests, and other centrifugal social forces were so aggressive that despotic control was necessary. Partisan organization became, consequently, a nationalizing influence second only to that of the Constitution and in some respects more effective than the Constitution."[66]

The moderating and conservative influence of party organizations, however, came at a price. There was a trade-off between the parties' capacity to build unity and to commit to clear and distinct positions on the vital questions of the day. American parties, it was often said, were distinct from their British counterparts in this regard.[67] The balance between party principle and the American party system's temperate character was made forthrightly by subsequent generations of political scientists. As Herbert Agar memorably observed in 1950,

> The party is intended to be an organization for "getting or keeping the patronage of government." Instead of seeking "principles," or "distinctive tenets," which can only divide a federal union, the party is intended to seek bargains between the regions, the classes, and the other interest groups. It is intended to bring men and women of all beliefs, occupations, sections, racial backgrounds, into a combination for the pursuit of power. The combination is too various to possess firm convictions. The members may have nothing in common except a desire for office. Unless driven by a forceful President they tend to do as little as possible. They tend to provide some small favor for each noisy group, and to call that a policy. They tend to ignore any issue that rouses deep passion. And by doing so they strengthen the Union.[68]

It is in the nature of American parties to sacrifice principle to assuage political differences and forge national unity. Yet for some analysts, the unifying effects of party organizations in the late nineteenth century were all too effective and complete. Party organizations, so the critique went, subordinated important questions of national policy and instead focused predominantly on the distribution of particularistic benefits to their supporters. Henry Adams drove to the heart of the problem when he observed that "Government" amounted to little more than "plundering the people in order to support party organizations. . . . No man," he said, "can name any well-defined question on which they are divided. Their paradise is power, and it furnishes the sole basis and inspiration of their contention."[69]

Woodrow Wilson developed this line of critique more forcefully and effectively than any other turn-of-the-century scholar. For Wilson, good government did not require the subordination of party spirit but rather a redefinition of the role of parties in public life. The parties of the late nineteenth century were inadequate because they were without principle: neither of the major parties united behind a set of coherent ideas or programmatic objectives. The machinery of the party organizations was hierarchical and closed, and the public was alienated from the democratic process. The people, as a result, respond in outbursts of discontent when they "happen to realize that under existing party machinery they have virtually no control at all over nominations for office, and that, having no real control over the choice of candidates, they are cut off from exercising real representative self-government,—that they have been solemnly taking part in a farce."[70] Popular resentment grew, as well it should; the voters, Wilson maintained, were entitled to a substantive choice on election day because the vote was their primary means for exercising control over their government.

The parties, as they were constituted, were fast becoming anachronisms in this rapidly modernizing polity. As Wilson explained, the development of industry and advances in communication and transportation technologies proved to be an unstoppable force for the political and economic integration of the nation. These progressive forces picked up where the parties left off: the adhesives of national communication, commerce, and transportation integrated the polity to such a degree that the nation could plausibly be treated as a single, extended community. Wilson noted in *Constitutional Government*, "Our life has undergone radical changes since 1787, and almost every change has operated to draw the nation together, to give it the common consciousness, the common interests, the common standards of conduct, the habit of concerted action, which will eventually impart to it in many more respects the character of a single community."[71] No longer needed to bind the nation together, the parties would have to be adapted to new ends to meet the changing needs of their country. Wilson accordingly embarked on a mission "to study new uses for our parties and to adapt them to new standards and principles."[72]

In his early work on late nineteenth-century parties, Wilson focused on Congress both because Congress was the locus of political power in the federal government in this period and because Congress was intended to be the most deliberative branch.[73] He trenchantly observed that the fragmentation of congressional parties boiled down to a matter of institutional organization: the organization and practices of Congress relegated all matters of public significance to the least public and least deliberative forums, the standing committees. The leadership in Congress was both divided and secretive. Power, in his view, "is nowhere concentrated; it is rather deliberately and of set policy scattered amongst many small chiefs [the chairmen of the standing committees]."[74] There were no great generals in Congress who could be recognized as spokesmen for their parties and held to account as such. The parties in Congress, as a result, were "like armies without officers, engaged upon a campaign which has no great cause at its back."[75]

Of equal concern was the proclivity of these "petty barons" to conduct their business out of view from the public eye.[76] The leadership of the standing committees successfully shifted "the theatre of debate upon legislation from the floor of Congress to the privacy of the committee-rooms." Wilson cynically quipped that "Congress in session is Congress on public exhibition, whilst Congress in its committee-rooms is Congress at work."[77] The public realm, as a result, was deprived of political power and emptied of significance: the political discussion that was in the open and witnessed by the public was meaningless because real power was wielded behind closed doors.[78] The exercise of power was unaccountable and therefore exercised "irresponsibly."

Wilson's understanding of "responsibility" was central to his theoretical outlook. Good government, in his view, could be reduced to a fairly simple formula involving several institutional attributes: freedom within the legislature for unfettered and open debate, the capacity for concerted action by recognizable party units, and the opportunity of the mass public to reward or censure those party units at the polls. As he explained, *"Power and strict accountability for its use* are the essential constituents of good government.

A sense of highest responsibility, a dignifying and elevating sense of being trusted, together with a consciousness of being in an official station so conspicuous that no faithful discharge of duty can go unacknowledged and unrewarded, and no breach of trust undiscovered and unpunished,—these are the influences, the only influences, which foster practical, energetic, and trustworthy statesmanship."[79] With lines of accountability clearly demarcated, the public could be relied on to ensure that the government operated in conformity with its interests and demands. Democracy, in other words, did not require mass participation but rather the institutional machinery that could make popular control of the government possible.[80] Wilson opined that the republic was ready for a new kind of party system that met these democratic standards: "The time is at hand when we can with safety examine the network of party in its detail and change its structure without imperiling its strength. This thing that has served us so well might now master us if we left it irresponsible. We must see to it that it is made responsible."[81] Wilson amended the view of responsible party government advanced in *Congressional Government* (1885), choosing in *Constitutional Government* (1908) to locate party government in the executive branch and to entrust the president with the responsibility of leadership. His vision for executive leadership effectively reordered the priorities of the executive in the American political system.[82] Indeed, the original president as defined by the Framers was an executive in the literal sense and not much more, charged with the responsibility to enforce the laws of the land and to guarantee the safety and sovereignty of the republic. He was a subordinate to Congress; his veto was a "power of restraint, not of guidance."[83] This job description had become an anachronism by the turn of the century: there was no mistaking, in Wilson's view, "the progress of the idea that the President is not merely the legal head but also the political leader of the nation."[84]

The modern Wilsonian president, unlike the executive of the nineteenth century, was an opinion leader who "interpreted" the will of the American people.[85] The highest aims of the American people could be found within the people themselves; yet the mass public, if left unto itself, could not fully grasp or articulate its own will. It required a master interpreter to make manifest what was latent in the people: "the business of every leader of government is to hear what the nation is saying and to know what the nation is enduring. It is not his business to judge *for* the nation, but to judge *through* the nation as its spokesman and as its voice."[86] The modern president was thus a principled opinion leader who advanced a national partisan program and was sub-ject to the people's approval or censure.[87]

Yet a paradox emerged within his conception of popular statesmanship, one that James Ceaser succinctly described: "Wilson accepted party compe-tition but continually alluded to a form of leadership that transcended partisanship and could unite the nation on the one 'right' interpretation." Wilson seemed to assume that "different interpretations are possible but only one is correct."[88] His political theory embraced the proposition that an ef-fective party opposition is essential to good government, knowing full well that the "right" interpretation might not always win the contest. His grounds for toleration were largely instrumental: he embraced an individual's right to be wrong because he believed that the protection of this right was the most expedient way to correct error. As he wrote in *Constitutional Government*, "the wisest thing to do with a fool is to encourage him to hire a hall and dis-course to his fellow citizens. Nothing chills nonsense like exposure to the air; nothing dispels folly like its publication; nothing so eases the machine as the safety valve."[89] This kind of pluralism, Wilson believed, achieved a sig-nificant measure of acceptance in the polity: "We are so accustomed to agi-tation, to absolutely free, outspoken argument for change, to an unrestrained criticism of men and measures carried almost to the point of licence, that to us it seems a normal, harmless part of the familiar processes of govern-ment."[90]

Wilson, at least as a political scientist, embraced this kind of pluralism. His commitment to diversity tacitly assumed that the risks of the "wrong" interpretation were not so great. He did not, to be sure, extend this princi-ple as far as Oliver Wendell Holmes did, who opined in *Gitlow v. New York* (1925) that if, "in the long run, the beliefs expressed in the proletarian dic-tatorship are destined to be accepted by the dominant forces of the com-munity, the only meaning of free speech is that they should be given their chance and have their way."[91] Holmes could entertain this kind of fatalistic pluralism because he lived in a polity where truly revolutionary movements were unlikely to succeed. Wilson's party pluralism was, in contrast, more limited: the process of interpretation allowed the president to pick and choose from the diversity of opinion in the public sphere and to extract from this diversity a singular vision of the national will. The president would then project this vision back to the people to mold opinion into its optimal form.[92]

Whether led by congressional leaders or the president, Wilson insisted that parties no longer needed to moderate antagonistic elements within the republic; they could safely afford to present the national public with rival, politically distinct alternatives. Moreover, the urgency for principled party competition grew as the forces of progress pushed the country forward. Yet Wilson's larger purpose to bring the great questions facing the nation into focus was plausible only in a polity where principled partisan divisions did not foreshadow separatist violence. The risk of such violence was diminishing with time: "we have come within sight of the end of the merely nationalizing process. Contrasts between region and region become every year less obvious, conflicts of interest less acute and disturbing. Party organization is no longer needed for the mere rudimentary task of holding the machinery together or giving it the sustenance of some common object, some single cooperative motive."[93]

Not all were on board with Wilson's call for more purposive and principled parties. Though they embraced a Wilsonian concept of responsible party government as an ideal, some notable political scientists doubted that this model of government could be implemented in a constitutional regime where powers were formally separated. Ford was one such skeptic. In his defense of the parties as they were constituted in the late nineteenth and early twentieth centuries, Ford made the case that the separation of powers would inevitably compromise party unity. Not only were partisans in the legislative and executive branches "free to use their own discretion as to the way in which they shall interpret and fulfill . . . party pledges"; they were also "shielded, by the constitutional partitions of privilege and distributions of authority, from any direct and specific responsibility for delay or failure in coming to an agreement for the accomplishment of party purposes." With authority divided, party responsibility was bound to be "uncertain and confused."[94] The structure of the Constitution itself, in other words, would undermine party discipline and thwart party programs. As former president of Harvard A. Lawrence Lowell explained in his *Essays on Government*, the British model of responsible government, of which Wilson was so fond, was "not in harmony with our institutions, and could not be introduced into the United States without destroying the entire fabric of the constitution."[95]

Wilson's peers had other grounds to object to his call for more principled parties. Indeed, parties without principle were also parties that refrained from divisive appeals to class and ethnic rivalries. Lowell, for example, emphasized the tendency of American parties to defuse class sympathies by highlighting other policy questions—especially disputes over the tariff and the distribution of spoils. He wrote in 1889 that the British demagogue

> will stir up class against class, and try to tempt the crowd to bear him on their shoulders by offering to scatter among them the money of the rich. But the American politician resorts to no such arts. He usually attempts, on the contrary, to conciliate all classes, and delights in such language as "a tariff for revenue only, so adjusted as to protect American industries;" an expression intended to win the votes of the free-traders without offending the protectionists. He is a member of an army of office-seekers, whose warfare is not directed against private rights, or the interests of particular classes, or even against what might be considered crying abuses, but is waged chiefly with a rival army of office-seekers; and the spoils of victory, in the form of public offices, . . . are allotted strictly to . . . persons more vulgarly called the workers or wire-pullers of the party. The result is, that party agitation in America does not in general involve any threat against the property or rights of private persons, and that those statutes which may be classed as socialistic rarely find a place in party programmes, and are not carried by party votes.[96]

Bryce, for his part, described this pattern as evidence of a kind of American exceptionalism. Writing in 1921, he averred,

> Class distinctions have during the last hundred years become in Continental Europe the forces which chiefly split and rend a people into antagonistic sections of opinion. This tendency has increased with the spread of the revolutionary school which preaches the so-called "class war" of the "proletariate" against the "bourgeois." It is only within the last three decades that this doctrine, brought from Europe by German and Russo-Jewish immigrants, has been making way [in the United States], and what support it receives comes almost wholly from the still unassimilated part of the immigrant population. America has been theretofore exempt from class antagonisms, because opinion has been divided, not horizontally along the strata of less or greater wealth, but vertically, so that each view, each political tenet, was common to men in every social

class. The employer and his workmen, the merchant and his clerks, were not led by their different social positions to think differently on politics any more than they would think differently on religion. They have been Republicans or Democrats for reasons unconnected with pecuniary means or station in life, neither of these two parties having any permanent affinity either with the richer or with the poorer. [97]

Faith in the capacity of the American party system to soften or deflect class antipathies was challenged in 1896 with the nomination of William Jennings Bryan as the standard bearer of the Democratic party. The election of 1896 represented for many "the first modern class-struggle political contest" to take place in industrial America.[98] This election, to the extent that it represented a battle over class, was a departure from the norm. For contemporaries, however, it appeared to be a harbinger for the future. Under Bryan, the Democrats staked out new ideological and policy commitments. Breaking with Grover Cleveland's conservative leadership, Bryan brought Populists into the fold of the Democratic party and ran on a platform supporting stronger railroad regulation, an end to federal repression of strikes, a constitutional amendment to restore the income tax, and, most important, the coinage of silver. Republican leaders and publicists responded to the nomination with a fusillade of attacks highlighting the alleged radicalism of the Democratic ticket.[99] Theodore Roosevelt, for example, accused Populists of "plotting a social revolution and the subversion of the American Republic"; he accused Illinois governor John Altgeld, an ally of Bryan's, of conspiring to inaugurate "a red government of lawlessness and dishonesty as phantastic and vicious as the Paris Commune itself."[100] John Hay, who would serve as secretary of state under McKinley and Teddy Roosevelt, campaigned in 1896 with the incendiary address "The Platform of Anarchy."[101] Conservative-minded elites were panicked, and their apprehension may have had an enduring impact: writing in 1913, Oliver Wendell Holmes opined, "When twenty years ago a vague terror went over the earth and the word socialism began to be heard, I thought and still think that fear was translated into doctrines that had no proper place in the Constitution or the common law."[102]

McKinley won the election thanks to an unusually well-funded campaign that emphasized the alleged threat that silver, "social revolution," and Populist demagoguery posed to the American way of life; this message successfully dissuading urban workers and silver Republicans from voting with the Democratic ranks.[103] The election was significant because it revealed voting patterns that were qualitatively different from those of previous presidential elections. The vote, as Sundquist explained, "was distributed in a wholly new configuration. Superimposed on the latitudinal pattern that had marked the party system since the 1850s was a longitudinal, East-West division resembling the schism expressed in so many congressional roll calls in the postwar decades."[104]

The outcome of the election has, for the reasons detailed by Sundquist, Burnham, and others, been treated as a watershed event in American electoral history—a "realigning" election comparable to the elections of 1860 and 1932.[105] The status of this election as a realigning event notwithstanding, there were important differences between what was said about the nature of the Democratic opposition during the heat of the electoral season (i.e., that it presented a threat to the industrial capitalist order) and what the Democratic party program actually represented. Indeed, the claim advanced by conservative contemporaries that Bryan's Democratic party threatened to undo the American system of free enterprise rests on questionable assumptions. The chief economic reforms sought by the Bryanites—a departure from the gold standard and an income tax—are today taken to be fully compatible with American capitalism. Bryan, moreover, dismissed proposals to nationalize the railroads and the telegraph—proposals that were near and dear to Populists across the country.[106] Bryan also attempted to build a regionally and economically diverse coalition including property owners committed to agrarian Jeffersonian ideals and hostile to statist, "socialistic" government policies.[107] His campaign rhetoric, moreover, advanced a Jacksonian defense of small business and labor, who in his view had been put-upon by monopolists and well-connected business interests that curried special favors from the federal and state governments. Bryan sought to extend the definition of a businessman to include the farmer and the wage earner and to make the case that the playing field for businessmen of all kinds needed to be leveled. This message yielded an electoral coalition that could not be fairly characterized as a legion of subversives and radicals: in addition to western Populists, it included, among others, southern Democrats, silver Republicans, and midwestern Prohibitionists.

The outer bounds of party legitimacy were slowly redrawn as questions concerning monetary policy, the income tax, and other redistributive policies took their place on the national political agenda. Herbert Croly called attention to this turn-of-the-century trend: "Anybody who squinted in the direction of economic and social reform was stigmatized as a Bryanite or at worst a Socialist, and was thereafter supposed to be excluded from the universe of polite political discourse. The remnant, who associated political with economic reorganization, were comprehensively condemned as "Populists." Once that sentence had been passed on a man, he was considered as much beyond the pale as a heretic would have been to the mediaeval church."[108] Croly wrote these words in 1914. The bounds of "polite political discourse" were even more vigilantly guarded in the years that followed.

Legitimate Opposition in Theory and Practice

As World War I broke out and the Bolshevik Revolution erupted, suspicion of political opposition concentrated in the cities and distributed in ethnic communities across the nation took on new force. Wilson's evolving pluralism provides a window into the changing nature of American ambivalence toward legitimate dissent. Indeed, Wilson's leadership stance as president was often at odds with the theoretical position he maintained as a scholar. As a political scientist, his political theory was relatively abstract and removed in important respects from the governing exigencies of the day. His model of party government was designed for "normal" times; he scarcely discussed the nature of leadership and the role of parties when fundamental interests were in the balance. In the few instances when he did, he focused his critique on the inability of a system of separated powers to act effectively during an emergency. He expressed no fear that parties or organized groups might themselves generate the emergency.[109]

Yet when forced to confront the apocalyptic violence of World War I and to manage the challenges of defining and enforcing a policy of neutrality at home, Wilson grew preoccupied with what he took to be the dangers of domestic "radicalism." Wilson's ire was directed first and foremost at immigrants, ethnic Americans, and those who embraced foreign and allegedly subversive ideologies. The political and state-sanctioned scrutiny of domestic opposition fell particularly hard on German Americans and Irish Americans. This was not surprising. German Americans, who constituted nearly 10 percent of the population at the time, were believed to harbor sympathies for their ancestral homeland; Irish Americans, many of them hostile to the interests of Britain, were also perceived to side with the Central Powers.

Opposition to Wilson's policy of neutrality moreover came predominantly, though by no means exclusively, from within the Democratic party. Opposition to Wilson's foreign policy measures also came from agrarian and middle-class isolationists as well as midwestern Republicans (including, for example, Senator Robert La Follette from Wisconsin). The preparedness advocates nevertheless wished to treat their diverse opposition as a "common enemy."[110]

Undisturbed by the outspoken pro-Allied constituency in America, Wilson stigmatized the foreign-born and others who criticized his neutrality policy or (by 1916) his program for military preparedness. For Wilson, the problem of nonneutral sentiment and action was a problem with the "hyphenates."[111] Wilson's admonitions to citizens "born under foreign flags" to maintain their neutrality was at first measured but grew progressively more hostile: in his 1915 address to Congress, Wilson warned that

> the gravest threats against our national peace and safety have been uttered within our own borders. There are citizens of the United States, I blush to admit, born under other flags but welcomed under our generous naturalization laws to the full freedom and opportunity of America, who have poured the poison of disloyalty into the very arteries of our national life; who have sought to bring the authority and good name of our Government into contempt, to destroy our industries wherever they thought it effective for their vindictive purposes to strike at them, and to debase our policies to the uses of foreign intrigue. . . . We should promptly make use of the processes of law by which we may be purged of their corrupt distempers. . . . Such creatures of passion, disloyalty, and anarchy must be crushed out.[112]

Expressing concern that a minority of America's foreign born do not always have the interests of America in mind, he proposed to the Daughters of the American Revolution that Americans should receive the foreign born into the United States in a manner not unlike the way college students haze freshmen: "I would a great deal rather be obliged to draw pepper up my nose than to observe the hostile glances of my neighbors. I would a great deal rather be beaten than ostracized. I would a great deal rather endure any sort of physical hardship if I might have the affection of my fellow-men. We constantly discipline our fellow-citizens by having an opinion about them. That is the sort of discipline we ought now to administer to everybody who is not to the very core of his heart an American. Just have an opinion about him and let him experience the atmospheric effects of that opinion!"[113] Opposition to his policy of neutrality, in this view, might be thwarted through the social intimidation of loyal and right-thinking Americans. This was a curious position for a president to maintain who, that same year, expounded upon the virtues of the free market of political ideas: "The market for ideas is a highly competitive market, and the rules of competition are necessarily fair. There is only one test for an idea and that is "Is it good?" . . . The best thing that is characteristic of countries like our own is that every man who has an idea is constantly invited to the platform. And there is nothing better for an idea by way of test than exposure to the atmosphere."[114] These positions led Wilson into a contradiction: the "atmospheric effects" of social intimidation should caution citizens before they publicize their ideas, but once these ideas were released into "the atmosphere," they would be weighed on their merits. Social intimidation, somehow, would not deter men from accepting the public's "[invitation] to the platform" in the first place.

As the United States commenced hostilities against the Central Powers, Wilson and leaders in Congress advanced new modes of surveillance to silence political opposition. Only days after Wilson delivered his address to Congress requesting a declaration of war, Wilson established the Committee on Public Information (CPI) to enforce "correct" opinion on matters relating to the conflict. A Board of Censorship was later instituted by executive order to regulate communications leaving the country.[115] More regulations of the scope of legitimate dissent followed in the wake of these executive actions. The Espionage Act, passed on 15 June 1917, included a measure that would punish, when the United States was at war, those who "willfully make or convey false reports or false statements with intent to interfere with the operation or success of the military or naval forces of the United States or to promote the success of its enemies." Those who "willfully cause or attempt to cause insubordination, disloyalty, mutiny, or refusal of duty, in the military or naval forces of the United States" were also liable for punitive measures.[116] Title XII of the Espionage Act empowered the postmaster general to suppress any material "advocating or urging treason, insurrection, or forcible resistance to any law of the United States."[117] The Espionage Act allotted to the postmaster general, Albert Burleson, considerable discretion to decide by his own lights what was permissible to publish. Using this discretion, Burleson embarked on a crusade to censor "radical" publications that went above and beyond the provisions of the law.[118]

The Sedition Act, which became law on 16 May 1918, took federal censorship one step further. This legislation prohibited speech of all kinds relating to the war effort. In particular, the Sedition Act made it a criminal offense to, among other things, "willfully utter, print, write, or publish any disloyal, profane, scurrilous, or abusive language about the form of government of the United States, or the Constitution of the United States, or the flag of the United States, or the uniform of the Army or Navy," to use any language intended to bring these same symbols and institutions "into contempt, scorn, contumely, or disrepute," to "incite, provoke, or encourage resistance to the United States," or to "advocate any curtailment of production in this country of any thing or things, product or products, necessary or essential to the prosecution of the war."[119] The debate in Congress over the Sedition Act was itself chilled by the spirit of censorship that prevailed in the legislative chambers. In fact, Republican senator Henry Cabot Lodge admitted that he has become "a little weary of having Senators get up here and say to those of us who happen to think a word had better be changed . . . that we are trying to shelter treason."[120]

Because of the reach and ambiguity of the Sedition Act, it was nearly impossible to lawfully criticize the management of the war effort or to speak out about the justice or wisdom of this effort. Writing just after the war, Special Assistant Attorney General John Lord O'Brian observed that the law "covered in all degrees of conduct and speech, serious and trifling alike, and, in the popular mind, gave the dignity of treason to what were often neighborhood quarrels or barroom brawls."[121]

After the successful passage of the Sedition Act, the Democratic Congress on 16 October 1918 passed an Alien Act—a coupling of measures that evoked the draconian laws passed by Federalist majorities in 1798. In accord with the contemporary prejudice that opposition to war came from hyphenates sympathetic to un-American ideologies, the Alien Act of 16 October 1918 authorized the federal government, upon the recommendation of the secretary of labor, to deport "aliens who are anarchists; aliens who believe in or advocate the overthrow by force or violence of the Government of the United States or of all forms of law; . . . [or] aliens who are members of or affiliated with any organization that entertains a belief in, teaches, or advocates" the same.[122]

With the draconian content of these measures in mind, one might wonder whether such repressive steps were warranted or proportionate given the nature of the opposition to the war. Indeed, opposition to American involvement in World War I was qualitatively different from antiwar sentiment of the late 1790s (during the Quasi War with France) or during the War of 1812. Though opposition tended to be concentrated in the South and the Midwest, neither of these regions entertained the idea of a separate peace or separate terms of neutrality with the Central Powers. Such measures were unthinkable in the early twentieth century. Nor was the Democratic party prepared (even if it had been unified in opposition to the war) to obstruct American military power through extralegal means. The direction of American policy could be altered only if opponents of the war or critics of the conduct of the war achieved a majority in Congress and passed legislation to this effect. The war, in other words, could be stopped only with the ballot; it could not be stopped with the bullet.

Wilson's fear of radicalism within the mass public did not soften once the war was over. The Bolshevik Revolution sent a chill and a panic through the country that lasted for years after the conclusion of the war. In December 1919, Wilson asked Congress to pass a peacetime Sedition Act: "the poison of disorder, the poison of revolt, the poison of chaos," he claimed, had entered "into the veins of this free people."[123] This poison required continued vigilance to be purged. In this spirit, Wilson refused, until the day before he left office, to terminate many of the security measures that he helped enact during the war—measures clearly limited by their text to the time of war.[124]

Wilson's fear that Bolshevism would make its way to the United States also prompted him to reconsider his views of domestic policy. American leaders, Wilson confided to his brother-in-law, must "think internationally as our labor masses are thinking. We can meet Bolshevism only with bold liberalism." The threat of global communism demanded domestic reforms that he might not consider otherwise: "It seems certain that some commodities will have to become the property of the state, the coal, the water powers and probably the railroads." Wilson qualified this statement with a rare acknowledgment that popular suspicions—suspicions that he himself promoted—had not only chilled the freedom of public debate, but also prompted him to censor himself. Referring to his support for the nationalization of several major industries, Wilson confessed in the same letter that "some people would call me a socialist for saying this."[125]

Conclusion

A new political and institutional setting took shape in the late nineteenth century, with sweeping ramifications for the development of party pluralism in America. Forces pushing for civil and political rights for blacks were steadily marginalized and, especially in the South, repressed outright. New questions gradually took center stage as labor violence spread in the industrial North, European immigrants flooded the cities, and agrarian "radicalism" became a force in national politics. The resurgence of white supremacist control in the South was callously ignored by many so long as this violence did not compromise the basic requirements of national sovereignty.[126] Though the central state's capacity to impose new controls on social and economic life in the South had failed, the postwar central state was able—unlike its early national and antebellum predecessor—to guarantee the territorial integrity of the Union and the collection of national revenues. The terms of legitimate party opposition evolved accordingly. Sectional parties were tolerated in the postbellum period because geographically concentrated partisan attachments no longer posed a credible threat to national unity.

With the Union secure, the standards for evaluating the role of party in American democracy changed. Party organizations were often represented as unaccountable and corrupting influences on the body politic. They were, nonetheless, widely taken to be innocuous creatures essential to the operations of a modern mass democracy. Lowell, in fact, went so far as to define party opposition in the modern world as something akin to an individual right. As he wrote in 1913, "In a modern popular government, where the whole people are never within reach of a man's voice, . . . the right of persuasion involves freedom of speech, of publication, and of organization." The "liberty of organization," in this view, was essential for the legitimacy of government more generally.[127]

Yet liberties, including the "liberty of organization," had their limits. The legitimacy of party opposition was delimited in the early national and antebellum periods, and so it was also in the postwar period. The terms of toleration were revised. Fresh lines were drawn in the late nineteenth and early twentieth centuries as leading political observers grew wary of organizations that politicized ethnic and class divisions. New boundaries demarcating the political mainstream from the politically marginal became clearer during World War I and as the domestic panic sparked by the Bolshevik Revolution spread. These international developments altered the nature of antipartisan discourse and shifted the target of political regulation. As we shall see in the concluding discussion to follow, limits on the legitimacy of political opposition were articulated in new ways in the twentieth century as minor parties came under special scrutiny and distinctions were drawn not only between mainstream and "radical" parties, but also between two-party and multi-party *systems*.

Epilogue:
Party Legitimacy, Then and Now

The defeat of the Confederacy and the passage of the Reconstruction amendments did not "solve" the problem of party. Though they did settle the intractable questions of slavery and separatism, the bounds of legitimate opposition were, instead, redefined in post-Reconstruction America. As we saw in Chapter 6, new anxieties emerged at the turn of the twentieth century as industrialism advanced and ideas challenging the hegemony of financial, manufacturing, and commercial interests gained ground in America. The following pages briefly examine how these anxieties were transposed onto critiques of third-party movements, which, many believed, would amplify subversive voices on the national stage. This epilogue glimpses beyond the long nineteenth century, offering a description of several institutional and geopolitical developments that altered the balance of electoral power between major and minor parties and recast the profile of party opposition in the United States. As I explain below, changing electoral rules and geopolitical conditions narrowed the electoral playing field, neutralizing the threat that a minor-party challenger might supplant one of the two major parties. Measures taken to set minor parties outside the American mainstream nonetheless opened space for the legitimation of *major* party opposition. Representative elites equated American democracy with the two-party system, and as they did, they identified the party in opposition as an institution not merely to be tolerated, but as a democratic prerequisite that conferred legitimacy on the governing regime itself.

* * *

Hostility to third-party movements gained force following World War I and the overthrow of the czarist government by Bolshevik revolutionaries.

Conservative elites in America felt increasingly vulnerable in these years as contentious challenges to capitalist modes of production and governance strengthened in Europe and Britain. A response to the threat of subversion "from below" appeared particularly urgent for many political and intellectual representatives of the governing establishment.[1]

To the good fortune of those who hoped to check the influence of third parties, electoral institutions set in place at the turn of the century laid the groundwork for a comprehensive assault on the status of minor-party competitors. The challenge to the role of third (or more) parties represented an important departure from the American electoral tradition. Minor parties played a regular and integral role in state and national politics during the long nineteenth century.[2] Before the turn of the twentieth century, minor parties hoping to cut into the major parties' vote share—or perhaps even supplant one of the two dominant parties—required only a printing press (to copy ballots) and a committed group of workers to distribute them at polling places.[3] Barriers to directly enter the electoral "market" at the local, state, and national levels were relatively low. Minor parties were also able to contest elections in a rather indirect manner: they could cross endorse major-party candidates, encouraging their supporters to nominate candidates supported by a major party.[4] Electoral fusion, where multiple parties nominate the same set of candidates, allowed minor parties to maintain a viable electoral "brand" in a single-member district voting system; it enabled them to consolidate their voting strength with another party to prevent the electoral victory of a least-favored major-party candidate. Greenbackers and Populists used this strategy most successfully, often fusing with the Democrats to defeat Republican candidates.[5]

The Australian secret ballot, adopted in states across the country in the 1890s, changed the electoral game. In addition to curbing partisan corruption and intimidation at the polls, the Australian ballot transferred control of the printing of ballots to state and local governments and made it possible for these governments to narrow the electoral playing field. The two dominant parties that controlled state and local governments across the country were able to make a novel strategic "play": they could, for the first time, limit minor parties' access to the ballot.[6] Ballot-access laws proliferated as a result; electoral fusion was banned in thirteen states in 1900 and in twenty-five states by 1920.[7]

These new legal contrivances (ballot access and antifusion laws) did not remove minor parties from the electoral playing field. Indeed, the most significant third-party challenge of the twentieth century came in 1912 when Eugene Debs's Socialist party garnered 6 percent of the national vote. The new rules of the game did, nonetheless, tilt the electoral playing field, reducing the "risk" that minor-party candidates might secure positions of governmental power. The two major parties, which automatically appeared on state-printed ballots in most districts, were placed at a distinct advantage.[8] New formal rules, moreover, made informal, rhetorical challenges to the status of minor parties more persuasive. As their ability to credibly challenge the major parties deteriorated, appeals for minor-party support were more readily dismissed as futile. The notion that votes for minor parties were irresponsible, "wasted" protests against an American way of conducting elections held greater weight in an electoral environment where minor parties were pressed to the periphery.[9]

The status of the major parties was elevated by default, cordoned off as a safe preserve for mature and responsible politics. As E. Pendleton Herring described them in 1940, "The major parties are conscious of their own limitations; the minor parties as a rule are not." Herring further surmised that "most of our minor parties in recent decades have inclined strongly to the devil theory of history. . . . Plutocracy, they insist, is the cause of all evil."[10] Political and intellectual elites of the postwar period, to be sure, did not believe that the major parties were pristine: the Democrats and Republicans did what they could to sully the reputations of their rivals for political gain. The major parties did not stand above the electoral fray; they set the parameters and produced the optics of an energetic and adversarial political atmosphere. Yet the major parties were, in a different and more fundamental sense, *against* the fray, largely committed to established modes of governmental operations and existing political arrangements. The major parties were not provocateurs of political dissent; their modus operandi was incremental and conservative, and their strength was in placating, accommodating, and—for their most outspoken critics—suffocating political differences.[11] The two-party system's establishmentarian bias was poorly disguised by some of its leading proponents, most notably the authors of the landmark report by the Committee on Political Parties of the American Political Science Association (APSA). Key to their appeal for a more "responsible two-party system" was the notion that programmatic major parties would help "*to consolidate public attitudes toward the work plans of government.*"[12] In the concluding sentences of their report, the authors were very explicit about the larger purpose of programmatic party competition: the aim was to set boundaries on the range of acceptable choices and avoid "unhealthy" divisions in the electorate. *"Orientation of the American two-party system along the lines of meaningful national programs,* far from producing an unhealthy cleavage dividing the electorate, *is* actually *a significant step toward avoiding the development of such a cleavage.* It is a way of keeping differences within bounds. It is a way of reinforcing the constitutional framework within which the voter may without peril exercise his freedom of political choice."[13] The major parties, in the account offered by the APSA report, needed to do the work of consolidating the people and delimiting their choices. This was important and, for many, strategically necessary work: in the tense geopolitical aftermath of World War II, elite preferences gathered in favor of institutions that would consolidate mass opinion. The parties were thus called on to consolidate public opinion, yet they also needed to offer a choice: in an international political arena where the United States was pitted against powerful foreign challengers boasting party systems of their own, a clear, bright line was essential to show that the American party system provided a meaningful choice—that it was qualitatively different from the sham single-party "systems" of the Soviet and Chinese regimes.

The fact of choice mattered more than the range of options, and the legitimacy of a single party in opposition (however modest or conservative it might be) preserved this fact. Political and intellectual elites leveraged the choice afforded by America's two-party pluralism to draw a clear contrast between the democratic polities of the West (the United States and the United Kingdom in particular) and the totalitarian, single-party regimes of the East. This difference between East and West endowed the American republic with a claim to exceptionalism.[14]

A double distinction thus emerged during the Cold War years. On the one hand, the American party system was advantageously contrasted with the closed, single-party "systems" of the Chinese Communist and Soviet regimes. The two-party system was also elevated above politically unreliable multiparty alternatives—unreliable because they opened the way for parties insufficiently committed to the struggle against global communism.[15] The contrast between major and minor parties, in other words, metastasized by midcentury into a distinction between different kinds of party systems.[16]

In the fraught geopolitical climate of midcentury America, major-party opposition achieved a standing that was never contemplated by the earliest generations of American statesmen and thinkers. Since the early national period, party opposition had been marked as one of the leading threats to the integrity and continuity of the republic. Yet in the aftermath of World War II, major-party opposition had become essential to the democratic legitimacy of the governing regime. This was a remarkable turnabout. Political and intellectual elites, mindful of the challenge that single-party communist regimes posed to American sovereignty and influence in the world, sought recourse in party legitimacy because they found in it the promise of a delimited, "responsible," democratic politics.

*   *   *

Modern party leaders are expected to adhere to a standard of toleration that was unknown to earlier generations of American statesmen. This standard, to be clear, is not very expansive. Stated in the antiseptic terms offered in the APSA report, it is the view that accountable government requires a (singular) opposition and that *"the opposition most conducive to responsible government is an organized party opposition*, produced by the organic operation of the two-party system."[17]

As I have argued in this study, this standard of toleration, however limited, was not the product of a progressive enlightenment of American political values. Rather, the historical evidence presented here suggests that the status of party opposition changed in accord, not only with liberal and republican currents of thought, but also with the developing capacities of the central state and the shifting position of the American polity in the international political arena. Elites, mindful of the state's limited capacity to contain domestic political conflict and insulate the polity from foreign influence, designed institutions to delimit the scope and content of partisan debate. The sphere of legitimate partisan contention was, to be sure, molded by partisan actors seeking electoral advantage, yet it was also molded to advance what many of these actors took to be (and what often were) vital governing purposes. The status of party opposition has thus undergone a dramatic transformation in sync with the changing exigencies of government; it has, in this sense, been the site of patterned change, political development. It may indeed be true that parties inevitably form in a free republic, but the *kinds* of parties that form and the scope of their rivalry is powerfully shaped by the institutional makeup of the regime itself and the leaders who wish to sustain it.

By some measures, party pluralism in the United States is, to this day, fairly limited. The range of choices presented to the American public, when compared to that on offer in other advanced, postindustrial polities, is quite narrow.[18] Yet the idea of legitimate party opposition has, nonetheless, come a long way since the American Founding. Party differences are today woven into the fabric of American life—they structure the way elite actors in Washington, D.C., pursue their ambitions, and they frame what Americans take to be the universe of acceptable political alternatives. They are embedded in Americans' everyday, lived reality—both for better and for worse.

The frustrations (rather than the benefits) often appear more salient.

From the vantage point of the voting decision, the grounds for popular discontent are understandable: voters are, after all, required to make difficult compromises. As they so often attest, they have no choice but to vote for a candidate that is insufficiently liberal or conservative for their tastes, deciding between two major parties they perceive to be too extreme, choosing a most-preferred minor-party candidate (at the risk of "wasting a vote"), or voting for a major-party candidate they dislike to prevent a least-favored candidate from winning.

These compromises are, by all appearances, uncomfortable; they are, nonetheless, familiar. Equally discomfiting and familiar is the emergent concern that party divisions are undermining lawmakers' efforts to respond to pressing domestic and foreign policy concerns. Doubts about the capacity of a government with separated powers and polarized parties to operate in a coordinated and efficient manner are raised today with a growing sense of urgency.[19] To be sure, the American system of government was intended to proceed methodically and to frustrate ambitious legislative programs; it was not designed to act with dispatch or to undertake grand programmatic visions. Most successful policy initiatives are today and have been in the past measured and incrementalist. The wheels of government may turn slowly, but they should in fact turn. The policy stalemate that prevails, insofar as it results from the ideological polarization of the parties in Congress, represents a highly salient frustration Americans experience with the fact of party differences.[20]

American ambivalence with party differences extends further, particularly when we consider the public theater that constitutes the day-to-day transactions of American politics. Stories of public officials consumed by partisan animus, unilaterally inhibiting the free exchange of ideas, make for good copy. When an Obama administration spokeswoman announced in October 2009 that the president would not grant any interviews to Fox News for the rest of the year, labeling it "the communications arm of the Republican Party," this struck some as an attempt to intimidate a media outlet. Whether the judgment was fair or not, denying a major media outlet access to an interview—a mere conversation—came across as a stubborn refusal to talk with others and to expose oneself to disagreement. Obama ultimately relented and granted the cable network an interview.[21] In a separate episode some four years later, the chairman of the House Committee on Oversight and Government Reform, Republican Darrell Issa, hastily concluded a hearing investigating allegations that the IRS targeted conservative Tea Party groups. Issa then silenced the microphone of the ranking Democrat on the committee, Elijah Cummings Jr., who wished to speak on the matter before the hearing was adjourned. Cummings continued to speak even though the microphone was turned off; he later described Issa's actions as "un-American." After a firestorm of criticism, Issa offered Cummings an apology.[22]

In these instances, Obama and Issa were censured for violating popular norms of communicative engagement. But did these breaches of decorum really warrant the public and media attention they attracted? One might wonder whether the "story" in both cases should have focused, not so much on the inappropriate actions of these public figures, but on the heightened political sensitivities of the American people themselves. Whether one supports or opposes President Obama or Congressman Issa, they both transgressed the norms of a public that is uncomfortable with "adversarial" discourse and action—a public that insists on the formality of giving "both sides" a full hearing. This standard, a mere formality to be sure, will at first blush strike the committed (small "d") democrat as a minimal requirement for free exchange. But set in comparative and historical perspective, it represents an important accomplishment.

From a comparative perspective (a perspective so often neglected by scholars who study polarization in the United States), one may argue that American party politics appears rather tame: in recent years, Europe has witnessed the emergence of a true Neo-Nazi party in Greece (the Golden Dawn), a party that openly embraces Nazi symbolism and has only gained in popularity over time, winning 7 percent of the popular vote in 2012, gaining eighteen seats in a Parliament of three hundred; since 2012, the Golden Dawn has registered as the third most popular party in the country, frequently polling above 10 percent. The Golden Dawn is, in fact, an "antisystem party" insofar as it sanctions vigilante violence against immigrants and political opponents.[23] Right-wing anti-immigrant parties have grown in popularity throughout Europe, particularly in the wake of austerity policies implemented in the aftermath of the Eurozone debt crisis. The Golden Dawn represents only the most extreme instance of a broader trend. Openly anti-Semitic, protofascist parties such as ATAKA in Bulgaria and Jobbik in Hungary have also gained considerable popular support in recent years.[24] In Austria, the anti-immigrant Freedom party has grown in strength in successive National Council (parliamentary) elections, receiving 11.2 percent of the vote in 2006, 17.5 percent in 2008, and 20.6 percent in 2013.[25] The National Front in France, a party that has been, at least in the recent past, openly racist and anti-Semitic, outpolled all other French parties, securing 25 percent of the vote in the 2014 European Parliamentary elections.[26] Glimpsing outside of Europe to the world's largest democracy, the people of India elected Hindu nationalist leader Narenda Modi in 2014 to the highest office in the land. As chief minister of the state of Gujarat in 2002, Modi failed, at the very least, to take even modest steps to thwart a pogrom in his state that resulted in the slaughter of over one thousand Muslim citizens; at worst, he and his subordinates in government supported the genocide.[27] The virulent racism and prejudice that has gained expression in representative bodies in Europe, India, and elsewhere should give those who are troubled by the incivility of partisan discourse in America pause. As off-putting as partisan posturing in Congress and in the media may be, this brand of politicking is delimited by electoral and institutional parameters that encourage pluralistic norms and discourage the public display of raw, ethno-racial and religio-nationalist animus found in other democratic polities around the world.[28]

In the American case, the popular argument that partisan rhetoric and practices have become appreciably more contentious in recent years typically elevates the period from midcentury to the late 1980s to the status of a golden age, when compromise in Congress was possible and professionalism reigned on the public airwaves.[29] It is certainly true that political elites (at least in Congress) were more ideologically moderate during this period than they are today; the evaluative judgment, however, that the rise in public contentiousness represents a deterioration of democratic values in America raises several basic problems. First, to the extent that this period exemplified a degree of public decorum in Congress and in the media, it masked underlying disagreements that periodically burst to the surface; these disagreements focused primarily, but not exclusively, on civil rights and the commitments of U.S. foreign policy. Organized movements mobilized a highly contentious brand of politics to protest government policies in these and other arenas. In

the case of Vietnam, leaders in Congress deferred to the Johnson administration and went to great lengths to keep the matter off the legislative agenda.
Congress, in other words, refused to publicly acknowledge the significant divisions forming both in Congress itself and in the polity at large over the
administration's war policy.[30] In the case of civil rights, when a meaningful
civil rights bill reached the floors of the House and Senate in 1964, legislators were in no mood for pragmatic negotiation. Instead, the civil rights bill
faced implacable opposition from southern senators and passed only after
supporters were able to marshal enough votes to invoke cloture, terminating
a filibuster that resulted in the longest continuous debate in Senate history.[31]
It is true that a collegial, cooperative atmosphere may indeed prevail in Congress when the most divisive (and for some, the most important) questions
of the day are set aside, studiously avoided, or actively subordinated. Yet this
is a significant price to pay for civil discourse and one that is not contemplated by those who claim that a change in governing norms will restore a
more pragmatic mode of policy making.[32]

Consensual appearances should always raise our suspicions.[33] Speaking
generally, consensus may be quite benign and constructive: it may entail either a prior agreement to disagree or an arrangement to set a divisive issue
of public concern aside where no settlement could be plausibly reached. Consensual appearances (or the absence of adversarial politics), however, may
also be the product of a strategic setting where the institutional rules of the
game stack the deck against challenges to the status quo so that potential dissenters are demoralized and effectively silenced. The absence of oppositional
politics may, moreover, entail an unspoken understanding, a deeper agreement that is simply "understood," that some subjects are out of order or inappropriate for public discussion. The lesson one cannot avoid from the study of
antebellum America is that sometimes, the most important questions in
politics lack an empirical trace; they are deliberately undiscussed.[34]

Returning to the politics of post–World War II America, it is also not
clear why this period, from midcentury through the 1980s, should be taken
as the standard for comparison, the norm against which other periods of
American history should be tested. One might, for the sake of argument, re-
verse this assumption: we might treat this period of public consensus as aberrant and a departure from a "normal" pattern of greater contentiousness
in the public sphere. If we were to change our point of view, to choose not to
prioritize one period over another (by treating one period as an exemplar of
democratic norms and others as aberrant), one might note that today's rules

of communicative engagement stand in sharp contrast to those of past eras. The polarized congresses of the Reconstruction and post-Reconstruction periods, for example, were not known for their comity or rhetorical pluralism; former Confederate and Union officers who had last met each other on the battlefield met again in the halls of Congress. Republicans did not hesitate to wave the "bloody shirt," and former Confederates returned the favor with conspiratorial talk of "Black Republican" plans to subdue the white man and build the foundations for "black supremacy" in the South.[35] Looking just a little further into the American past, we do not see today veiled (let alone manifest) threats of violence such as those witnessed on the floor of Congress during the antebellum years. One can reference here the caning of William Sumner on the floor of the Senate in 1856, but this case is so widely known that it almost does a disservice to the problem: it appears to stand as an exception and, as such, to imply that the halls of Congress were innocuous spaces. As new research from Joanne Freeman shows, violence was in the background, and periodically, the foreground, of congressional debate as legislators came to chambers armed, brandishing weapons in debate and signaling threats in less conspicuous ways that were, nonetheless, understood by all on the floor. To use the jargon of the time, legislators divided between "fighting men" and "noncombatants." Freeman counted in the thirty-year period from 1830 to 1860 approximately 120 physical clashes in the House and Senate and their immediate surroundings—these involving bowie knives, pistols, bricks, and canes.[36]

Americans, however, are so far removed from this history and from political violence more generally that uncivil and illiberal acts such as refusing an interview or silencing a microphone are what today pass for "adversarial" behavior. Viewed from a historical perspective, dissensus has been defined down. Even relatively innocuous modes of partisan politicking that once may not have been given a second thought are today carefully policed and ritually censured. Insults and abuse were, in other times, freely exchanged among legislators; today, when a congressman calls the president a liar during the State of the Union address, it triggers an apology, a disavowal from the leaders of the congressman's party, and a moment of national "soul-searching."[37]

Many Americans expect a greater degree of public civility, and this is understandable: the political theater consumed by millions of American citizens on a day-to-day basis is an unpleasant spectacle to behold. One must be mindful, nonetheless, that America's polarized extremities are not as illiberal as what one might find in other democracies around the world or in the American past. Their relative moderation is itself a historical phenomenon: it is a product of a constricted electoral and institutional landscape that was constructed over time, from the Founding of the republic to the development of the two-party system. Because they operate in a two-party system and aim, as a result, to become majority parties, they face strong incentives to reach out to a great diversity of economic and political interests. It should therefore come as no surprise that both major parties, the Democrats and the Republicans, are market capitalist parties that rely for their support on a diverse range of private business interests.[38] Both parties possess ethnically and racially heterogeneous coalitions and face strong electoral incentives to make their national coalitions even more heterogeneous than they presently are. Thanks to these electoral incentives and to the courts' constructions of the religious establishment and free exercise clauses of the First Amendment, neither party is a theocratic party, embracing a single, true national faith. The two major parties, in other words, are polarized within a truncated ideological continuum.[39] American parties are today restrained by institutions designed to moderate policy position-taking and to stabilize what was once a structurally fragile republic.

The stakes of this polarization, such as it is, are not so great. As I have argued in this book, political parties in America no longer possess the capacity to compromise the structural integrity of the republic. Polarized parties can produce unseemly mischief, but their posturing doesn't threaten political violence, nor does it risk radical policy change. If anything, the central tendency of party competition in recent years has been to prevent meaningful policy change. The parties in Congress have deep disagreements, but these disagreements produce, at worst, policy stalemate. This can be, in some cases, a highly undesirable outcome. But it is not a catastrophic one. In a governing regime where the executive branch is equipped with at least temporary authority to address emergencies, a period of policy deadlock is unlikely to do existential harm to the republic.[40]

Polarized party opposition simply does not pose the kind of grave risk to the well-being of the American regime that it once did. Some elected officials and opinion leaders still nonetheless wonder whether the United States, with its geopolitical responsibilities, can afford to tolerate a vigorous partisan debate about its foreign policy commitments. The distinguished political scientist James Q. Wilson addressed this concern in an essay written in 2006. "Sharpened debate . . . is arguably helpful with respect to domestic issues, but not for the management of important foreign and military matters. . . . Denmark or Luxembourg can afford to exhibit domestic anguish and uncertainty over military policy; the United States cannot. A divided America encourages our enemies, disheartens our allies, and saps our resolve—potentially to fatal effect. What General Giap of North Vietnam once said of us is even truer today. America cannot be defeated on the battlefield, but it can be defeated at home. Polarization is a force that can defeat us."[41] Polarized party opposition, in Wilson's rendering, will compromise American influence in the world and its prospects for success in a conflict abroad. Wilson explains that America cannot "afford" vigorous partisan debate on vital matters of U.S. foreign policy—politics must, as the old saying goes, "stop at the water's edge." On vital questions of defense policy, what is needed is not active public debate involving citizens and leaders in Congress, but consensus or the appearance of consensus. The parties should simply find other grounds for differentiation.

As we saw in Chapter 5, partisan divisions at home can, no doubt, present significant strategic disadvantages when a polity is engaged in a hot war. Wilson called the legitimacy of party opposition into question as the United States was engaged in the Iraq War, a small war to remove a relatively weak tyrant, unlike the American Civil War, a war begun to preserve the union of the states. Wilson may be correct to suggest that division at home altered perceptions of America's strength and commitment among its enemies and allies alike.[42] At stake, however, was the image of America in the world and not the integrity or the fundamental security of the republic.[43]

In this sense, the Iraq War was qualitatively different from the Civil War. Yet Wilson's formulation seems untroubled by the difference, as if all wars begun must collapse free space for debate at home. Anticipating this very problem—that public perceptions of foreign threat may endanger republican liberty—Madison observed over two hundred years ago that it is, perhaps, "a universal truth that the loss of liberty at home is to be charged to provisions against danger, real or pretended, from abroad."[44]

To be sure, one can imagine circumstances when party opposition might be "out of order." There were occasions in the not too distant past—the Cuban Missile Crisis comes to mind—that called for consensus and a pause in partisan posturing. One must remember, nonetheless, that the United States is not the institutionally vulnerable republic it once was. The structure and capacities of American government have changed, and these changes should afford a wider and less inhibited partisan debate. Vigorous political rivalry will not shake the foundations of the country. Yet the notion that the republic cannot sustain an oppositional politics—that polarization will, in fact, destabilize the country—has a receptive audience. This is troubling, not only because this belief prepares citizens to embrace policy ideas packaged as nonpartisan or bipartisan by politically interested groups, but also because it valorizes the idea of consensus and deprives it of the suspicion it deserves.

NOTES

Chapter 1. Legitimate Party Opposition and the Early American State

1. "Speech by Secretary Seward: The Military and Political Situation Reviewed," *New York Times*, 7 September 1864.

2. John Adams to Thomas Jefferson, 30 June 1813, in *The Adams-Jefferson Letters*, ed. Lester J. Cappon (Chapel Hill: University of North Carolina Press, 1959), 2: 346–47.

3. George Washington "Farewell Address," 17 September 1796, in *Messages and Papers of the Presidents*, ed. James D. Richardson (New York: Bureau of National Literature, 1897), 1: 218.

4. See Stanley M. Elkins and Eric L. McKitrick, *The Age of Federalism* (New York: Oxford University Press, 1993), 490–94.

5. I am echoing E. E. Schattschneider's noted quip that "modern democracy is unthinkable save in terms of the parties." E. E. Schattschneider, *Party Government* (New York: Farrar and Rinehart, 1942), 1.

6. Richard Hofstadter, *The Idea of a Party System: The Rise of Legitimate Party Opposition in the United States, 1780–1840* (Berkeley: University of California Press, 1969).

7. For my purposes, "structural integrity" refers to the territorial unity of the nation-state and the capacity of the central government to extract revenue from the territory's population.

8. On the growing literature that builds bridges between American political development and American political thought, see the symposium in *American Political Thought* 3 (Spring 2014): 114–76; also see Ruth O'Brien, "Finding a Nexus Between APD and American Political Thought," *Clio: Newsletter of Politics and History* 22 (Spring/Summer 2012–13): 3.

9. Hofstadter, *Idea of a Party System*, 8.

10. See Hofstadter, *Idea of a Party System*, 16–33. As I explain below, antipartisan figures were not uniformly opposed to party legitimacy. Quite a few antipartisan "progressive" statesmen and thinkers of the late nineteenth and early twentieth centuries maintained that party spirit was undesirable and a detriment to the common good. These same figures, nonetheless, acknowledged that party affiliation (which at the time

was defined by divisions over tariff protection, monetary policy, and the distribution of the spoils of government) was reasonable; progressives rarely spoke of partisanship as a fundamental threat to the integrity and civil peace of the republic.

11. Diana C. Mutz, "Effects of 'In-Your-Face' Television Discourse on Perceptions of a Legitimate Opposition," *American Political Science Review* 101 (November 2007): 621.

12. Engel draws a distinction between a loyal opposition and a legitimate opposition. A legitimate opposition, in his rendering, is the view held by those in power that though opposition is "natural, unavoidable, and manageable," it is, nonetheless, believed to present a threat to the republic. In this definitional arrangement, legitimate opposition is the less inclusive category. Engel, *American Politicians Confront the Court: Opposition Politics and Changing Responses to Judicial Power* (Cambridge: Cambridge University Press, 2011), 5–6.

13. Paul Krugman, "It's Witch-Hunt Season," *New York Times*, 29 August, 2010; Thomas E. Mann and Norman J. Ornstein, *It's Even Worse Than It Looks: How the Constitutional System Collided with the New Politics of Extremism* (New York: Basic Books, 2012), xiv, 62, 185.

14. To be more precise, I use Sartori's concept as a foundation, which I build on and modify to suit the needs of this study. Giovanni Sartori, *Parties and Party Systems: A Framework for Analysis* (Cambridge: Cambridge University Press, 1976). I was tempted to rely instead on Robert Dahl's concept of polyarchy. Polyarchy refers to a kind of governing regime that guarantees the right to oppose and organize in opposition, institutionalizing an unfettered competition among party (and other) organizations. The concept of polyarchy also, however, envisions the institutionalization of a broad range of other democratic rights. It is therefore a wider and more encompassing concept. Sartori's notion of party pluralism is more helpful for our purposes because it narrows our focus to the role that party opposition plays in a regime. Robert A. Dahl, *Polyarchy: Participation and Opposition* (New Haven, Conn.: Yale University Press, 1971), 1–9.

15. Sartori, *Parties and Party Systems*, 13. Also see Nancy L. Rosenblum, *On the Side of the Angels: An Appreciation of Parties and Partisanship* (Princeton, N.J.: Princeton University Press, 2008), 6–7.

16. "Party pluralism" and "legitimate party opposition" will henceforth be used interchangeably. I employ both terms because the expressions "legitimate opposition," "legitimate dissent," and "legitimate party opposition" are fairly commonplace in popular and scholarly discourse—perhaps because of the close association between "legitimate opposition" and "loyal opposition." "Legitimate opposition," "legitimate dissent," and "legitimate party opposition" are also useful because they are familiar. These expressions are, nonetheless, rarely defined. Sartori's party pluralism, by contrast, is relatively unfamiliar; he does, however, give the concept a relatively clear definition. His definition of party pluralism, moreover, captures what scholars typically mean when they refer to opposition as "legitimate."

17. For examples of alleged partisan bullying by George W. Bush, see E. J. Dionne, *Stand Up and Fight Back: Republican Toughs, Democratic Wimps, and the Politics of Revenge* (New York: Simon and Schuster, 2004). For allegations of partisan intimidation by Barack Obama, see Ben Shapiro, *Bullies: How the Left's Culture of Fear and Intimidation Silences Americans* (New York: Simon and Schuster, 2013).

18. Rosenblum, *On the Side of Angels*, 6.

19. The notion that the legitimacy of government requires the opposition of only one major party emerged with the advent of the modern discipline of political science in the late nineteenth century. The discipline itself identified multipartyism as a problem in the early to mid-twentieth century. Minor political parties, in point of fact, played a consistent and central role in electoral politics during the nineteenth century. See Lisa Jane Disch, *The Tyranny of the Two-Party System* (New York: Columbia University Press, 2002), and Richard Franklin Bensel, *The American Ballot Box in the Mid-Nineteenth Century* (Cambridge: Cambridge University Press, 2004). For a discussion of the two-party pattern in the United States, i.e., the tendency for two major parties to dominate electoral politics at a time, see Chapter 2. The identification of multipartyism as a problem is discussed in the Epilogue.

20. Sartori, *Parties and Party Systems*, 13.

21. Note that Hofstadter omits any reference here to nullification or secession. Hofstadter, *Idea of a Party System*, 4.

22. To be clear, I do not use the expression "boundary condition" as J. David Greenstone does in his classic work, *The Lincoln Persuasion: Remaking American Liberalism* (Princeton, N.J.: Princeton University Press, 1993). For my purposes, the expression refers only to the terms that circumscribe party legitimacy.

23. The most recent and notable works that focus on the philosophical objections to partisanship are Rosenblum's *On the Side of the Angels* and Russell Muirhead's *The Promise of Party in a Polarized Age* (Cambridge, Mass.: Harvard University Press, 2014).

24. On the doctrine of content neutrality in free speech law, see Geoffrey R. Stone, "Content Regulation and the First Amendment," *William and Mary Law Review* 25 (1983): 189–252; also see Steven H. Shiffrin, *Dissent, Injustice, and the Meanings of America* (Princeton, N.J.: Princeton University Press, 1999), 10–11.

25. Hofstadter, *Idea of a Party System*; Ronald P. Formisano, "Political Character, Antipartyism, and the Second Party System," *American Quarterly* 21 (Winter 1969): 683–709; Ronald P. Formisano, "Deferential-Participant Politics: The Early Republic's Political Culture, 1789–1840," *American Political Science Review* 68 (June 1974): 473–87; Marc W. Kruman, "The Second American Party System and the Transformation of Revolutionary Republicanism," *Journal of the Early Republic* 12 (Winter 1992): 509–37. On the unevenness of this transition, see Glenn Altschuler and Stuart Blumin, *Rude Republic: Americans and their Politics in the Nineteenth Century* (Princeton, N.J.: Princeton University Press, 2000), 3–13; Major Wilson, "Republicanism and the Idea of Party in the Jacksonian Period," *Journal of the Early Republic* 8 (Winter 1988):

419–42; Engel, *American Politicians Confront the Court*, 87–96 and 138–45; Daniel Peart, *Era of Experimentation: American Political Practices in the Early Republic* (Charlottesville: University of Virginia Press, 2014).

26. As Frank Sorauf notes, "Writers on American parties have tended to consider them as independent agencies in the political system—as some *élan vital*, some autonomous, ordering force set loose in the system. It has been customary, for example, to speak of the parties as 'democratizing' American politics as if they were reforming missionaries from some far-off places." "Political Parties and Political Analysis," in *The American Party Systems: Stages of Political Development*, ed. William Nisbet Chambers and Walter Dean Burnham (New York: Oxford University Press, 1967), 49. For additional criticism of this trend in historical scholarship, see Ronald Formisano, "Deferential-Participant Politics," 473–75; Kenneth Kolson, "Party, Opposition, and Political Development," *Review of Politics* 40 (1978): 163–82; Gerald Leonard, *The Invention of Party Politics: Federalism, Popular Sovereignty, and Constitutional Development in Jacksonian Illinois* (Chapel Hill: University of North Carolina Press, 2002); Engel, *American Politicians Confront the Court*, 87–96 and 138–45; Peart, *Era of Experimentation*; Jeffrey S. Selinger, "Rethinking the Development of Legitimate Party Opposition in the United States," *Political Science Quarterly* 127 (Summer 2012): 263–87.

27. Paul Goodman, "The First American Party System," in *American Party Systems*, Chambers and Burnham, 57–58.

28. Joseph Charles, *The Origins of the American Party System: Three Essays* (New York: Harper and Row, 1961), 85. John F. Hoadley remarks that acceptance of the idea of legitimate party opposition "came reluctantly as their inevitability became more apparent.... Gradually," he points out, "people realized that unanimity was impossible in a diverse society and that the right of opposition had to be recognized." "The Emergence of Political Parties in Congress, 1789–1803," *American Political Science Review* 74 (1980): 778. For more recent iterations of this sentiment, see Charles Stewart III, "Congress and the Constitutional System," in *The Legislative Branch*, ed. Paul J. Quirk and Sarah A. Binder (New York: Oxford University Press, 2005), 6, and Sean Wilentz, *The Rise of American Democracy: Jefferson to Lincoln* (New York: Norton, 2005), 516–17.

29. Hofstadter, *Idea of a Party System*, xii.

30. This observation was in reference to Washington's criticism of the Democratic-Republican Societies. Hofstadter, *Idea of a Party System*, 99. Hofstadter adopts a similarly dismissive tone toward Jefferson and James Monroe, see ibid. 203–5.

31. This theme is evident in some of the landmark studies of the early republic. See, for example, Wilentz, *Rise of American Democracy*, 516–17; Gordon S. Wood, *The Radicalism of the American Revolution* (New York: Vintage Books, 1993), 87–92, 293–305; Hofstadter, *Idea of a Party System*, 240–43; Harry L. Watson, *Liberty and Power: The Politics of Jacksonian America* (New York: Hill and Wang, 1990), chs. 1, 6, and 8; Joel Silbey, *The Partisan Imperative: The Dynamics of American Politics Before the*

Civil War (New York: Oxford University Press, 1985), ch. 4; James Sterling Young, *The Washington Community, 1800–1828* (New York: Columbia University Press, 1966), 251–54. For a more focused study that maintains a similar premise, see William G. Shade, "Political Pluralism and Party Development: The Creation of a Modern Party System: 1815–1852," in *The Evolution of American Electoral Systems*, ed. Paul Kleppner, Walter Dean Burnham, Ronald P. Formisano, Samuel P. Hays, Richard Jensen, and William G. Shade (Westport, Conn.: Greenwood Press, 1981), 77–111.

32. The most noted English commonwealthmen were John Trenchard and Thomas Gordon, who authored the highly influential *Cato's Letters* in the early 1720s. For more on Trenchard and Gordon's influence on the Revolutionary generation, see Bernard Bailyn, *The Ideological Origins of the American Revolution* (Cambridge, Mass.: Harvard University Press, 1992), 35–54. For a helpful survey of the emergence of republicanism as a theme in the study of early American political culture and thought, see Robert Shalhope, "Republicanism and Early American Historiography," *William and Mary Quarterly* 39 (April 1982): 334–56.

33. For discussions of the way in which classical republican norms and practices gave way to more boldly partisan and publicly self-interested social and political routines, see Wood, *Radicalism of the American Revolution*, 87–92, 293–305, and Ralph Ketchum, *Presidents Above Parties: The First American Presidency, 1789–1829* (Chapel Hill: University of North Carolina Press, 1984).

34. This achievement, to be sure, came at the expense of black freedmen who were disenfranchised in many states as white males were enfranchised. See William Shade, "Politics and Parties in Jacksonian America," *Pennsylvania Magazine of History and Biography* 110 (October 1986): 483–508. On the gradual (and nonlinear) elimination of property qualifications and other restrictions on white male suffrage, see Alexander Keyssar, *The Right to Vote: The Contested History of Democracy in the United States* (New York: Basic Books, 2009).

35. Wood, *Radicalism of the American Revolution*, see especially 77–92 and 169–89.

36. Scholars of American political development are increasingly studying the impact of foreign affairs on American institutional development. See in particular Ira Katznelson and Martin Shefter, eds., *Shaped by War and Trade: International Influences on American Political Development* (Princeton, N.J.: Princeton University Press, 2002).

37. For analyses that reflect these assumptions, see Joel H. Silbey, *Partisan Imperative*, ch. 4, and James Sundquist, "Needed: A Political Theory for the New Era of Coalition Government in the United States," *Political Science Quarterly* 103 (Winter 1988): 613–35.

38. Sundquist, "Needed," 617.

39. Arthur M. Schlesinger Jr., *The Age of Jackson* (Boston: Little, Brown, 1945), 424, 422–33.

40. See especially E. E. Schattschneider, *Semi-Sovereign People: A Realist's View of Democracy in America* (Chicago: Holt, Rinehart, and Winston, 1960), ch. 4. To be

sure, not all elites sought to avoid the most polarizing questions all the time. Alexander Hamilton and his followers, the "High Federalists," hoped to meet head-on the thorniest problem leaders confronted in the 1790s: how to engage Great Britain and France during the French Revolutionary Wars. As we shall see in Chapter 3, the limited coercive reach of the central state defined a strategic landscape where any attempt to decisively settle this foreign policy question ran the risk of civil war.

41. Ibid., 3.

42. A number of important historical studies that highlight the relationship between parties and the state explore how party organizations patterned the development of America's administrative and governing institutions. The present study, by contrast, examines how the federal government's limited coercive capacity vis-à-vis the states shaped the scope and content of partisan dispute. See especially Martin Shefter, *Political Parties and the State: The American Historical Experience* (Princeton, N.J.: Princeton University Press, 1994); Stephen Skowronek, *Building a New American State: The Expansion of National Administrative Capacities, 1877–1920* (Cambridge: Cambridge University Press, 1982); Sidney M. Milkis, *The President and the Parties: The Transformation of the American Party System Since the New Deal* (New York: Oxford University Press, 1993); Sidney M. Milkis, *Political Parties and Constitutional Government* (Baltimore: Johns Hopkins University Press, 1999). Other notable party scholars in the American field examine institutions and institutional development, but their focus strongly favors the study of electoral and legislative institutions. See, for example, Aldrich, *Why Parties? A Second Look* (Chicago: University of Chicago Press, 2011), 16–24; Leon Epstein, *Political Parties in the American Mold* (Madison: University of Wisconsin Press, 1986); Mark D. Brewer and Jeffrey M. Stonecash, *Dynamics of American Political Parties* (Cambridge: Cambridge University Press, 2009); Alan Ware, *The American Direct Primary: Party Institutionalization and Transformation in the North* (Cambridge: Cambridge University Press, 2002); Kathleen Bawn, Martin Cohen, David Karol, Seth Masket, Hans Noel, and John Zaller, "A Theory of Political Parties: Groups, Policy Demands and Nominations in American Politics," *Perspectives on Politics* 10 (September 2012): 571–97. The impact of state capacities on party development figures more prominently in the comparative literatures on democratization and party systems. See, for example, Adrienne LeBas, *From Protest to Parties: Party-Building and Democratization in Africa* (Oxford: Oxford University Press, 2011); Dankwart Rustow, "Transitions to Democracy: Towards a Dynamic Model," *Comparative Politics* 2 (1970): 337–63.

43. John Aldrich, *Why Parties? The Origin and Transformation of Political Parties in America* (Chicago: Chicago University Press: 1995); Aldrich, *Why Parties? A Second Look* (Chicago: Chicago University Press, 2011). All references to *Why Parties?* hereinafter are to the 2011 edition.

44. Aldrich, *Why Parties?* 5, 15.

45. See ibid., chs. 3, 4, and 5.

46. Ibid., 67.

47. When Aldrich uses the expression "the great principle," he is describing a dimension of policy in dispute. This dimension might be better described as a "question" than as a "principle" since there were rival principles at stake. Aldrich and Ruth Grant more aptly describe this dimension as the "regime question" in "The Antifederalists, the First Congress, and the First Parties," *Journal of Politics* 55 (May 1993): 299.

48. Ibid., 75.

49. Taken together, these issues raised what Madison believed to be the "great division of interests" in the United States. As he explained to the delegates at the Constitutional Convention in Philadelphia, "the States were divided into different interests not by their difference in size, but by other circumstances; the most material of which resulted partly from climate, but principally from (the effects of) their having or not having slaves. These two causes concurred in forming the great division of interests in the U. States. It did not lie between the large & small States: it lay between the Northern & Southern. and if any defensive power were necessary, it ought to be mutually given to these two interests." *The Records of the Federal Convention of 1787* (hereafter *RFC*), rev. ed., ed. Max Farrand (New Haven, Conn.: Yale University Press, 1966), 1: 486.

50. The first party system featured a noticeable sectional skew, with the South strongly (but not solidly) Republican and New England leaning heavily in favor of the Federalists. These divisions, however, were not too sharply drawn: the Republicans had supporters in the North just as the Federalists had a contingent of support in the South. The middle states, moreover, were closely divided. See Mary P. Ryan, "Party Formation in the United States Congress, 1789 to 1796: A Quantitative Analysis," *William and Mary Quarterly* 28 (1971): 532–33; John Hoadley, "The Emergence of Political Parties in Congress, 1789–1803," *American Political Science Review* 74 (1980): 772–73.

51. Aldrich, *Why Parties?* 75.

52. Ibid. To be sure, the Framers did not anticipate that war between Britain and France, commenced several years after ratification, would exaggerate and inflame divisions structured by the great principle.

53. Aldrich, to be sure, does discuss the politics of the ratification process, but his analysis does not detail the efforts the Framers undertook to contain the contentious politics of the mid-1780s and to narrow the scope of conflict for future generations. Ibid., 71–79; also see Aldrich and Grant, "Antifederalists, the First Congress, and the First Parties"; Ryan, "Party Formation in the United States Congress"; John Hoadley, "The Emergence of Political Parties in Congress, 1789–1803," *American Political Science Review* 74 (1980): 757–79; Epstein, *Parties in the American Mold*; Milkis, *Political Parties and Constitutional Government*; Bawn et al., "Theory of Political Parties."

54. The view that the second party system was designed, first and foremost, to contain the question of slavery was advanced most recently by Robert Pierce Forbes. Forbes, *The Missouri Compromise and Its Aftermath: Slavery and the Meaning of America* (Chapel Hill: University of North Carolina Press, 2007), 8.

55. See, for example, Skowronek, *Building a New American State*; Richard Franklin Bensel, *Yankee Leviathan: The Origins of Central State Authority in America, 1859–1877* (New York: Cambridge University Press, 1990); Theda Skocpol, *Protecting Soldiers and Mothers: The Political Origins of Social Policy in United States* (Cambridge, Mass.: Harvard University Press, 1995).

56. On the federal government's support for economic development, see William D. Adler and Andrew J. Polsky, "Building the New American Nation: Economic Development, Public Goods, and the Early U.S. Army," *Political Science Quarterly* 125 (Spring 2010): 87–110. On the federal government's capacity to defend the Northwest Territory, as well as its neglect of the southwestern frontier, see Andrew R. L. Cayton, "'Separate Interests' and the Nation-State: The Washington Administration and the Origins of Regionalism in the Trans-Appalachian West," *Journal of American History* 79 (June 1992): 39–67. On the development of a communications and civic infrastructure, see Richard John, *Spreading the News: The American Postal System from Franklin to Morse* (Cambridge, Mass.: Harvard University Press, 1995), and, more generally, Daniel Walker Howe, *What Hath God Wrought: The Transformation of America, 1815–1848* (Oxford: Oxford University Press, 2007).

57. Brian Balogh, *Government Out of Sight: The Mystery of National Authority in Nineteenth Century America* (Cambridge: Cambridge University Press, 2009), 4; also see Peter Baldwin, "Beyond Weak and Strong: Rethinking the State in Comparative Policy History," *Journal of Policy History* 17 (2005): 12–33; William Novak, "The Myth of the 'Weak' American State," *American Historical Review* 113 (June 2008): 752–72.

58. See especially Ira Katznelson, "Flexible Capacity: The Military and Early American Statebuilding," in Katznelson and Shefter, *Shaped by War and Trade*, 82–110; Novak, "Myth of the 'Weak' American State."

59. For a comparable balance-of-power perspective, though one that does not focus on the role of political parties, see Daniel H. Deudney, "The Philadelphian System: Sovereignty, Arms Control, and Balance of Power in the American States-Union," *International Organization* 49 (Spring 1995): 191–228.

60. John M. Murrin, "The Great Inversion, or Court Versus Country: A Comparison of the Revolution Settlements in England (1688–1721) and America (1776–1816)," in *Three British Revolutions, 1641, 1688, 1776*, ed. J. G. A. Pocock (Princeton, N.J.: Princeton University Press, 1980), 425.

61. There were only 3,578 enlisted men and approximately 235 officers in the army in 1794 (3,813 total), many of whom were stationed to defend the western frontier from invasion by neighboring Indian tribes. In 1801, the total number of men enlisted rose to 4,051. This figure dropped to 2,873 in 1802, and would not exceed four thousand until 1808. Total uniformed army personnel plateaued at or below approximately 10,500 from the conclusion of the War of 1812 to 1835 and did not exceed 12,500 men until the Mexican War. See the appendix in Russell F. Weigley, *History of the United States Army* (Bloomington: Indiana University Press, 1984) for data on the strength of the active army since 1789.

62. Katznelson, "Flexible Capacity," 84, 86.

63. Ibid., 84–90.

64. See ibid., 90–91, 94–97.

65. This is a crucial problem addressed by scholars like Richard Franklin Bensel and Stephen Skowronek, who detail the limitations of the early American central state. Given their narrower focus, it is not so clear how Bensel and Skowronek have "underestimated badly" (in Katznelson's words) the capacities of their chosen subject matter (the federal government). See ibid., 86; Bensel, *Yankee Leviathan*; Skowronek, *Building a New American State*.

66. *The Federalist Papers*, 1788, ed. Isaac Kramnick (New York: Penguin, 1987), no. 46, 301.

67. See Rosenblum, *On the Side of the Angels*, 7.

68. Sally E. Hadden, *Slave Patrols: Law and Violence in Virginia and the Carolinas* (Cambridge, Mass.: Harvard University Press, 2001), 168–70; Jason Kaufman, "Americans and Their Guns: Civilian Military Organizations and the Destabilization of American National Security," *Studies in American Political Development* 15 (Spring 2001): 88.

69. On the republican critique of standing armies, see Lawrence Cress, *Citizens in Arms: The Army and the Militia in American Society to the War of 1812* (Chapel Hill: University of North Carolina Press, 1982), 17–21, 97–102; Max M. Edling, *A Revolution in Favor of Government: Origins of the U.S. Constitution and the Making of the American State* (Oxford: Oxford University Press, 2003), 73–88 and 101–14.

70. *U.S. Statutes at Large* 1 (1792): 271.

71. Militias in the New England states were typically better equipped and trained than their counterparts elsewhere. H. Richard Uviller and William G. Merkel, *The Militia and the Right to Arms; or, How the Second Amendment Fell Silent* (Durham, N.C.: Duke University Press, 2002), 285 n. 78; John K. Mahon, *History of the Militia and the National Guard* (New York: Macmillan, 1983), 58–59. For a general discussion of the poor training and preparation of the state militias, see Marcus Cunliffe, *Soldiers and Civilians: The Martial Spirit in America, 1775–1865* (Boston: Little, Brown, 1968), 179–212. On the distinctive role and limited capacities of the territorial militias, see Mark Pitcavage, "Ropes of Sand: Territorial Militias, 1801–1812," *Journal of the Early Republic* 13 (Winter 1993): 481–500.

72. Uviller and Merkel, *Militia and the Right to Arms*, 109–24; Mahon, *History of the Militia and the National Guard*, 78–83; Cunliffe, *Soldiers and Civilians*, 205–12; Howe, *What Hath God Wrought*, 491. The data that is available, which is drawn from state reports to the secretary of war and likely includes in its count volunteer militia memberships, is not considered reliable given the wide variation in reporting standards from state to state. This data, nonetheless, suggests that militia memberships—including members of state and volunteer militias—kept pace with the rapidly growing population of antebellum America. Though one cannot say for certain, increases in the number of volunteer militiamen, in all likelihood, compensated for declines in state

militia participation rates. *American Almanac and Repository of Useful Knowledge*, ed. Jared Sparks (Boston: Charles Bowen, 1830), 1: 222; Katznelson, "Flexible Capacity," 91; Lyle D. Brundage, "The Organization, Administration, and Training of the United States Ordinary and Volunteer Militia, 1792–1861" (Ph.D. diss., University of Michigan, 1958), 421–22.

73. Uviller and Merkel, *Militia and the Right to Arms*, 109–24; Mahon, *History of the Militia and the National Guard*, 78–83; Howe, *What Hath God Wrought*, 491.

74. Hadden, *Slave Patrols*, 42, 46–47.

75. Mahon, *History of the Militia and the National Guard*, 83–96; Cunliffe, *Soldiers and Civilians*, 215–41; Kaufman, "Americans and Their Guns," 88–102.

76. Uviller and Merkel, *Militia and the Right to Arms*, 125–27; Mahon, *History of the Militia and the National Guard*, 84; Cunliffe, *Soldiers and Civilians*, 220. As Jason Kaufman persuasively argues, the proliferation of civilian military organizations contradicts the assumption, commonplace among scholars, that "there is a clean analytical divide between state and civil society when it comes to military matters." "Americans and Their Guns," 88.

77. James MacPherson, *Battle Cry of Freedom: The Civil War Era* (Oxford: Oxford University Press, 1988), 317–18. Hadden, *Slave Patrols*, 167–75; Mahon, *History of the Militia and the National Guard*, 101–2. On the aptly named Minute Men for the Defense of Southern Rights and the mobilization of secessionist militia companies in South Carolina, see Steven A. Channing, *Crisis of Fear: Secession in South Carolina* (New York: Simon and Schuster, 1970), 269–73, 278.

78. *RFC*, Farrand, 1: 164–65.

79. For a penetrating analysis of this strategic problem, see David C. Hendrickson's *Peace Pact: The Lost World of the American Founding* (Lawrence: University Press of Kansas, 2003), and *Union, Nation, or Empire: The American Debate over International Relations, 1789–1941* (Lawrence: University Press of Kansas, 2009).

80. *Federalist Papers*, no. 7, 113. That the states did ratify the Constitution provided little comfort to Hamilton. The principle of state sovereignty was carried over from the Articles into the Constitution. For Hamilton, this principle was one of the new charter's fatal defects—a defect that exposed the new American Union to the kind of security challenges he described in the *Federalist Papers*. Indeed, Hamilton offered a plan at the convention for a consolidated government that did not accord any sovereignty to the states. For his plan, see *RFC*, Farrand, 1: 291–93. The risk that foreign powers might seize on differences between the states and the federal government played an important role in the party politics of the 1790s as well as the War of 1812 and the Civil War. See Chapters 3 and 5 below.

81. As we shall see in Chapter 4, this problem presented itself quite clearly during the Nullification Crisis. In the midst of the standoff between the Jackson administration and the Nullifiers, the governor of Virginia was ready to mobilize the militia to prevent federal troops from passing through the state to enforce federal law in South Carolina. As cooler heads in the Jackson administration (Van Buren in particular)

knew, any attempt to coerce South Carolina would risk a wider conflict. See Richard Ellis, *The Union at Risk: Jacksonian Democracy, States' Rights, and the Nullification Crisis* (New York: Oxford University Press, 1987), 130, 138.

82. To be sure, the elimination of the threat of exit does not provide a complete explanation for why the Republican party did not commit to a southern wing in the postbellum period. It was, however, a necessary condition for the subsequent decision to abandon early efforts to build a wing of the Republican party in the South. This matter will be discussed in greater detail in Chapter 6.

83. Sartori, *Parties and Party Systems*, 16.

Chapter 2. Economic Collapse and the Constitutional Construction of Party Politics

1. *RFC*, Farrand, 1: 48.

2. Ibid., 1: 289.

3. Ibid., 1: 288.

4. The story of the Constitution has been written with an emphasis on republican and liberal values; it has also been told through the lens of key policy problems, e.g., western territorial expansion, slavery, and the conduct of foreign affairs. See, for example, Gordon Wood, *The Creation of the American Republic, 1776–1787* (Chapel Hill: University of North Carolina Press, 1969); Joyce Appleby, *Liberalism and Republicanism in the Historical Imagination* (Cambridge, Mass.: Harvard University Press, 1992); Peter Onuf, *The Origins of the Federal Republic: Jurisdictional Controversies in the United States, 1775–1787* (Philadelphia: University of Pennsylvania Press, 1983); George William Van Cleve, *A Slaveholders' Republic: Slavery, Politics, and the Constitution in the Early Republic* (Chicago: University of Chicago Press, 2010); Robin Einhorn, *American Taxation, American Slavery* (Chicago: University of Chicago Press, 2006); Hendrickson, *Peace Pact.*

5. As Madison confessed shortly after the convention, "The evils issuing" from the states "contributed more to that uneasiness which produced the convention, and prepared the public mind for a general reform, than those which accrued to our national character and interest from the inadequacy of the Confederation to its immediate objects." Madison to Thomas Jefferson, 24 October 1787, in *The Writings of James Madison*, ed. Gaillard Hunt (New York: G. P. Putnam's Sons, 1901) 5: 27.

6. The devastation wrought by years of war is generally underappreciated by historically minded political scientists. David Brian Robertson, *The Constitution and America's Destiny* (Cambridge: Cambridge University Press, 2005), 52, is a notable exception. For a helpful survey of the economic toll taken by the war, see Allan Kulikoff, "'Such Things Ought Not to Be': The American Revolution and the First National Great Depression," in *The World of the Revolutionary American Republic: Land, Labor, and the Conflict for a Continent*, ed. Andrew Shankman (New York: Routledge, 2014),

134–64. For a vivid description of the anarchy that ensued in the Lower South during the war, see Ira Berlin, *Many Thousands Gone: The First Two Centuries of Slavery in North America* (Cambridge, Mass.: Belknap Press of Harvard University Press, 1998), 290–304.

7. Stanley L. Engerman and Robert E. Gallman, "U.S. Economic Growth, 1783–1860," *Research in Economic History* 8 (1983): 19.

8. John J. McCusker and Russell R. Menard, *The Economy of British America, 1607–1789* (Chapel Hill: University of North Carolina Press, 1985), 373–74. Peter Lindert and Jeffrey Williamson offer a more modest estimate, suggesting that the decline in per capita GDP from 1774 to 1790 was likely between 18 and 30 percent. Claudia Goldin and Frank Lewis, for their part, found an average annual decline in per capita income of 0.34 percent from 1774 to 1793. These estimates range widely, reflecting the limitations of the available data. They also utilize different indices. A consensus is nonetheless taking shape among economic historians that, though the proportions of the depression may be open for dispute, the economic calamity of the period can no longer be ignored. Lindert and Williamson argue that it has been overlooked for so long because scholars "have emphasized the strong growth experienced across the 1790s, perhaps due to the wisdom of Alexander Hamilton and other founding fathers and/or due to the recovery of foreign markets. Yet, the more we come to accept their sanguine view of the 1790s, the more we must infer a true economic disaster between 1774 and 1790." Lindert and Williamson, "American Incomes 1774–1860," *National Bureau of Economic Research Working Papers Series* 18396 (September 2012): 22–23; Claudia D. Goldin and Frank D. Lewis, "The Role of Exports in American Economic Growth During the Napoleonic Wars, 1793 to 1807," *Explorations in Economic History* 17 (1980): 22–23.

9. Terry Bouton, "Getting, Keeping, and Losing the Land: The Importance of Money, Credit, and Political Economy to Early American Farmers" (paper presented at conference "The Problem of Land in the History of North America, 1700–1850," Montreal, Canada, April 2011), 3. For a detailed analysis of economic developments from the 1770s to 1800, see Allan Kulikoff, "'Such Things Ought Not to Be.'"

10. Terry Bouton, *Taming Democracy: "The People," the Founders, and the Troubled Ending of the American Revolution* (Oxford: Oxford University Press, 2007), 18.

11. Terry Bouton, "A Road Closed: Rural Insurgency in Post-Independence Pennsylvania," *Journal of American History* 87 (December 2000): 864. To calculate interest rates, Bouton converted values in pounds into dollars using the methods practiced by government officials at the time.

12. Ibid., 859–60. As Bouton explains, these figures represent the number of foreclosure orders processed and not the actual number of properties foreclosed; sheriffs typically made several trips to the home of a debtor before a foreclosure order was finalized. For details on the rash of bankruptcies in Philadelphia in 1785 and 1786, see Thomas M. Doerflinger, *A Vigorous Spirit of Enterprise: Merchants and Economic De-*

velopment in Revolutionary Philadelphia (Chapel Hill: University of North Carolina Press, 1986), 262.

13. Woody Holton, "'From the Labours of Others': The War Bonds Controversy and the Origins of the Constitution in New England," *William and Mary Quarterly* 61 (April 2004): 276.

14. See Doerflinger, *Vigorous Spirit of Enterprise*, 261–62. As Gordon Bjork sums up, the crucial chain of economic events that led to unrest in the years just prior to the ratification of the Constitution were as follows: "Prices were falling both because of the outflow of specie and because of the behavior of European prices of important export staples. The differential effects of a falling general price level on the community are well-known. The burden of governmental debt becomes heavier. The dissatisfaction of the debtor class with the resultant redistribution of income is expressed in civil unrest." Bjork, "The Weaning of the American Economy: Independence, Market Changes, and Economic Development," *Journal of Economic History* 24 (December 1964): 558–59. Also see Roger H. Brown's excellent summary in *Redeeming the Republic: Federalists, Taxation, and the Origins of the Constitution* (Baltimore: Johns Hopkins University Press, 2000), 39.

15. Max Edling and Mark Kaplanoff, "Alexander Hamilton's Fiscal Reform: Transforming the Structure of Taxation in the Early Republic," *William and Mary Quarterly* 61 (2004): 734–35.

16. For figures describing the concentration of ownership of government debt, see E. James Ferguson, *The Power of the Purse: A History of American Public Finance, 1776–1790* (Chapel Hill: University of North Carolina Press, 1961), 273, 276, 278, 280, and 283.

17. What is remarkable is not that there was so much war debt, but that state governments were in such haste to retire it. State legislative decisions to retire the debt rapidly led to significant postwar tax increases. Direct taxes levied in Massachusetts between 1772 and 1775 amounted to $391,880; between 1785 and 1788, direct taxes amounted to $1,297,534. In Rhode Island, direct taxes rose from £4,000 per year in 1773 and 1774 to approximately £27,500 annually from 1785 to 1788. Property taxes in New Jersey tripled. New York, which did not levy direct taxes from 1768 to 1784, levied $310,000 between 1785 and 1788. Delaware's direct taxes, which were "infrequent and insubstantial" in the 1770s and early 1780s, were close to $120,000 in the period from 1785 to 1788. Edling and Kaplanoff, "Alexander Hamilton's Fiscal Reform," 729. Roger Brown found a similar pattern in Pennsylvania and South Carolina. Though he did not present a comparison between prewar and postwar tax levels, Brown identifies Virginia, New Hampshire, and Maryland as states eager to retire their war debt rapidly. Brown, *Redeeming the Republic*, 33–34, 122–31, 137.

18. Holton, "From the Labours of Others," 283. Land disputes were also a consistent source of strife. In his study of the Maine frontier, for example, Alan Taylor details the contentious relations between great proprietors who speculated in land and

settlers who cleared the land and made it productive. Animating this social rift was what Taylor described as a "dread of tenancy" commonplace in the eighteenth-century backcountry. This was the fear that elites meant to reduce freehold farmers to tenants serving, in a feudalistic fashion, under the lordship of a landed aristocracy. Taylor, *Liberty Men and Great Proprietors: The Revolutionary Settlement on the Maine Frontier, 1760–1820* (Chapel Hill: University of North Carolina Press, 1990), 13–14.

19. "A Friend to the Public," *Newport* (R.I.) *Mercury,* 27 January 1786. Quoted in Holton, "From the Labours of Others," 278.

20. "Jonas, Junior," *Hampshire Herald* (Springfield, Mass.), 17 May 1785. Quoted in Holton, "From the Labours of Others," 278.

21. Ibid.; Holton, "Did Democracy Cause the Recession That Led to the Constitution?" *Journal of American History* 92 (September 2005); Brown, *Redeeming the Republic*, chs. 7 and 8.

22. Though they consistently divided along a socioeconomic class cleavage, I do not agree with Main that these legislative blocs constituted political parties. Parties are more than opinion groups: they possess organization and engage in electioneering activities. Organization and electioneering, Main admits, are not the focus of his study. "The precise attributes and the significance of these preparty "parties" in America form the subject of our investigation. With a couple of exceptions, we will not describe organizations, nor must we expect systematic electioneering, though we will discover a little of it. We will find no platforms, though we will devote much space to principles of concert." *Political Parties Before the Constitution* (Chapel Hill: University of North Carolina Press, 1973), xviii.

23. This polarity was evident in every state, though there were important variations on the dominant pattern that are worthy of note. States with active ports such as New York, for example, had relatively little difficulty making payments to retire state debt and paying congressional requisitions because state tariffs provided a reliable source of revenue. In southern states such as Virginia, Maryland, and South Carolina, representatives of highly indebted plantation owners tended to side with the less affluent, agrarian elements on matters touching debtor-creditor relations. Ibid., 138, 220–21, 280, 365–407; Norman K. Risjord and Gordon DenBoer, "The Evolution of Political Parties in Virginia, 1782–1800," *Journal of American History* 60 (March 1974): 961–84; Robert Becker, "Salus Populi Suprema Lex: Public Peace and South Carolina Debtor Relief Laws, 1783–1788," *South Carolina Historical Magazine* 80 (January 1979): 68–69.

24. This connection between the position taking of representatives and the socioeconomic status of constituents is one of the key findings of Main's comprehensive study of roll-call data in the states. As he explains, "The most important single influence [on delegates' political alignments] was the delegates' residence, which included their own environment and the kind of constituency they represented. Although the situation varied state to state, and New Jersey seems an exception [where a sectional, East versus West divide prevailed], the differences based upon residence may be de-

scribed by three sets of adjectives [urban v. rural; commercial v. agrarian; cosmopolitan v. localist]." According to Main, the key tension at the time was between "agrarian-localist" parties and "commercial-cosmopolitan" parties. Main, *Political Parties Before the Constitution*, 387–88.

25. As Alan Taylor reminds us in his study of agrarian settlers on the Maine frontier, "To understand agrarian resistance in the early Republic, we should avoid two misconceptions: that settlers were a proletariat, and that there can be no class conflict without one." Taylor, *Liberty Men and Great Proprietors*, 7. For a broader discussion of the category of class in the seventeenth and eighteenth centuries, see E. P. Thompson, "Eighteenth-Century English Society: Class Struggle Without Class," *Social History* 3 (May 1978): 133–65.

26. I argue here that class divisions were highly salient in the mid- to late 1780s and that America's leading statesmen went to great lengths to assuage these divisions. In making this argument, I do not share the assumption made by Charles Beard that the debate surrounding the framing and ratification of the Constitution reflected the private material or class interests of the participants. While it is true that most of the delegates at the Constitutional Convention identified strongly with the affluent, proprietary classes of late eighteenth-century society, many articulated a coherent (and in some instances, quite compelling) vision of how a new national charter could enable positive-sum policy solutions that would end unnecessary conflict between states, regions, and classes of property owners, and benefit the country as a whole. Charles A. Beard, *An Economic Interpretation of the Constitution of the United States* (New York: Macmillan, 1913).

27. James Madison, "Vices of the Political System of the U. States," April 1787, in *Writings of James Madison*, Hunt, 2: 363. This statement was issued nearly verbatim at the convention in Philadelphia. See *RFC*, Farrand, 1: 318–19.

28. Madison appears to have the political violence taking place across the country, most notably in Massachusetts with Shays' Rebellion, in mind.

29. On Dunmore's decree, see Alan Taylor, *The Internal Enemy: Slavery and War in Virginia, 1772–1832* (New York: W. W. Norton, 2013), 23–27. For a discussion of the impact of Dunmore's decree on slaves in Virginia as well as the disparate responses of whites of different social and class backgrounds, see Michael McDonnell and Woody Holton, "Patriot vs. Patriot: Social Conflict in Virginia and the Origins of the American Revolution," *Journal of American Studies* 34 (August 2000): 231–56; Woody Holton, "Rebel Against Rebel: Enslaved Virginians and the Coming of the American Revolution," *Virginia Magazine of History and Biography* 105 (April 1997): 157–92. On the impact of Dunmore's decree on South Carolina's planter elites, see Robert A. Olwell, "'Domestick Enemies': Slavery and Political Independence in South Carolina, May 1775–March 1776," *Journal of Southern History* 55 (February 1989): 41–45.

30. Quoted in Ronald Hoffman, "'The Disaffected' in the Revolutionary South," in *The American Revolution: Explorations in the History of American Radicalism*, ed. Alfred F. Young (DeKalb: Northern Illinois University Press, 1976), 282.

31. Douglas R. Egerton, *Gabriel's Rebellion: The Virginia Slave Conspiracies of 1800 and 1802* (Chapel Hill: University of North Carolina Press, 1993), 5, 7.

32. See Paul Bourke, "The Pluralist Reading of James Madison's Tenth Federalist," *Perspectives in American History* 9 (1975): 271–95; Douglas Adair, "The Tenth Federalist Revisited" and "'That Politics May Be Reduced to a Science': David Hume, James Madison, and the Tenth Federalist," in *Fame and the Founding Fathers*, ed. Trevor Colbourn (New York: Norton, 1974): 75–106.

33. Wood, *Radicalism of the American Revolution*.

34. Taylor, *Liberty Men and Great Proprietors*, 5.

35. On prerevolutionary land riots in New Jersey and New York, see Edward Countryman, "'Out of the Bounds of the Law': Northern Land Rioters in the Eighteenth Century," in *American Revolution*, 37–69. For an excellent survey of the diverse incarnations of "backcountry resistance," see Taylor, *Liberty Men and Great Proprietors*, 4–6. "Contentious politics" broadly refers to group political struggle that occurs outside of regular, institutionalized channels for political participation. For a formal definition of "contentious politics," see Doug McAdam, Sidney Tarrow, and Charles Tilly, *Dynamics of Contention* (Cambridge: Cambridge University Press, 2001), 5.

36. On this point, see Pauline Maier's seminal essay "Popular Uprisings and Civil Authority in Eighteenth-Century America," *William and Mary Quarterly* 27 (1970): 3–35; also see Gordon Wood, "A Note on Mobs in the American Revolution," *William and Mary Quarterly* 23 (1966): 635–42; Arthur M. Schlesinger Sr., "Political Mobs in the American Revolution, 1765–1776," *Proceedings of the American Philosophical Society* 99 (1955): 244–50.

37. Wood, "Note on Mobs in the American Revolution," 639.

38. Ibid., 641.

39. David P. Szatmary, *Shays' Rebellion: The Making of an Agrarian Insurrection* (Amherst: University of Massachusetts Press, 1980), 124.

40. Aedanus Burke, *Charleston Morning Post*, 22 February 1786. Quoted in Becker, "Salus Populi Suprema Lex," 71.

41. Quoted in ibid., 69.

42. Quoted in ibid., 72.

43. The nine states were Pennsylvania, South Carolina, Rhode Island, Massachusetts, Maryland, Virginia, New Hampshire, New Jersey, and possibly Delaware. Most of these states, in fact, later retreated from their firm stances on tax collections. Brown, *Redeeming the Republic*, 122.

44. These were Connecticut, New York, Georgia, and North Carolina. Brown points out that tax "reliefer" majorities in the lower houses of the legislatures thwarted efforts by these states to coerce hard money collections. Brown, *Redeeming the Republic*, 122–38; Szatmary, *Shays' Rebellion*, 126.

45. See Szatmary, *Shays' Rebellion*, 80.

46. Alexis de Tocqueville, *Democracy in America*, trans. George Lawrence, ed. J. P. Mayer (New York: Harper Perennial, 1969), 193.

47. *Federalist Papers*, no. 14, 141.

48. See James A. Morone, *The Democratic Wish: Popular Participation and the Limits of American Government* (New Haven, Conn.: Yale University Press, 1998), 53–62.

49. "Impartial Examiner," (Trenton) *New Jersey Gazette*, 13 January 1779. Quoted in Main, *Political Parties Before the Constitution*, 398.

50. For an analysis of the conceptual distinctions between "insurrection," "riot," and "mob," see David Grimsted "Rioting in Its Jacksonian Setting," *American Historical Review* 77 (April 1972): 361–97.

51. *Federalist Papers*, no. 50, 318.

52. *Radicalism of the American Revolution*, 5–8.

53. For a helpful analysis of the idea of a natural aristocracy, see Saul Cornell, "Aristocracy Assailed: The Ideology of Backcountry Anti-Federalism," *Journal of American History* 76 (March 1990): 1157–59.

54. *Radicalism of the American Revolution*, 213, 294–98.

55. Edling, *Revolution in Favor of Government*.

56. The Federalist party of the 1790s should not be confused with the Federalists of the Confederation period (1781–88) and the ratification process (1787–88). The Federalists of the Confederation period and the ratification process were the nationalists who advocated in favor of the constitutional charter framed at the Constitutional Convention in Philadelphia and were opposed by Anti-Federalists. These Federalists counted among their leaders both Hamilton and Madison. The Federalist *party* of the 1790s, by contrast, was formed by Hamilton to defend the Washington and Adams administrations and stood in favor of expanded national authority. This party was opposed by the first American opposition party, the Democratic-Republicans or Republicans, led by Jefferson and Madison. All references to the Federalists in this chapter are to the nationalists of the Confederation period and the ratification process. References to the Federalists in subsequent chapters, unless otherwise indicated, are to supporters of the Federalist party led by Hamilton.

57. *Federalist Papers*, no. 9, 119.

58. Robertson, *Constitution and America's Destiny*, 44–45.

59. See Hendrickson, *Peace Pact*.

60. *U.S. Statutes at Large* 8 (1783): 80.

61. *Federalist Papers*, no. 21, 173–74.

62. *RFC*, Farrand, 2: 48.

63. *Federalist Papers*, no. 10, 126–27.

64. The way Madison arrived at this insight may be as important as the insight itself. Indeed, Madison famously framed the challenge of managing political conflict as a problem of managing faction. He handled the subject in *Federalist* 10 with the analytical clarity and deductive sensibility befitting a natural scientist. It is little wonder that these papers have inspired generations of political analysts to fashion their study in equally scientific terms. See Paul Bourke, "The Pluralist Reading of James Madison's

Tenth Federalist," *Perspectives in American History* 9 (1975); Douglas Adair, "The Tenth Federalist Revisited" and "'That Politics May Be Reduced to a Science,'" in *Fame and the Founding Fathers*, Colbourn, 75–106.

65. Wilson and Rush are quoted in Bouton, *Taming Democracy*, 179 and 179 n. 17.

66. Woody Holton, "'Divide et Impera': 'Federalist 10' in a Wider Sphere," *William and Mary Quarterly* 62 (April 2005): 175–212.

67. *Federalist Papers*, no. 10, 128.

68. *Lochner v. New York*, 198 U.S. 45 (1905).

69. Hofstadter, *Idea of a Party System*, ch. 2.

70. The expression is from Epstein, *Political Parties in the American Mold*.

71. Richard P. McCormick, *The Presidential Game: The Origins of American Presidential Politics* (New York: Oxford University Press, 1982), 9, 11.

72. See, for example, Gouverneur Morris's and Elbridge Gerry's comments on this point. *RFC*, Farrand, 2: 53–54, 114; also see Shlomo Slonim, "The Electoral College at Philadelphia," *Journal of American History* 73 (1986): 35–58.

73. Andrew Jackson, who won a plurality (but not a majority) of the electoral votes in 1824, was deprived of the presidency as the contest was decided in the House. A "corrupt bargain" was allegedly struck between John Quincy Adams and Henry Clay that gave Adams the presidency and made Clay the secretary of state.

74. Charles O. Jones, *The Presidency in a Separated System* (Washington, D.C.: Brookings Institution Press, 2005): 1–34; Robertson, *The Constitution and America's Destiny*, 256–59.

75. Aldrich, *Why Parties?* 72.

76. Einhorn, *American Taxation, American Slavery*, ch. 4.

77. *RFC*, Farrand, 2: 307.

78. *Federalist Papers*, no. 12, 135–37.

79. *RFC*, Farrand, 2: 223.

80. Einhorn, *American Taxation, American Slavery*, ch. 4.

81. For details on the federal assumption of state debts, see Edwin J. Perkins, *American Public Finance and Financial Services, 1700–1815* (Columbus: Ohio State University, 1994), 215; Ferguson, *Power of the Purse*, 321.

82. See Hamilton's "Report on the Public Credit," reprinted in *Documentary History of the First Federal Congress*, ed. Linda Grant De Pauw (Baltimore: Johns Hopkins University Press, 1972) 5: 743–98.

83. As I explain in greater detail below, the bank proposal is widely credited with having crystallized political opposition to the Washington administration.

84. On the creation of a capital market based on the exchange of U.S. government bonds and stock certificates of the First Bank of the United States, see Perkins, *American Public Finance and Financial Services*, 199–234.

85. To Robert Morris, 30 April 1781, in *The Papers of Alexander Hamilton*, ed. Harold Syrett et al. (New York: Columbia University Press, 1969) 2: 635.

86. *RFC*, Farrand, 2: 327.

87. Edling and Kaplanoff, "Alexander Hamilton's Fiscal Reform," 732. The northern and middle states include Massachusetts, New Hampshire, Rhode Island, Connecticut, New York, New Jersey, Pennsylvania, and Delaware.

88. Ibid., 716–17, 738–39.

89. Economic developments in the 1790s also helped to reconcile agrarians to the new order. Crop failures in Europe and political disorder surrounding the French Revolution boosted demand and prices for U.S. food exports. Improved credit, thanks in part to Hamilton's new fiscal regime, also contributed to the economic recovery. Brown, *Redeeming the Republic*, 235.

90. See ch. 4, "Taxers and Reliefers," in Brown, *Redeeming the Republic*.

91. As Taylor notes, "Few Jeffersonians were agrarian ideologues. Most meant to give just enough ground to popular discontents to assure a domestic stability that would permit every white man to pursue his commercial ambitions." Taylor, *Liberty Men and Great Proprietors*, 229–30. On the character and coalitional structure of the Jeffersonian Republicans, see Lance Banning, *The Jeffersonian Persuasion: Evolution of a Party Ideology* (Ithaca, N.Y.: Cornell University Press, 1978); Joseph Charles, *The Origins of the American Party System: Three Essays* (New York: Harper and Row, 1961); Goodman, "First American Party System"; Hoadley, "Emergence of Political Parties in Congress, 1789–1803"; Noble Cunningham, *The Jeffersonian Republicans: The Formation of Party Organization, 1789–1801* (Chapel Hill: University of North Carolina Press, 1957); Aldrich, *Why Parties?* ch. 3.

92. The proposed legislative language offered that "the present holders of public securities, which have been alienated, shall be settled with according to the highest market rate of such securities; and that the balance of the sums due from the public, be paid in such proportion to the original holder of such securities." 2 *Annals of Cong.* 1196 (1790). For a helpful discussion of this debate, see Perkins, *American Public Finance and Financial Services*, 222.

93. 2 *Annals of Cong.* 1263 (1790).

94. 2 *Annals of Cong.* 1263 (1790).

95. See, for example, *Federalist Papers*, no. 44.

96. See Holton, "From the Labour of Others"; Brown, *Redeeming the Republic*, ch. 4, "Taxers and Reliefers."

97. De Pauw, *Documentary History of the First Federal Congress*, 5: 724.

98. Ferguson, *Power of the Purse*, 299; Irving Brant, *James Madison, Father of the Constitution, 1787–1800* (Bobbs-Merrill, 1950), 298–99.

99. See debate on 2 February 1791, 2 *Annals of Cong.* 1896–1902 (1791).

100. 2 *Annals of Cong.* 1918 (1791).

101. 2 *Annals of Cong.* 1930 (1791). For an insightful analysis of the anxieties surrounding Hamilton's fiscal program, see Edling, *Revolution in Favor of Government*, chs. 13 and 14.

102. Aldrich and Grant provide a contrasting account of the Jeffersonians, calling attention to the continuities in thought between the Anti-Federalists and the bloc of

legislators from the First Congress that formed in opposition to the Washington administration. Aldrich and Grant, however, did not have the benefit of Saul Cornell's 1999 study, which disaggregates the diverse strands of Anti-Federalist thought. Aldrich and Grant identify important continuities between Anti-Federalism and Jeffersonian Republicanism but overlook the possibility that the Jeffersonian Republicans may have drawn selectively from a diverse Anti-Federalist tradition. Indeed, the Jeffersonian Republicans prioritized themes raised by the more philosophical "middling" Anti-Federalists like Brutus and the Federal Farmer, and elite Anti-Federalists like Elbridge Gerry, George Mason, and Richard Henry Lee. The more radical, plebeian populist Anti-Federalists, however, were effectively marginalized in the new national structure. Cornell, *The Other Founders: Anti-Federalism and the Dissenting Tradition in America, 1788–1828* (Chapel Hill: University of North Carolina Press, 1999), 11–15, Aldrich and Grant, "Antifederalists, the First Congress, and the First Parties."

103. *Liberty Men and Great Proprietors*, 229.

104. *Liberty Men and Great Proprietors*, 229.

105. Hamilton anticipated when he took up his position as secretary of the treasury that, as crucial as the impost would be to America's fiscal future, the federal government would require further revenue to service state debts. He sought out Madison for advice on the question, asking him, "What further taxes will be *least* unpopular?" Hamilton to James Madison, 12 October 1789, in *Papers of Alexander Hamilton*, Syrett et al., 5: 439. See Chapter 3 for further discussion of the Whiskey Rebellion.

106. See, for example, Luther Martin in *RFC*, Farrand, 1: 438; also see Madison's essay, *Federalist Papers*, no. 46.

Chapter 3. The French Revolutionary Wars and the Ordeal
of America's First Party System

1. Brown, *Redeeming the Republic*, 241.

2. Ibid. To be sure, the salience of taxation as a flashpoint for conflict did not simply disappear. The benefits of the positive-sum solutions identified above were not felt immediately in the Pennsylvania backcountry, for example, where agrarians mounted a significant resistance to a new national excise tax on domestically distilled spirits—the episode we commonly refer to as the Whiskey Rebellion. As I explain below, however, fiscal policy, including resistance to new taxes, was colored by new divisions over the European conflict abroad.

3. The war between Britain and France ended temporarily with the Treaty of Amiens, signed 27 March 1802, only to resume again in 1803.

4. The expression "party to end all parties" is Hofstadter's, *Idea of a Party System*, 151. Also see David Waldstreicher's discussion of "partisan anti-partisanship," *In the Midst of Perpetual Fetes: The Making of American Nationalism, 1776–1820* (Chapel Hill: University of North Carolina Press, 1997), 201–7.

5. Describing the rhetorical violence of this period, Ronald Formisano explained, "'Violence' tended to be used in the early republic to mean uncontrolled, excessive, and distorting energy of expression and emotion. The connotation of physical violence is more characteristic of our own time." "Deferential-Participant Politics," 485. Also see John R. Howe Jr., "Republican Thought and the Political Violence of the 1790s," *American Quarterly* 19 (1967): 147–65.

6. See Jeffrey S. Selinger, "Making Sense of Presidential Restraint: Foundational Arrangements and Executive Decision-Making Before the Civil War," *Presidential Studies Quarterly* 44 (March 2014): 27–49.

7. The French Revolutionary Wars are conventionally dated from 1793 to 1815; the first party system is usually periodized from 1795 to 1815. See Formisano, "Deferential-Participant Politics," 477; Hoadley, "Emergence of Political Parties in Congress, 1789–1803," 757–79.

8. For an examination of the Jeffersonian ideas that were mobilized to oppose Hamilton's political-economic program, see Drew R. McCoy, *The Elusive Republic: Political Economy in Jeffersonian America* (New York: Norton, 1982).

9. To Gouverneur Morris, 13 October 1789, *The Papers of George Washington*, ed. W. W. Abbot (Charlottesville: University of Virginia Press, 2005) 4: 177.

10. To Lafayette, 6 October 1789, *Papers of Alexander Hamilton*, Syrett et al., 5: 425. For a helpful discussion of the French Revolution in America, see Gordon S. Wood, *Empire of Liberty: A History of the Early Republic, 1789–1815* (New York: Oxford University Press, 2009), 174–208.

11. Alexander DeConde, *Entangling Alliance: Politics and Diplomacy Under George Washington* (Durham, N.C.: Duke University Press, 1958), 186.

12. Hamilton himself referred to the spread of such ideas as the "French disease." See John C. Miller, *Alexander Hamilton and the Growth of the New Nation* (New Brunswick, N.J.: Transaction, 2004), 365.

13. Jefferson to James Monroe, 4 June 1793, in *The Papers of Thomas Jefferson*, ed. John Catanzariti (Princeton, N.J.: Princeton University Press, 1995) 26: 190.

14. Bawn et al. argue that the first opposition party was formed by the emergence of the Democratic-Republican societies. Party scholars, however, have amassed extensive evidence that highlights the party-building role played by Madison and other *congressional* critics of the Washington administration. Bawn et al., "Theory of Political Parties," 580. See Aldrich, *Why Parties?*, ch. 3; Wood, *Empire of Liberty*, 162; Hoadley, "Emergence of Political Parties in Congress, 1789–1803"; Harry Ammon, "The Genet Mission and the Development of American Political Parties," *Journal of American History* 52 (March 1966): 725–41. Matthew Schoenbacher's study of the Democratic-Republican societies dispels the myth that these associations constituted the organizational basis of the Jeffersonian Republican party. Schoenbacher, "Republicanism in the Age of the Democratic Revolution: The Democratic-Republican Societies of the 1790s," *Journal of the Early Republic* 18 (1998): 239.

15. DeConde, *Entangling Alliance*, 269.

16. This last provision would have required the United States to help defend the French West Indies in the war with Britain.

17. DeConde, *Entangling Alliance*, 88, 91.

18. Elkins and McKitrick, *Age of Federalism*, 340.

19. "Opinion on the French Treaties," 28 April 1793, in *Papers of Thomas Jefferson*, Catanzariti, 25: 613.

20. DeConde, *Entangling Alliance*, 89 n. 61, 190–91.

21. "Pacificus No. 1–7," in *Papers of Alexander Hamilton*, Syrett et al., 15: 33–43, 55–63, 65–69, 82–86, 90–95, 100–106, 130–35; "Helvidius No. 1–5," in *Letters and Other Writings of James Madison* (New York: Worthington, 1884), 1: 607–54.

22. "Defense of the President's Neutrality Proclamation," c. May 1793, *Papers of Alexander Hamilton*, Syrett et al., 14: 504; for the Proclamation itself, see "Neutrality Proclamation," 22 April 1793, in *The Papers of George Washington*, vol. 12, ed. Philander Chase (Charlottesville: University of Virginia Press, 2005), 472–73.

23. *Papers of Alexander Hamilton*, Syrett et al., 14: 506.

24. Washington to Thomas Jefferson, 12 April 1793, in *Papers of George Washington*, ed. Chase 12: 448. Several years later, Washington lamented the failure of the people to remain neutral: "the difficulties with which we are threatened: which, assuredly, will have been brought on us by the misconduct of some of our own intemperate people; who seem to have preferred throwing themselves into the Arms of France (even under the present circumstances of that Country) to that manly, and Neutral conduct which is so essential, and would so well become us, as an Independent Nation." To Alexander Hamilton, 8 May 1796, in *The Writings of George Washington from the Original Manuscript Sources, 1745–1799*, ed. John C. Fitzpatrick (Washington, D.C.: U.S. GPO, 1931) 35: 41.

25. Elkins and McKitrick, *Age of Federalism*, 333. See, more generally, Harry Ammon, *The Genet Mission* (New York: Norton, 1973).

26. Robert W. Coakley, *The Role of Federal Military Forces in Domestic Disorders, 1789–1878* (Washington, D.C.: Center of Military History, 1988), 26.

27. Coakley, *Role of Federal Military Forces in Domestic Disorders*, 26–27.

28. On Genêt's role in extending Republican partisanship outside the confines of the national legislature to the mass public, see Harry Ammon, "Genet Mission and the Development of American Political Parties." On the contest between Genêt, Republican leaders, and the Washington administration to sway public opinion, see Christopher J. Young, "Connecting the President and the People: Washington's Neutrality, Genet's Challenge, and Hamilton's Fight for Public Support," *Journal of the Early Republic* 31 (Fall 2011): 435–66.

29. To repeat from Chapter 1: "You certainly never felt the Terrorism excited by Genêt, in 1793, when ten thousand People in the Streets of Philadelphia, day after day threatened to drag Washington out of his House, and effect a Revolution in the Government, or compell it to declare War in favour of the French Revolution and against

England." John Adams to Thomas Jefferson, 30 June 1813, in *Adams-Jefferson Letters*, Cappon, 2: 346–47.

30. In a letter to Henry Lee, Washington refers to Genêt as the "father" of the Democratic-Republican societies. Washington to Henry Lee, 26 August 1794, in *The Papers of George Washington*, ed. Theodore J. Crackel (Charlottesville: University of Virginia Press, 2005) 16: 602.

31. Genêt's words, quoted in DeConde, *Entangling Alliance*, 252. On the Democratic-Republican societies, see Schoenbacher, "Republicanism in the Age of the Democratic Revolution," 237–62; Eugene Perry Link, *Democratic-Republican Societies, 1790–1800* (New York: Columbia University Press, 1942).

32. Washington to Burges Ball, 25 September 1794, in *Papers of George Washington*, ed. Crackel, 16: 722–23, emphasis in original.

33. "Farewell Address." John Adams sounded similar themes just a few years after Washington issued this address: "Republics are always divided in opinion, concerning forms of governments, and plans and details of administration. These divisions are generally harmless, often salutary, and seldom very hurtful, except when foreign nations interfere, and by their arts and agents excite and ferment them into parties and factions. Such interference and influence must be resisted and exterminated, or it will end in America, as it did anciently in Greece, and in our own time in Europe, in our total destruction as a republican government and independent power." To the citizens of Baltimore City and County, Maryland, 2 May 1798, in *The Works of John Adams, Second President of the United States*, ed. Charles Francis Adams (Boston: Little, Brown, 1850) 9: 186–87.

34. A series of British orders-in-council directed the British navy to take neutral ships carrying provisions to French colonies. Furthermore, news arrived in December 1793 that the British negotiated a treaty between Portugal and Algeria enabling the Portuguese to assist in the fight against France. This left the United States at the mercy of the Algerian pirates who would be free to prey on American ships in the Atlantic. See Samuel Flagg Bemis, *A Diplomatic History of the United States*, 5th ed. (New York: Holt, Rinehart and Winston, 1965), 99–100; Jerald A. Combs, *The Jay Treaty: Political Battleground of the Founding Fathers* (Berkeley: University of California Press, 1970), 116, 121; DeConde, *Entangling Alliance*, 94.

35. "Treaty of Amity Commerce and Navigation," *Treaties and Other International Agreements of the United States of America, 1776–1949*, ed. Hunter Miller (Washington, D.C.: U.S. GPO, 1931), 3: 245–64.

36. Elkins and McKitrick note that "for hostility of feeling against a measure of government, and for violence of language, nothing comparable had been seen on so wide a scale since the founding of the Republic." *Age of Federalism*, 421. Alexander DeConde observes that " 'Sir John Jay' became the most hated man in America. Seldom in time of peace had a treaty aroused such violent public reaction." *Entangling Alliance*, 114. Some historians identify the Jay Treaty as the landmark controversy that

brought forth the clearest articulation of America's first party system. See Elkins and McKitrick, *Age of Federalism*, 415; Charles, *Origins of the American Party System*, 83.

37. DeConde, *Entangling Alliance*, 133.

38. Bemis, *Diplomatic History of the United States*, 96-97.

39. Irish immigrants, who harbored strong sympathies for the French republican struggle against the British, were as suspect as the French in this political climate. See Alexander DeConde, *The Quasi-War: The Politics and Diplomacy of the Undeclared War with France 1797-1801* (New York: Scribner, 1966), 86, 94-95. The Sedition Act imposed a $2,000 fine and a two-year sentence for "false, scandalous and malicious" accusations against the president, Congress, or the government. It additionally set a maximum fine of $5,000 and a maximum sentence of five years for those who would "combine or conspire together, with intent to oppose any measure or measures of the government of the United States." See *U.S. Statutes at Large* 1 (1798): 596. There were three "alien acts" in all. The Naturalization Act raised the period of residence required for an alien to qualify for citizenship from 5 to 14 years; it also required aliens to register with government authorities and subjected aliens to surveillance, *U.S. Statutes at Large* 1 (1798): 566. The Act Concerning Aliens, the "Alien Friends Act," authorized the President to deport any alien considered dangerous to the public peace, *U.S. Statutes at Large* 1 (1798): 570-71. The Act Respecting Alien Enemies authorized the President to deport citizens of any country with which the United States was at war, *U.S. Statutes at Large* 1 (1798): 577.

40. For the Provisional Army Act, see *U.S. Statutes at Large* 1 (1798): 558; for the New Army Act, see *U.S. Statutes at Large* 1 (1798): 604. The Provisional Army, though authorized by Congress, was never in fact organized; the Department of War was able to enlist fewer than half of the authorized force for the New Army. Richard H. Kohn, *Eagle and Sword: The Federalists and the Creation of the Military Establishment in America, 1783-1802* (New York: Free Press, 1975), 229, 248. Owing to difficulties with recruitment, Russell Weigley notes, "the Army of 1798" was "a shadow rather than a substance." See Weigley, *History of the United States Army*, 103, 119-21.

41. Quoted in Ralph A. Brown, *The Presidency of John Adams* (Lawrence: University Press of Kansas, 1975), 117. For a helpful summary of the distinct measures that authorized this military build-up (even though many of the newly authorized forces were never, in fact, organized), see Kohn, *Eagle and Sword*, 229.

42. Hamilton to Theodore Sedgwick, 2 February 1799, in Syrett et al., *Papers of Alexander Hamilton*, 22: 453. Whether Hamilton intended to provoke Virginia to resist remains to this day a subject of controversy. For a helpful historiography of this debate, see John L. Harper, *American Machiavelli: Alexander Hamilton and the Origins of U.S. Foreign Policy* (Cambridge: Cambridge University Press, 2004), 227-28. Setting Hamilton's intentions aside, the strategic circumstances did not bode well for his belligerent solution. Indeed, one might well wonder whether a federal force that was preparing for war with France could subdue a "*refractory* & powerful *State*" without igniting a protracted civil conflict. Virginia might have, for example, declared a sepa-

rate peace in the conflict with France. Hamilton and his followers would then have a far more complex problem on their hands.

43. Manning Julian Dauer, *The Adams Federalists* (Baltimore: Johns Hopkins University Press, 1968), 228–29. Jefferson anticipated this popular response when he observed, "This disease of the imagination [Federalism] will pass over, because the patients are essentially republican. Indeed, the Doctor is now on his way to cure it, in the guise of a taxgatherer." Jefferson to John Taylor, 26 November 1798, in *The Papers of Thomas Jefferson*, ed. Barbara B. Oberg (Princeton, N.J.: Princeton University Press, 2003) 30: 588.

44. High Federalists at this time began to differentiate themselves from the more moderate supporters of Adams or Adams Federalists.

45. Brown, *Presidency of John Adams*, 119; Dauer, *Adams Federalists*, 202.

46. To the Boston Marine Society, MA, 7 September 1798, *Works of John Adams*, Adams, 9: 221.

47. DeConde, *Quasi-War*, 90–91.

48. For the act that created the new department, see *U.S. Statutes at Large* 1 (1798): 553–54.

49. Gerry's Minutes of a Conference with the President 26 March 1799. Quoted in Elkins and McKitrick, *Age of Federalism*, 617.

50. Adams to Francis Adrian Van der Kemp, 25 April 1808. Quoted in Brown, *Presidency of John Adams*, 76.

51. "Mr. Adams's Correspondence," *Boston Patriot*, 10 June 1809.

52. Kohn, *Eagle and Sword*, 266–67.

53. Charles, *Origins of the American Party System*, 62. Adams, to be sure, believed (and historian Stephen Kurtz agrees) that the president could have won in 1800 without the support of Hamilton's faction. Kurtz notes, nonetheless, that Adams pursued a suboptimal reelection strategy, pointing out that Adams's "re-election would have been assured had he followed the Hamiltonian line." As Kurtz explains, Adams pursued peace with France to avert domestic conflict: "To sacrifice both conscience and domestic peace for another term of office seemed too high a price [for Adams]." Stephen G. Kurtz, *The Presidency of John Adams: The Collapse of Federalism, 1795–1800* (Philadelphia: University of Pennsylvania Press, 1957), 394.

54. To be sure, there were other developments that came into play as Adams decided to soften relations with France. The French had begun to back off of their aggressive position on trade and maritime policy: on 31 July 1798, the French Directory lifted a temporary embargo imposed on American vessels, revoked the commissions of privateers which preyed on American ships in the West Indies, and repealed earlier directives requiring American ships to carry a *role d'equipage*. DeConde, *Quasi-War*, 153.

55. Margaret Bayard Smith to Susan B. Smith on the day of Jefferson's inauguration, 4 March 1801, *The First Forty Years of Washington Society: Portrayed by the Family Letters of Mrs. Samuel Harrison Smith (Margaret Bayard)*, ed. Gaillard Hunt (New York: Charles Scribner's Sons, 1906), 25.

56. See, for example Daniel Sisson's study *The American Revolution of 1800*, where he concluded that the Jeffersonians "had achieved what no other group of revolutionaries had gained in the entire course of western political history: a change in the power of government, from one party to another, without a tremendous cost in violence and bloodshed." Sisson, *The American Revolution of 1800* (New York: Alfred A. Knopf, 1974), 436; also see Hofstadter, *Idea of a Party System*, 128–32.

57. James E. Lewis Jr., "'What Is to Become of Our Government?,'" in *The Revolution of 1800: Democracy, Race, and the New Republic*, ed. James Horn, Jan Ellen Lewis, and Peter S. Onuf (Charlottesville: University of Virginia Press, 2002), 10–11.

58. James Roger Sharp, *American Politics in the Early Republic: The New Nation in Crisis* (New Haven, Conn.: Yale University Press, 1993), 227.

59. Hamilton to John Jay, 7 May 1800, in *Papers of Alexander Hamilton*, Syrett et al., 24: 465.

60. In the words of one notable Republican, the consequences of an Adams victory would be to leave power in the hands of "a party extended throughout the union, both active and powerful [and] . . . utterly devoted to a monarchical system." Elbridge Gerry quoted in Sharp, *American Politics in the Early Republic*, 226–27; also see Edward J. Larson, *A Magnificent Catastrophe: The Tumultuous Election of 1800, America's First Presidential Campaign* (New York: Free Press, 2007), 188–89. For discussion of the hyperbolic discourse of the election, see John Ferling, *Adams v. Jefferson: The Tumultuous Election of 1800* (Oxford: Oxford University Press, 2004), 143–56.

61. Hamilton to John Jay, 7 May 1800, in *Papers of Alexander Hamilton*, Syrett et al., 24: 464–66.

62. In Virginia, for example, Republicans passed a "general ticket" law to thwart Federalist strength in urban settings. See Cunningham, *Jeffersonian Republicans*, 150–52; Joanne B. Freeman, "Corruption and Compromise in the Election of 1800: The Process of Politics on the National Stage," in *Revolution of 1800*, Horn et al., 95–96.

63. Next in line was the Speaker of the House; this position was occupied at the time by Federalist Theodore Sedgwick of Massachusetts.

64. See Larson, *Magnificent Catastrophe*, 259.

65. James E. Lewis Jr., "'What Is to Become of Our Government?'" in *Revolution of 1800*, Horn et al., 14.

66. Sharp, *American Politics in the Early Republic*, 271.

67. Quoted in Michael A. Bellesiles, "'The Soil Will Be Soaked with Blood': Taking the Revolution of 1800 Seriously," in *Revolution of 1800*, Horn et al., 65.

68. Jefferson to James Monroe, 15 February 1801, in *Papers of Thomas Jefferson*, Oberg, 32: 594.

69. John Quincy Adams to Thomas Adams, 30 December 1800, in *Writings of John Quincy Adams*, ed. Worthington Chauncey Ford (New York: Macmillan, 1913) 2: 490–91; also see John Quincy Adams to William Vans Murray, 17 and 27 January 1801, ibid. 2: 494–98.

70. Sharp, *American Politics in the Early Republic*, 269.

71. According to an informant sent by Monroe, federal officers on site had received notice that the arms were ordered to be moved. Sharp, *American Politics in the Early Republic*, 269–70; Harry Ammon, *James Monroe: The Quest for National Identity* (New York: McGraw-Hill, 1971), 193.

72. Hamilton to Rufus King, 5 January 1800, in *Papers of Alexander Hamilton*, Syrett et al., 24: 167–68.

73. Bellesiles, "'The Soil Will Be Soaked with Blood,'" in *Revolution of 1800*, Horn et al., 73–74.

74. The plan resembled, in crucial respects, the positions staked out by Madison and Jefferson in the Virginia and Kentucky Resolutions. "Plan at Time of Balloting for Jefferson and Burr. Communicated to Nicholas and Mr. Jefferson" [early February 1801], in *The Writings of Albert Gallatin*, ed. Henry Adams (Philadelphia: J. B. Lippincott, 1879) 1: 18–23.

75. Ibid., 1: 20. For a discussion of this memorandum, see Bellesiles, "'The Soil Will Be Soaked with Blood,'" 73; Lewis, "'What Is to Become of Our Government?'" 17–18.

76. Jefferson to James Madison, 18 February 1801, in *Papers of Thomas Jefferson*, Oberg, 33: 16. Jefferson may have been correct that defecting Federalists feared such a scenario. We will never know whether this scenario would have come to pass; in light of the available historical evidence, however, violent resistance organized by the Republican leadership appears to have been improbable. One must remember, though, that Republican elites did not hold sway over all Republican and dissenting groups. Political violence may have erupted, and it might have been widespread even if Republican leaders had chosen a moderate course.

77. Bayard to Richard Bassett, 16 February 1801, "Papers of Bayard," in *American Historical Association Annual Report for the Year 1913*, ed. Elizabeth Donnan (Washington, D.C.: American Historical Association, 1915): 126–27.

78. Ibid., 129–30. Lewis, "'What Is to Become of Our Government?'" 23. For a discussion of Bayard's role in resolving the crisis, see Cunningham, *Jeffersonian Republicans*, 245.

79. Bellesiles, "'The Soil Will Be Soaked with Blood,'" 68–72.

80. Leonard D. White, *The Federalists: A Study in Administrative History* (New York: Macmillan, 1948): 271–78; Cress, *Citizens in Arms*, 145–46; Weigley, *History of the U.S. Army*, 97–104.

81. Egerton, *Gabriel's Rebellion*, ix.

82. On the impact of Caribbean slave insurrections on the formation of black identity in the South, see James Sidbury, *Ploughshares into Swords: Race, Rebellion, and Identity in Gabriel's Virginia, 1730–1810* (Cambridge: Cambridge University Press, 1997), 39–48.

83. Egerton, *Gabriel's Rebellion*, 64–65.

84. James Monroe to Thomas Jefferson, 15 September 1800, in *Papers of Thomas Jefferson*, Oberg, 32: 144.

85. Egerton, *Gabriel's Rebellion*, 49–51, 65.

86. Ibid., 38–41.

87. Ibid., 38.

88. Ibid., 37.

89. Laurent Dubois, "'Troubled Water': Rebellion and Republicanism in the Revolutionary French Caribbean," in *Revolution of 1800*, Horn et al., 291–95.

90. Jefferson to Monroe, 14 July 1793, in *Papers of Thomas Jefferson*, Catanzariti, 26: 503; also see Jefferson to St. George Tucker, 28 August 1797, in *Papers of Thomas Jefferson*, Oberg, 29: 519–20. For an analysis of the impact of revolutionary developments in the Caribbean on the Antebellum South, see Alfred N. Hunt, *Haiti's Influence on Antebellum America: Slumbering Volcano in the Caribbean* (Baton Rouge: Louisiana State University Press, 1988), 107–46.

91. Egerton, *Gabriel's Rebellion*, 164–67; Sidbury, *Ploughshares into Swords*, 130–31.

92. Bellesiles, "'The Soil Will Be Soaked with Blood,'" 77.

93. Hofstadter, *Idea of a Party System*, 151.

94. Inaugural Address, 4 March 1801, in *Papers of Thomas Jefferson*, Oberg, 33: 149.

95. Jefferson to Joel Barlow, 3 May 1802, in *Papers of Thomas Jefferson*, Oberg, 37: 400. For Madison's views on this subject, see "Parties," 23 January 1792, in *Writings of James Madison*, Hunt, 6: 86.

96. On the weakness of the American navy, see Bradford Perkins, *Prologue to War: England and the United States, 1805-1812* (Berkeley: University of California Press, 1961), 50–52.

97. Jefferson to Albert Gallatin, 3 December 1807, in *The Writings of Albert Gallatin*, ed. Henry Adams (Philadelphia: J. B. Lippincott, 1879), 367. As Jefferson explained the policy, "The embargo keeping at home our vessels, cargoes & seamen, saves us the necessity of making their capture the cause of immediate war: for if going to England, France has determined to take them; if to any other place, England was to take them. Till they return to some sense of moral duty therefore, we keep within ourselves. This gives time, time may produce peace in Europe: peace in Europe removes all causes of difference, till another European war: and by that time our debt may be paid, our revenue clear, & our strength increased." Jefferson to John Taylor, 6 January 1808, in *The Writings of Thomas Jefferson*, ed. Albert Ellery Bergh (Washington, D.C.: Thomas Jefferson Memorial Association of the United States, 1905) 11: 414.

98. See Henry Adams, *History of the United States During the Administrations of Thomas Jefferson* (1889; New York: Library of America, 1986), 1066–67, 1082–98.

99. Pickering to G. H. Rose [British Minister at Washington], 13 March 1808, Henry Adams, *Documents Relating to New-England Federalism* (Boston: Little, Brown, 1877), 367.

100. For the original embargo act, see U.S. *Statutes at Large* 2 (1807): 451. For an analysis of subsequent amendments, see Leonard Williams Levy, *Jefferson and Civil Liberties: The Darker Side* (Cambridge: Belknap Press of Harvard University Press, 1963), 97–98.

101. See Bennett Milton Rich, *The Presidents and Civil Disorder* (Washington, D.C.: Brookings Institution Press, 1941), 11, 34, and Coakley, *Role of Federal Military Forces in Domestic Disorders*, 88–89.

102. See Coakley, *Role of Federal Military Forces in Domestic Disorders*, 90.

103. Gallatin to Thomas Jefferson, 29 July 1808, in *Writings of Albert Gallatin*, Adams, 397–99.

104. Ibid., emphasis added.

105. Jefferson to Henry Dearborn, 9 August 1808, in *Writings of Thomas Jefferson*, Bergh, 12: 119. Also see Jefferson to Albert Gallatin, 11 August 1808, in ibid., 12: 121.

106. Allegations of this sort were not unfounded; however, it appears that such activity was limited to the actions of a select few. Most notably, Timothy Pickering, the High Federalist and secretary of state under Washington and Adams, maintained a correspondence with British envoy George Rose throughout the duration of the embargo. Adams, *Administrations of Thomas Jefferson*, 1082–98, esp. 1090. Years later, during the War of 1812, Federalists coordinated with the British navy along the Connecticut coast using blue lights to allow sympathetic vessels to break the British blockade. Consequently, burning blue lights became a symbol of Federalism. David Hackett Fischer, *The Revolution of American Conservatism: The Federalist Party in the Era of Jeffersonian Democracy* (New York: Harper and Row, 1965), 178.

107. Jefferson to Doctor Thomas Leib, 23 June 1808, in *Writings of Thomas Jefferson*, Bergh, 12: 76–77, emphasis added.

108. See Bradford Perkins, *Prologue to War: England and the United States, 1805–1812* (Berkeley: University of California Press, 1961), 162, 166–68.

109. Bradford Perkins echoes this conclusion: "Successful coercion required the almost unanimous support of the American people, both to enforce self-denial and make it clear to Great Britain that the United States did not flinch." Perkins, *Prologue to War*, 158. Also see Levy, *Jefferson and Civil Liberties*, 94. Richard Hofstadter disparages Jefferson's desire for partisan unanimity, failing to relate Jefferson's aversion to party opposition with the policy exigencies Jefferson confronted at the time. Jefferson's hope for unanimity, though it may have been unreasonable, was at least intelligible when viewed in light of the challenges he faced in enforcing his signature foreign policy initiative. *Idea of a Party System*, 204–5.

110. According to Monroe (secretary of state under Madison), France seized 307 American vessels under the Berlin and Milan decrees (of 1806 and 1807, respectively) and forty-five after the repeal of these decrees. Great Britain seized 389 after November, 1807; in 1805 and 1806, British seizures far outnumbered French seizures. Figures based on a report from Monroe, 6 July 1812, *American State Papers: Documents, Legislative and Executive, of the Congress of the United States*, 38 vols. (Washington, D.C., 1832), *Foreign Relations*, 3: 583–85.

111. Perkins, *Prologue to War*, 287–88.

112. On the sectional motives for seizing Canada, see ibid., 289. Congressman Felix Grundy of Tennessee expressed these sentiments in a speech to the House: "I am

willing to receive the Canadians as adopted brethren. It will have beneficial political effects; it will preserve the equilibrium of the government. When Louisiana shall be fully peopled, the Northern States will lose their power; they will be at the discretion of others; they can be depressed at pleasure, and then this Union might be endangered. I therefore feel anxious not only to add the Floridas to the South, but the Canadas to the North of this empire." Quoted in Henry Adams, *History of the United States During the Administrations of James Madison* (1901; New York: Library of America, 1986), 392.

113. James Madison to Thomas Jefferson, 25 May 1812, in *Letters and Other Writings of James Madison*, 2: 535.

114. Pickering to Edward Pennington, 12 July 1812, in *Documents Relating to New-England Federalism*, ed. Henry Adams (Boston: Little, Brown, 1877), 390.

115. Pickering to George Logan, 4 July 1813, in ibid., 391.

116. Quoted in Adams, *Administrations of James Madison*, 1109–10.

117. Quoted in James M. Banner, *To the Hartford Convention: The Federalists and the Origins of Party Politics in Massachusetts, 1789–1815* (New York: Knopf, 1970), 307.

118. Quoted in Adams, *Administrations of James Madison*, 1111.

119. See Madison to John Nicholas, 2 April 1813, in *Letters and Other Writings of James Madison*, 2: 562.

120. Pickering to Gouverneur Morris, 21 October 1814, in *Documents Relating to New-England Federalism*, Adams, 400–401.

121. Marshall Smelser, *The Democratic Republic, 1801–1815* (New York: Harper and Row, 1968), 291; J. C. A. Stagg, *Mr. Madison's War: Politics, Diplomacy, and Warfare in the Early American Republic, 1783–1830* (Princeton, N.J.: Princeton University Press, 1983), 477.

122. Quoted in Adams, *Administrations of James Madison*, 1100–1101.

123. Coles, *War of 1812*, 242. Also see Adams, *Administrations of James Madison*, 1098, 1105–6.

124. See Adams, *Administrations of James Madison*, 1106–7.

125. *U.S. Statutes at Large* 3 (1813): 88.

126. Adams, *Administrations of James Madison*, 1108–23.

127. Quoted in Banner, *To the Hartford Convention*, 332.

128. Ibid., 338.

129. On the proposed amendments, see ibid., 341–42. The original is reprinted in Henry Steele Commager, *Documents of American History*, 6th ed. (New York: Appleton-Century-Crofts, 1958), 209–11.

130. Quoted in Banner, *To the Hartford Convention*, 339.

131. Ibid., 342.

132. Caleb Strong, governor of Massachusetts, in fact sent an emissary to Canada in November 1814 to inquire about the prospects for a separate peace; see J. S. Martell, "A Side Light on Federalist Strategy During the War of 1812," *American Historical Review* 43 (1938): 553–66.

133. Taylor uses this expression to highlight *four* intersecting conflicts that defined the politics of the borderland with Canada (the subject of Taylor's analysis): in addition to the bitter partisanship between Republicans and Federalists, there was the struggle for control of Upper Canada, the Irish republicans' resistance against the British Empire, and the divisions between native peoples who allied with the British and the Americans. Alan Taylor, *The Civil War of 1812: American Citizens, British Subjects, Irish Rebels and Indian Allies* (New York: Knopf, 2010), 9.

134. Shaw Livermore, *The Twilight of Federalism: The Disintegration of the Federalist Party, 1815-1830* (Princeton, N.J.: Princeton University Press, 1962), 12.

135. Jefferson to Marquis de Lafayette, 14 May 1817, in *Writings of Thomas Jefferson*, Bergh, 15: 114-15.

136. See Livermore, *Twilight of Federalism*, 13.

Chapter 4. The Second Party System and the Politics of Displacing Conflict

1. See, for example, Hofstadter, *Idea of a Party System*; Joel H. Silbey, *Martin Van Buren and the Emergence of American Popular Politics* (Lanham, Md.: Rowman and Littlefield, 2002), preface, xii–xiii; Silbey, *Partisan Imperative*; Robert V. Remini, *Martin Van Buren and the Making of the Democratic Party* (New York: Columbia University Press, 1959), 56; and Wilentz, *Rise of American Democracy*, 309–10.

2. See Hofstadter, *Idea of a Party System*, xii, Goodman, "First American Party System," 57–58; and Stewart, "Congress and the Constitutional System," 6–7. In sharp contrast to the idea-driven approach to party legitimization offered by Hofstadter and others, Scott James advances a materialist account of this development in his "Patronage Regimes and American Party Development from 'The Age of Jackson' to the Progressive Era," *British Journal of Political Science* 36 (January 2006): 55–56.

3. Other social and institutional developments have contributed to the timing and structure of the Jacksonian Democratic party and the second party system more generally. The expansion of the electorate, for example, has been examined both as a cause and an effect of the modern party system. Wilentz, *Rise of American Democracy*; Wood, *Radicalism of the American Revolution*. Richard John, for his part, notes the vital role of the postal system which created a civic infrastructure essential for the construction of mass party organizations. *Spreading the News*, 206–56. The literature on the development of the second party system is extensive. See, among numerous others, Formisano's studies of political change in Michigan and Massachusetts, McCormick's state-by-state survey of party development, and Michael Holt's essays on voting behavior and the changing forturnes of the Whig party. Ronald P. Formisano, *The Birth of Mass Political Parties: Michigan, 1827-1861* (Princeton, N.J.: Princeton University Press, 1971); Formisano, *The Transformation of Political Cultures: Massachusetts Parties, 1790s-1840s* (Oxford: Oxford University Press, 1983); Richard P. Mc-

Cormick, *The Second American Party System: Party Formation in the Jacksonian Era* (Chapel Hill: University of North Carolina Press, 1966); Michael F. Holt, *Political Parties and American Political Development from the Age of Jackson to the Age of Lincoln* (Baton Rouge: Louisiana State University Press, 1992); Michael F. Holt, *The Rise and Fall of the American Whig Party: Jacksonian Politics and the Onset of the Civil War* (New York: Oxford University Press, 1999).

4. Ammon, *James Monroe*, 409.

5. In his seminal article on party development, Michael Wallace observes that a "lack of ideological fervor . . . contributed to a lowering of the political temperature" in the 1820s. Wallace's study focuses on domestic political developments; his analysis does not associate the moderation of party ideology with the end of hostilities in Europe. "Changing Concepts of Party in the United States: New York, 1815–1828," *American Historical Review* 74 (1968): 479.

6. Tariff and bank politics during this period are familiar and well documented. On the growth of direct federal spending during the "era of internal improvements," 1825–37, see Stephen Minicucci, "Internal Improvements and the Union, 1790–1860," *Studies in American Political Development* 18 (Fall 2004): 160–85; see more generally John Lauritz Larson, *Internal Improvement: National Public Works and the Promise of Popular Government in the Early United States* (Chapel Hill: University of North Carolina Press, 2001).

7. See Van Buren's discussion of this and related matters in "Autobiography of Martin Van Buren," *American Historical Association, Annual Report for the Year 1918*, ed. John C. Fitzpatrick (Washington, D.C., 1920) 2: 122–27.

8. Hofstadter, *Idea of a Party System*, 190–204.

9. "Inaugural Address," 4 March 1817, *The Political Writings of James Monroe*, ed. James P. Lucier (Washington, D.C.: Regnery, 2001), 493.

10. Monroe to Andrew Jackson, 14 December 1816, in ibid., 475.

11. See Martin Van Buren, *Inquiry into the Origin and Course of Political Parties in the United States* (New York: Hurd and Houghton, 1867), 3–5, 229.

12. "Old Party Distinctions," *Albany Argus*, 8 October 1824. Discussed in Wallace, "Changing Concepts of Party," 482. Also see Fitzpatrick, "Autobiography of Martin Van Buren," 2: 122–27. The expression "Era of Good Feelings" was promoted by Federalists after the election of 1816, apprehensive that Monroe would push a strident Republican agenda. George Dangerfield, *The Era of Good Feelings* (New York: Harcourt Brace and World, 1963), 104.

13. The Bucktails took their name from the emblem of Tammany Hall.

14. Wallace, "Changing Concepts of Party," 457.

15. The candidates were Andrew Jackson of Tennessee, William Crawford of Georgia, John Quincy Adams of Massachusetts, and Henry Clay of Kentucky. The notion that the lack of party discipline undermined efforts to distinguish Republicans from political enemies during the election of 1824 can be found in the July 1835 "Statement

by the Democratic Republicans of the United States." Reprinted in Joel Silbey, "The Election of 1836," in *History of American Presidential Elections, 1789–1968*, ed. Arthur Schlesinger Jr. and Fred Israel (New York: Chelsea House, 1971) 1: 616–38.

16. "New Parties and New Expedients," *Albany Argus*, 1 August 1823.

17. "The Republican Party and the Designs of Its Opponents," *Albany Argus*, 9 April 1824, emphasis in original. The *Albany Argus*'s claims that politicians opposed to party distinctions hoped to divide Republicans against one another is discussed in Wallace, "Changing Concepts of Party," 490.

18. This talk, to be sure, was not always below the surface: in the *Argus*'s narrative, slavery was one of the "irrelevant subjects" that Federalists utilized to regain power, and talk of "the grand division of a *northern* and *southern* confederacy, was applied wherever it could be." "New Parties and New Expedients," emphasis in original.

19. The slavery question, to be sure, was raised in 1790 when Quakers and the Pennsylvania Abolition Society petitioned Congress to abolish the slave trade and slavery more generally. The Senate refused to consider these petitions at all. For a recent examination of this debate, see George Van Cleve, *A Slaveholders' Union: Slavery, Politics, and the Constitution in the Early American Republic* (Chicago: University of Chicago Press, 2010), ch. 5.

20. James Cobb, *Niles' Weekly Register*, 15 February 1819, supplement to volume 16, "Missouri Question," 172.

21. James Tallmadge, *Niles' Weekly Register*, 15 February 1819, supplement to volume 16, "Missouri Question," 163. For an illuminating discussion of this debate, see Forbes, *Missouri Compromise and Its Aftermath*, 36–44. For an analysis of what was at stake during this episode in American political history, see Richard H. Brown, "The Missouri Crisis, Slavery, and the Politics of Jacksonianism," *South Atlantic Quarterly* 65 (1966): 55–72.

22. See, for example, Monroe to Thomas Jefferson, 7 February, 19 February, and 20 May 1820, in *Political Writings of James Monroe*, Lucier, 516–21.

23. Ammon, *James Monroe*, 454; Stephen Skowronek, The *Politics Presidents Make: Leadership from John Adams to Bill Clinton* (Cambridge, Mass.: The Belknap Press of Harvard University Press, 1997), 103.

24. Jefferson to the Marquis de Lafayette, 4 November 1823, in *Writings of Thomas Jefferson*, Bergh, 15: 492. Madison sounded the same themes in his communications with Monroe. In his view, "the zeal wth. which the extension, so called, of slavery is opposed, has, with the coalesced *leaders*, an object very different from the welfare of the slaves, or the check to their increase; and that their real object is, as you intimate, to form a new state of parties founded on local instead of political distinctions; thereby dividing the Republicans of the North from those of the South, and making the former instrumental in giving to the opponents of both an ascendancy over the whole." Madison to James Monroe, 10 February 1820, in *Writings of James Madison*, Hunt, 9: 21–22, emphasis in original. Also see "Autobiography of Martin Van Buren," Fitzpatrick, 2: 137–38. These reflections notwithstanding, the argument that the Missouri

issue was a Federalist plot did not hold water: as historian Robert Forbes points out, Republicans in the middle and northern states had initiated the controversy and led the debate in the Fifteenth Congress. The legislatures of key mid-Atlantic states where the Republican party was strong (New York, New Jersey, Delaware, and Pennsylvania), moreover, had all issued unanimous resolutions opposing the extension of slavery into Missouri. Forbes, *Missouri Compromise and Its Aftermath*, 57–58, 75.

25. Forbes, *Missouri Compromise and Its Aftermath*, 50.

26. Van Buren to Thomas Ritchie, 13 January 1827, in *The Papers of Martin Van Buren*, ed. Lucy Fisher West et al. (Alexandria, Va.: Chadwyck-Healey, 1987), reel 6. The notion that intraparty attachments had frayed in the absence of a clear partisan opponent was substantiated for party stalwarts like Van Buren by the fact that Tallmadge was a New York Republican—a supporter of Van Buren's archrival, DeWitt Clinton. Tallmadge, however, broke with Clinton over personal differences several months after he proposed his amendment to the Missouri Enabling Act. Glover Moore, *The Missouri Controversy, 1819–1821* (Lexington: University of Kentucky Press, 1953), 38.

27. Van Buren to Thomas Ritchie, 13 January 1827, in *Papers of Martin Van Buren*, West et al., reel 6.

28. These tactics are meticulously documented in Forbes, *Missouri Compromise and Its Aftermath*, 69–70, 91, and more generally, chs. 2 and 3. Also see Harry Ammon, "The Richmond Junto, 1800–1824," *Virginia Magazine of History and Biography* 61 (1953): 395–418, and Ammon, *James Monroe*, 449–61.

29. For an account which similarly situates Martin Van Buren as a pivotal political entrepreneur, see Brown, "Missouri Crisis, Slavery, and the Politics of Jacksonianism," 58–64.

30. Van Buren to Thomas Ritchie, 13 January 1827, in *Papers of Martin Van Buren*, West et al., reel 6.

31. "Statement by the Democratic Republicans of the United States," reprinted in Silbey, "The Election of 1836," in Schlesinger and Israel, *History of American Presidential Elections*, 1: 626.

32. See Douglas W. Jaenicke, "The Jacksonian Integration of Parties into the Constitutional System," *Political Science Quarterly* 101 (1986): 87, 91.

33. "Brutus" [Robert J. Turnbull], "The Crisis; or, Essays on the Usurpations of the Federal Government." Quoted in Forbes, *Missouri Compromise and Its Aftermath*, 225.

34. On the influence of this essay, see Forbes, *Missouri Compromise and Its Aftermath*, 225–26.

35. John, *Spreading the News*, 263–77.

36. Jaenicke, "Jacksonian Integration of Parties into the Constitutional System," 87, 91. John M. McFaul, "Expediency vs. Morality: Jacksonian Politics and Slavery," *Journal of American History* 62 (June 1975): 24–39. On the importance of constructing an electoral message to assuage southern fears of a nonsouthern president (Van Bu-

ren) in the years following Jackson's tenure, see William G. Shade, "'The Most Delicate and Exciting Topics': Martin Van Buren, Slavery, and the Election of 1836," *Journal of the Early Republic* 18 (Autumn 1998): 459–84.

37. Quoted in Donald B. Cole, *Martin Van Buren and the American Political System* (Princeton, N.J.: Princeton University Press, 1984), 150.

38. Jackson's support for Monroe's idea of amalgamation, prior to his election, was an important cause for concern within the Albany Regency. Wallace, "Changing Concepts of Party," 487. On the tariff see Cole, *Martin Van Buren and the American Political System*, 112.

39. This message was conveyed through Van Buren's associate James Hamilton. Van Buren to James Hamilton, 21 February 1829, in *Papers of Martin Van Buren*, West et al., reel 7; Remini, *Martin Van Buren and the Making of the Democratic Party*, 126.

40. First Annual Message to Congress, 8 December 1829, in *A Compilation of the Messages and Papers of the Presidents, 1789–1897*, ed. James D. Richardson (Washington, D.C.: U.S. GPO, 1897) 2: 449; John, *Spreading the News*, 219–21. The expression "to the victor belong the spoils" was, in fact, coined by Bucktail William Marcy. Hofstadter, *Idea of a Party System*, 250.

41. Engel offers a thoughtful alternative interpretation of Van Buren and Jackson's thought, one that shares the assumption advanced here that the second generation of American statesmen did not conceive of party rivalry as a stable and regular "system." In Engel's account, Van Buren identified an aristocratic or "courtly" faction as the essential source of system instability. The present account, which is compatible with Engel's, focuses attention on the slavery question as the crucial source of instability. Engel, *American Politicians Confront the Courts*, 138–45; also see Leonard, *Invention of Party Politics*.

42. John Quincy Adams, for example, refused after his election to "exhibit himself" to the public in a vain attempt for popularity. Quoted in Hofstadter, *Idea of a Party System*, 233.

43. On the problem of demagoguery and electioneering, see James Ceaser, *Presidential Selection: Theory and Development* (Princeton, N.J.: Princeton University Press, 1979), 166–67 and 318–27.

44. McCormick, *Presidential Game*, 12; also see Altschuler and Blumin, *Rude Republic*, 47–86.

45. Howe, *What Hath God Wrought*, 510–12.

46. Holt, *Rise and Fall of the American Whig Party*, 44, 95–96, 99, 952–53.

47. Two party competition became national in scope, where elections were contested by Democrats and Whigs in every state, by the late 1830s. Branches of these parties were nonetheless active in numerous states since the early 1820s. McCormick, *Second American Party System*, 340–41.

48. Van Buren to Thomas Ritchie, 13 January 1827, in *Papers of Martin Van Buren*, West et al., reel 6.

49. The balance rule was the practice of pairing the admission of a new slaveholding state with the admission of a new nonslaveholding state to ensure representative parity of the sections in the Senate. See Charles Stewart III and Barry R. Weingast, "Stacking the Senate, Changing the Nation: Republican Rotten Boroughs, Statehood Politics, and American Political Development," *Studies in American Political Development* 6 (Fall 1992): 223–71.

50. McCormick, *Second American Party System*, 346–49.

51. Theodore J. Lowi, "Party, Policy, and Constitution in America," in Chambers and Burnham, *American Party Systems*, 247–48.

52. For Van Buren's shifting positions on the tariff, see Cole, *Martin Van Buren and the American Political System*, 111–12, 160–62, 167–69, 236–38, and Remini, *Martin Van Buren and the Making of the Democratic Party*, 150–52, 184–85.

53. Remini, *Martin Van Buren and the Making of the Democratic Party*, 185.

54. Quoted in Noble Cunningham Jr., "Nathaniel Macon and the Southern Protest Against National Consolidation," *North Carolina Historical Review* 32 (July 1955): 380.

55. Turnbull, "Crisis," quoted in Forbes, *Missouri Compromise and Its Aftermath*, 223.

56. William W. Freehling, *Prelude to Civil War: The Nullification Controversy in South Carolina, 1816–1836* (New York: Harper and Row, 1966), 255.

57. The nullifiers did not confront the threat to slavery directly because the question might unite opposition in the northern states and abroad in condemnation of the institution. There was, moreover, no powerful abolitionist movement at the time, to confront. Ibid., 257–58.

58. Calhoun to Virgil Maxcy, 11 September 1830, in *The Papers of John C. Calhoun*, ed. Clyde Norman Wilson (Columbia: University of South Carolina Press, 1978) 11: 229.

59. Freehling, *Prelude to Civil War*, 95, 131, 133.

60. Ibid., 157–58 and 292.

61. Calhoun to Virgil Maxcy, 11 September 1830, in *Papers of John C. Calhoun*, Wilson, 11: 229.

62. Annual Message of 4 December 1832, in *Compilation of the Messages and Papers of the Presidents 1789–1897*, Richardson, 2: 597–99. Jackson's strategy was to remove any pretext the nullifiers might use to continue in opposition. Merrill D. Peterson, *Olive Branch and Sword: The Compromise of 1833* (Baton Rouge: Louisiana State University Press, 1982), 22–23.

63. Many of Jackson's states' rights supporters were also unsettled by his expansive definition of treason, which encompassed the support of state laws aimed to obstruct the execution of federal law. Van Buren cautiously brought this concern to his attention. Van Buren to Andrew Jackson, 27 December 1832, in *Correspondence of Andrew Jackson*, ed. John S. Bassett (Washington, D.C.: Carnegie Institution, 1929), 4: 506–7. Also see C. C. Cambreleng to Van Buren, 18 December 1832, in ibid., 4: 505 n.

3. States' rights advocates, moreover, were troubled by Jackson's requests for expanded executive authority to stifle resistance to the tariff. Message of 16 January 1833 (later known as the "Force Bill Message"), *Messages and Papers of the Presidents, 1789–1897*, Richardson, 2: 610–32.

64. Skowronek, *Politics Presidents Make*, 144–47.

65. At one critical juncture during the standoff, Floyd entered into his diary that "if [Jackson] uses force, I will oppose him with a military force." Quoted in Ellis, *Union at Risk*, 130.

66. Van Buren to Andrew Jackson, 27 December 1832, in *Correspondence of Andrew Jackson*, Bassett, 4: 507.

67. Donald B. Cole, *The Presidency of Andrew Jackson* (Lawrence: University Press of Kansas, 1993), 174.

68. See 20 February 1833, in *Correspondence of Andrew Jackson*, Bassett, 5: 19–21.

69. Cole, *Presidency of Andrew Jackson*, 179.

70. Freehling, *Prelude to Civil War*, 270–71, 293.

71. Peterson, *Olive Branch and Sword*, 18.

72. Ibid., 66. The convention in South Carolina that passed the state's Nullification Ordinance (which declared the tariffs of 1828 and 1832 null and void in the state of South Carolina) also endorsed a proposal that insisted that a just and equitable tariff would tax protected and unprotected goods equally, at a rate no higher than 12 percent. Freehling, *Prelude to Civil War*, 262.

73. Clay to Thomas Speed, 9 June 1833. Quoted in Peterson, *Olive Branch and Sword*, 66.

74. Ibid., 81; Cole, *Presidency of Andrew Jackson*, 174.

75. A vote on the Force bill might have undermined Clay's role as a compromiser. Clay said of the Force bill: "I could not vote against the measure; I would not speak in its behalf." Clay never, in fact, voted on the bill. Peterson, *Olive Branch and Sword*, 79.

76. Freehling, *Prelude to Civil War*, 294. Not all scholars accord Jackson the same credit. See, for example, Peterson, *Olive Branch and Sword*, 86. Skowronek maintains that Jackson's position was more confused than centrist: "Far from holding the center and isolating the extremists, Jackson's double message seem [*sic*] to abandon the center to embrace the opposing poles." Skowronek, *Politics Presidents Make*, 146.

77. Peterson, *Olive Branch and Sword*, 27, 99.

78. Jackson to General John Coffee, 9 April 1833, in *Correspondence of Andrew Jackson*, Bassett, 5: 56. Also see Jackson to Rev. Andrew Crawford, 1 May 1833, in ibid., 5: 72.

79. Calhoun to John Bauskett and others, 3 November 1837, *Papers of John C. Calhoun*, Wilson, 13: 639.

80. See Theodore J. Lowi, "American Business, Public Policy, Case-Studies, and Political Theory," *World Politics* 16 (July 1964): 690.

81. See Eric Foner, *Free Soil, Free Labor, Free Men: The Ideology of the Republican Party Before the Civil War* (New York: Oxford University Press, 1970), 57–64; Gavin

Wright, *Slavery and American Economic Development* (Baton Rouge: Louisiana State University Press, 2006), 50–51.

82. See Howe, *What Hath God Wrought*, 342–57.

83. See Skowronek, *Politics Presidents Make*, 159.

84. Michael A. Morrison, *Slavery and the American West: The Eclipse of Manifest Destiny and the Coming of the Civil War* (Chapel Hill: University of North Carolina Press, 1997), 14–15.

85. Morrison, *Slavery and the American West*, 14–16.

86. On Whig opposition to the annexation of Texas, see Morrison, *Slavery and the American West*, 19–26.

87. Michael A. Morrison, " 'New Territory Versus No Territory': The Whig Party and the Politics of Western Expansion, 1846–1848," *Western Historical Quarterly* 23 (1992): 28, 37, 45–47.

88. Skowronek, *Politics Presidents Make*, 155–76.

89. Howe, *What Hath God Wrought*, 742.

90. Morrison, " 'New Territory Versus No Territory;' " Howe, *What Hath God Wrought*, 764, 828.

91. In fact, before Lincoln became a war president, he was best known as an anti-war congressman: he introduced into the House of Representatives in 1847 what became known as the Spot Resolutions, proposals to determine whether the spot of soil where the Mexican government began its assault was on American soil, or ground controlled by Spain until the Mexican Revolution. Critics of the Mexican War suspected that President James Polk sought to draw the Mexicans into a war by venturing into Mexican territory. Polk claimed that American forces were attacked by the Mexicans on American soil. See *Collected Works of Abraham Lincoln* (hereafter *CWAL*), ed. Roy P. Basler (New Brunswick, N.J.: Rutgers University Press, 1953), 1: 420–22.

92. Strictly speaking, the Missouri Compromise line permitting slavery south of 36°30′ applied only to the Missouri Territory—it did not apply to the far West. Many, however, viewed the compromise line as the definitive boundary between free and slave territory not just for the Missouri Territory, but for all of America's western territorial possessions.

93. Paul Bergeron, *The Presidency of James K. Polk* (Lawrence: University Press of Kansas, 1987), 208.

94. Eugene Irving McCormac, *James K. Polk: A Political Biography* (Berkeley: University of California Press, 1922), 639–40.

95. James K. Polk, *The Diary of James K. Polk During His Presidency, 1845 to 1849* (Chicago: A. C. McClurg, 1910) 4: 300.

96. Ibid., 4: 299.

97. "Speech in Lexington, Ky.," 13 November 1847, in *The Papers of Henry Clay*, ed. Melba Porter Hay (Lexington: University of Kentucky Press, 1991), 10: 371.

98. According to one sympathetic historian, Van Buren's "revolt in 1848 was designed to right the balance between the sections of the party." Max M. Mintz, "'The Political Ideas of Martin Van Buren,'" *New York History* 3 (1949): 439–42.

99. Joel H. Silbey, *The Shrine of Party: Congressional Voting Behavior, 1841–1852* (Pittsburgh: University of Pittsburgh Press, 1967), 142–46.

100. Southern Whigs, to offer one illustration, resisted Calhoun's efforts in the late 1830s to recruit them to the party most committed to states' rights—the Democratic party. Those that did follow Calhoun's lead were punished at the polls. Calhoun may have been surprised to learn that Southern Whigs were not uniformly preoccupied (as he and his circle were) with states' rights. Charles Sellers Jr., "Who Were the Southern Whigs?" *American Historical Review* 59 (January 1954): 339.

101. Van Buren to Moses Y. Tilden [Samuel Tilden's eldest brother], 1 September 1856, in *Letters and Literary Memorials of Samuel J. Tilden*, ed. John Bigelow (New York: Harper and Brothers Publishers, 1908) 1: 119–21. Discussed in Michael Holt, *Political Crisis of the 1850s*, ch. 1.

102. McCormick, *Presidential Game*, 174–75.

103. Stephen Skowronek describes Van Buren's approach to party and governance in similar terms: "Holistic policy programs would only have exacerbated sectional cleavages and threatened national unity. In Martin Van Buren's master scheme, American government could be made to work only by two constituent parties competing across the major sectional divisions of the nation. In this way, the conflicting interests of all sections would be given an "equal opportunity" to gain national services and support within one governmental order. Such parties would not articulate a clear policy linkage between citizens and government, but they would bind together a radically decentralized state and a faction-ridden nation." Skowronek, *Building a New American State*, 26.

Chapter 5. Union, Emancipation, and Party Building

1. *RFC*, Farrand, 1: 164–65.

2. Message to Congress, 17 July 1862, in *CWAL*, Basler, 5: 330.

3. For the argument that the Union government might be equated with the Republican party organization itself, see Bensel, *Yankee Leviathan*, 3–4. See also Andrew Polsky's analysis of the relationship between partisanship and Union command appointments. Polsky, "'Mr. Lincoln's Army' Revisited: Partisanship, Institutional Position, and Union Army Command, 1861–1865," *Studies in American Political Development* 16 (Fall 2002): 176–207.

4. See, for example, James M. McPherson, *Abraham Lincoln and the Second American Revolution* (New York: Oxford University Press, 1991); Allen C. Guelzo, *Lincoln's Emancipation Proclamation: The End of Slavery in America* (New York: Simon and Schuster, 2004).

5. Don E. Fehrenbacher, *The South and Three Sectional Crises* (Baton Rouge: Louisiana State University Press, 1980), 41–42.

6. See Bensel, *Yankee Leviathan*, 24.

7. In addition to the well-documented divisions it introduced in the Whig party, the Kansas-Nebraska Act divided the Democratic party as well: northern Democrats in the House were divided evenly. More than 70 percent of these members lost their seats in the following elections. Fehrenbacher, *South and Three Sectional Crises*, 49. On the divisions that formed in both parties in response to the Kansas-Nebraska Act, see Michael F. Holt, *The Political Crisis of the 1850s* (New York: W. W. Norton, 1978), 148–51.

8. "Appeal of the Independent Democrats to the People of the United States," 19 January 1854, *Congressional Globe*, 33rd Cong., 1st Sess. (1853–54), 281–82. See Mildred C. Stoler, "Insurgent Democrats of Indiana and Illinois in 1854," *Indiana Magazine of History* 33 (March 1937): 1–31.

9. Nine southern Whigs voted for final passage; one, John Bell, joined the six northern Whigs in opposition. The following account of the impact of the Kansas-Nebraska Act on the Whig party draws on Holt, *Rise and Fall of the American Whig Party*, 815–21.

10. Quoted in ibid., 821.

11. Ibid., 839.

12. According to Millard Fillmore, the conservative New York Whig (and former president) who hoped to head such a coalition, the Know Nothing order represented "the only hope of forming a truly national party, which shall *ignore* the constant and disturbing agitation of slavery." Quoted in ibid., 911. The Know-Nothings, by 1855, called themselves the American party.

13. For a detailed analysis of the events that led to the Republicans' coalescence as the alternative to the Democracy, see William E. Gienapp, *The Origins of the Republican Party, 1852–1856* (New York: Oxford University Press, 1987), 295–303, 439–43.

14. 16 October 1854, in *CWAL*, Basler, 2: 270.

15. Speech at Cincinnati, 17 September 1859, in ibid., 3: 449.

16. This condition required that any extension of the South's "peculiar institution" come as a result of negotiation and compromise between the free and slave states. A "system of equivalents"—of reciprocal exchange of benefits between the free and slave states—had, according to Lincoln, governed past compromises. Speech on the Kansas-Nebraska Act at Peoria, Illinois, 16 October 1854, in ibid., 2: 259.

17. See James Rawley, *Race and Politics: "Bleeding Kansas" and the Coming of the Civil War* (New York: J. B. Lippincott, 1969), 79–99.

18. He described the conjunction of the Kansas-Nebraska Act and the Dred Scott decision as an "almost complete legal combination—piece of *machinery* so to speak." "House Divided" Speech, 16 June 1858, Springfield, Illinois, in *CWAL*, Basler, 2: 462, emphasis in original. Since the Kansas-Nebraska Act and the Dred Scott decision so neatly complemented one another, Lincoln suspected that they had been coordinated

by Douglas, Pierce, Buchanan, and Taney. For a brief discussion of this conspiracy allegation, see James M. McPherson, *Battle Cry of Freedom: The Civil War Era* (New York: Oxford University Press, 1988), 178–79.

19. "House Divided" Speech, 16 June 1858, in *CWAL*, Basler, 2: 464–65, emphasis in original.

20. See ibid., 2: 466–67.

21. Eric Foner, *Free Soil, Free Labor, Free Men: The Ideology of the Republican Party Before the Civil War* (New York: Oxford University Press, 1970), 73–102; Gienapp, *Origins of the Republican Party*, 358–65.

22. Speech on the Kansas-Nebraska Act at Peoria, Illinois, 16 October 1854, in *CWAL*, Basler, 2: 273–74.

23. The First Congress later reaffirmed the antislavery tenets of the Northwest Ordinance. Lincoln neglected to mention that the Founders, just as they prohibited slavery from the Northwest, also permitted it to expand into the Southwest. See Fehrenbacher, *South and Three Sectional Crises*, 12.

24. Speech on the Kansas-Nebraska Act at Peoria, Illinois, 16 October 1854, in *CWAL*, Basler, 2: 275.

25. Speech at Leavenworth, Kansas, 3 December 1859, in ibid., 3: 502.

26. To Edward Wallace, 11 October 1859, in ibid., 3: 487.

27. Speech at New Haven, Connecticut, 6 March 1860, in ibid., 4: 14, emphasis in original; also see McPherson, *Battle Cry of Freedom*, 182.

28. David Wilmot, quoted in Foner, *Free Soil*, 116. For a discussions of the limitations of this theory, see Roger L. Ransom, *Conflict and Compromise: The Political Economy of Slavery, Emacipation, and the American Civil War* (New York: Cambridge University Press, 1989), 53–60, and Bensel, *Yankee Leviathan*, 27–33.

29. As Lincoln opined in the first Lincoln-Douglas Debate, "I believe if we could arrest the spread, and place it where Washington, and Jefferson, and Madison placed it, it *would be* in the course of ultimate extinction, and the public mind *would*, as for eighty years past, believe that it was in the course of ultimate extinction." 21 August 1858, in *CWAL*, Basler, 3: 18, emphasis in original. Also see Speech at Springfield, 17 July 1858, in ibid., 2: 513–14.

30. He was less certain in private. Indeed, he suggested on several occasions that slavery was unlikely to end without a fight. See especially, "Fragment on Sectionalism" ca. 23 July 1856, in ibid., 2: 349–53. Also see Lincoln to George Robertson, 15 August 1855, in ibid., 2: 317–18. For Seward's landmark address on the subject, see "The Irrepressible Conflict," 25 October 1858, in *The Works of William H. Seward*, ed. George E. Baker (New York: Houghton Mifflin, 1889) 4: 289–302.

31. *CWAL*, Basler, 2: 461–62, emphasis in original.

32. Address at Cooper Institute, New York City, New York, 27 February 1860, in ibid., 3: 547.

33. Seward sent a memo to Lincoln recommending that the administration demand answers from Spain and France for their improper interventions in the

Americas (à la the Monroe Doctrine). Should their answers prove unsatisfactory, Seward recommended that the United States should declare war. Seward further recommended that agents should be sent into "*Canada, Mexico* and *Central America*, to rouse a vigorous continental *spirit of independence* on this continent against European intervention." Lincoln ignored Seward's recommendation to unite the sections by contriving a foreign, military distraction. Seward to Abraham Lincoln, 1 April 1861, in ibid., 4: 317–18, emphasis in original. See McPherson, *Battle Cry of Freedom*, 270–71.

34. 4 March 1861, in *CWAL*, Basler, 4: 271, emphasis in original.

35. Inaugural Address, in ibid., 4: 269. Lincoln also enumerated a number of political and commercial disadvantages that would result from a permanent separation—many of the points reminiscent of the concerns raised by Federalists should the Constitution fail to secure ratification. The prospect that a successful secession movement would encourage attempts by *other* regions of the country to secede, though not explicitly mentioned in Lincoln's speech, was also a crucial consideration in the North's decision to repress the rebellion. As Richard Bensel observes, "the choice for the North posed by southern secession was never between one nation and two but between one nation and many." Bensel, *Yankee Leviathan*, 62. Also see McPherson, *Battle Cry of Freedom*, 246–47.

36. Quoted in McPherson, *Battle Cry of Freedom*, 250.

37. The Crittenden Compromise Plan, proposed during the secession crisis, may be treated as a fair approximation of what many northern Democrats would accept but moderate Republicans would not. This plan was a series of constitutional amendments that would have, among other things, prohibited slavery north of 36°30′ and protected it south of that line in all territories presently held or acquired in the future, denied Congress the authority to regulate the interstate slave trade, severely limited Congress's authority to prohibit slavery in the District of Columbia, and required compensation for slaveholders who were prevented in northern states from recovering fugitive slaves. Crucially, these amendments, like the provision allocating equal representation of each state in the Senate, would be valid for all time and not subject to change by future amendments to the Constitution. *Congressional Globe*, 36th Cong., 2nd Sess. (1860), 114. For a discussion of the compromise plan, see McPherson, *Battle Cry of Freedom*, 253.

38. Seward to Abraham Lincoln, 27 January 1861, in Abraham Lincoln Papers at the Library of Congress, Memory.loc.gov, accessed 27 June 2014. As historian Michael Holt explained, "Lincoln almost from the moment he was elected set out to destroy the Republican party as it existed in 1860, that is, as an exclusively northern party whose sole basis of cohesion was hostility toward the South and the Democratic party. Instead, Lincoln wanted to create a new national coalition with support in both sections, a party built around the issue of restoring the Union, rather than the issue of crushing the Slave Power or abolishing slavery as congressional Republicans wanted." Michael Holt, "Abraham Lincoln and the Politics of Union," in *Abraham Lincoln and the*

American Political Tradition, ed. John L. Thomas (Amherst: University of Massachusetts Press, 1986), 117–18. For a sustained and incisive treatment of the Union party as a stridently patriotic and nationalistic movement, as a "righteous crusade of national redemption" that did not recognize the legitimacy of the Democratic opposition, see Adam I. P. Smith, *No Party Now: Politics in the Civil War North* (Oxford: Oxford University Press, 2006), 162.

39. Geoffrey R. Stone, *Perilous Times: Free Speech in Wartime from the Sedition Act of 1798 to the War on Terrorism* (New York: W. W. Norton, 2004), 80.

40. There were exceptions to this general pattern. He famously defended General Burnside's arrest of Clement Vallandigham under the authority of Burnside's General Order No. 38, issued without Lincoln's knowledge or approval, which prohibited speech expressing sympathy for the enemy. Lincoln's justification for Vallandigham's arrest rested on a rhetorically appealing, though constitutionally suspect position: "Long experience has shown that armies can not be maintained unless desertion shall be punished by the severe penalty of death. . . . Must I shoot a simple-minded soldier boy who deserts, while I must not touch a hair of a wiley agitator who induces him to desert?" There was no evidence, however, that Vallandigham had directly encouraged others to dodge the draft or otherwise defy federal authority. Lincoln to Erastus Corning and others, 12 June 1863, in *CWAL*, Basler, 6: 266; Mark E. Neely, *The Fate of Liberty: Abraham Lincoln and Civil Liberties* (New York: Oxford University Press, 1991), 65–68. Lincoln later overturned an order issued by Burnside to close the *Chicago Times*, insisting that the publicity such an act would attract would do more harm than the publication itself, Stone, *Perilous Times*, 118.

41. Lincoln to John C. Frémont, 2 September 1861, in *CWAL*, Basler, 4: 506. General David Hunter in May 1862 issued a similar directive without Lincoln's approval, declaring martial law and abolishing slavery in three states, South Carolina, Georgia, and Florida. Lincoln revoked this order as well. Proclamation Revoking General David Hunter's Order of Military Emancipation, 19 May 1862, in ibid., 5: 222–23. Lincoln held that Union forces possessed the authority to confiscate enemy property only if there was a military necessity requiring such action. Lincoln to Orville Browning, 22 September 1861, in ibid., 4: 532.

42. Lincoln to Orville Browning, 22 September 1861, in ibid., 4: 532. If these states were to join the rebellion, they would significantly increase the population and industrial capacity of the Confederacy. Washington, D.C., which was bordered on three sides by Maryland and Confederate Virginia on the fourth, would also be surrounded by rebel territory.

43. "The Prayer of Twenty Millions," *New York Tribune*, 20 August 1862, reprinted in ibid., 5: 389.

44. He was careful to remind Greeley and his readers of the *Tribune* that he spoke only of his understanding of his official duty; "I intend no modification of my oft-expressed *personal* wish that all men every where could be free." Lincoln to Horace Greeley, 22 August 1862, in ibid., 5: 388–89, emphasis in original.

45. Message to Congress, 6 March 1862, in ibid., 5: 144–45. Also see his appeal to border state representatives to support the federal plan for compensated emancipation, 12 July 1862, in ibid., 5: 317–19.

46. Lincoln to Horace Greeley, 24 March 1862, in ibid., 5: 169.

47. Message to Congress, 6 March 1862, in ibid., 5: 144–45.

48. Proclamation Revoking General David Hunter's Order of Military Emancipation, 19 May 1862, in ibid., 5: 223.

49. Slaves held in the border states still loyal to the Union, namely Missouri, Kentucky, Maryland, and Delaware, were therefore excluded. Preliminary Emancipation Proclamation, 22 September 1862, in ibid., 5: 433–36.

50. The purpose of the Preliminary Emancipation Proclamation, as Michael Holt perceptively argues, was to pressure states in rebellion to hold elections to *avoid* emancipation. Emancipation, in other words, was used as a "stick" to encourage reunion. Holt, "Abraham Lincoln and the Politics of Union," in Thomas, *Abraham Lincoln and the American Political Tradition*, 119.

51. McPherson, *Battle Cry of Freedom*, 700.

52. Lincoln to Andrew Johnson, 26 March 1863, in *CWAL*, Basler, 6: 149–50, emphasis in original. These comments came nearly four months after the Emancipation Proclamation. Six days after the Preliminary Emancipation Proclamation was issued, however, Lincoln was unsure what impact freedom would have on the Union effort. As he wrote to his vice president, "We have fewer troops in the field at the end of six days than we had at the beginning—the attrition among the old outnumbering the addition by the new. The North responds to the proclamation sufficiently in breath; but breath alone kills no rebels." Lincoln to Hannibal Hamlin, 28 September 1862, in ibid., 5: 444.

53. Lincoln to Andrew Johnson, 3 July 1862, in ibid., 5: 303, emphasis added.

54. Holt, "Abraham Lincoln and the Politics of Union," in Thomas, *Abraham Lincoln and the American Political Tradition*, 119.

55. Ibid., 135.

56. Jennifer L. Weber, *Copperheads: The Rise and Fall of Lincoln's Opponents in the North* (Oxford: Oxford University Press, 2006), 99–100.

57. "Copperheads" was first used as a term of derision in an Ohio newspaper in 1861. Antiwar Democrats soon embraced the name, wearing badges with copper pennies (which featured lady liberty). Charles Coleman, "The Use of the Term 'Copperhead' During the Civil War," *Mississippi Valley Historical Review* 25 (1938): 263–64.

58. Weber, *Copperheads*, 9.

59. Eric L. McKitrick, "Party Politics and the Union and Confederate War Efforts," in Chambers and Burnham, *American Party Systems,*141.

60. Mark E. Neely, *The Union Divided: Party Conflict in the Civil War North* (Cambridge, Mass.: Harvard University Press, 2002), 21.

61. Quoted in Weber, *Copperheads*, 15.

62. *U.S. Statutes at Large* 12 (1863): 731.

63. See Iver Bernstein, *The New York City Draft Riots: Their Significance for American Society and Politics in the Age of the Civil War* (New York: Oxford University Press, 1990).

64. Quoted in Oscar A. Kinchen, *Confederate Operations in Canada and the North: A Little-Known Phase of the American Civil War* (North Quincy, Mass.: Christopher, 1970), 93.

65. Quoted in Weber, *Copperheads*, 168.

66. The platform committee was headed by the most prominent Copperhead, former Ohio congressman Clement Vallandigham. The platform itself was adopted with only four dissenting votes. Weber, *Copperheads*, 170–74; Joel Silbey, *A Respectable Minority: The Democratic Party in the Civil War Era, 1860–1868* (New York: W. W. Norton, 1977), 118–34.

67. Weber, *Copperheads*, 4, 155–56. Also see Charles R. Wilson, "McClellan's Changing Views on the Peace Plank of 1864," *American Historical Review* 38 (April 1933): 498–505.

68. Weber, *Copperheads*, 173.

69. 3 September 1864, in *Works of William H. Seward*, Baker, 5: 496–97.

70. Memo, 23 August 1864, in ibid., 7: 514. Some of his most ardent supporters equally expected a McClellan victory. See Thurlow Weed to William H. Seward, 22 August 1864, in ibid., 7: 514–15.

71. Interview with Alexander W. Randall and Joseph T. Mills, 19 August 1864, in ibid., 7: 506–8. "The party who could elect a President on a War & Slavery Restoration platform, would, of necessity, lose the colored force; and that force being lost, would be as powerless to save the Union as to do any other impossible thing. It is not a question of sentiment or taste, but one of physical force." Lincoln to Charles Robinson, 17 August 1864, in ibid., 7: 500.

72. "Perseverance in War," 7 November 1864, in *Works of William H. Seward*, Baker, 5: 510–11. Also see "An Armistice—What It Signifies—New and Dangerous Trick to Secure a Final Rebel Triumph," *New York Times*, 16 September 1864.

73. Lincoln to Isaac Schermerhorn, 12 September 1864, in *CWAL*, Basler, 8: 1–2.

74. He continued, "Nor do I think we should in this connection make nice distinctions between those who declare for peace unconditionally and those who advocate it as a means of restoring the Union however much we may prefer the former.

"We should bear in mind that the friends of peace at the North must make concessions to the earnest desire that exists in the minds of their countrymen for a restoration of the Union, and that to hold out such a result as an inducement is essential to the success of their party.

"Should the belief that peace will bring back the Union become general, the war would no longer be supported, and that after all is what we are interested in bringing about. When peace is proposed to us it will be time enough to discuss its terms . . . the desire of our people for a distinct and independent national existence will prove as steadfast under the influence of peaceful measures as it has shown itself in the midst of war." Lee to Jefferson Davis, 10 June 1863, in *The Wartime Papers of Robert E. Lee*, ed. Clifford Dowdey and Louis H. Manarin (New York: Da Capo, 1987), 507–9. See more generally Larry E. Nelson, *Bullets, Ballots, and Rhetoric: Confederate Policy for the United States Presidential Contest of 1864* (Tuscaloosa: University of Alabama Press, 1980), 18–30; McPherson, *Battle Cry of Freedom*, 721.

75. Message to Congress, 4 July 1861, in *CWAL*, Basler, 4: 439.

76. This line of argumentation originated with historian David Potter's essay "Jefferson Davis and the Political Factors in Confederacy Defeat," in *Why the North Won the Civil War*, ed. David Herbert Donald and Richard Nelson Current (Baton Rouge: Louisiana State University Press, 1960). The most thorough exposition of this view is made by McKitrick, "Party Politics and the Union and Confederate War Efforts." For a discussion of the historiography of this debate, see Neely, *Union Divided*, ch. 7.

77. McKitrick, "Party Politics and the Union and Confederate War Efforts," 141–42.

78. Ibid., 141.

79. Ibid.

80. Ibid.

81. Neely, *Union Divided*, 184–85. Also see Smith, *No Party Now*, 157–62.

82. Both legislatures brought resolutions that called for a convention of state commissioners to be held in Louisville in the spring to arrange terms for peace and called on Congress to seek an armistice. Allan Nevins, *The War for the Union* (New York: Scribner, 1960), 2: 391–92; James G. Randall, *Lincoln the President: Midstream* (New York: Dodd, Mead, 1952) 3: 252–53.

83. Lincoln claimed the authority to do so under the constitutional provision that guarantees to all state governments a republican form. Lincoln to Andrew Johnson, 11 September 1863 and 19 September 1863, in *CWAL*, Basler, 6: 440, 469. Also see McPherson, *Battle Cry of Freedom*, 702–3.

84. Congress could influence war policy by withholding funds for the war, but Democrats, mindful of the example set by the Federalists during the War of 1812, knew that to do so would be tantamount to political suicide. Even if Congress did possess the authority to control war policy, the Peace Democrats simply did not hold enough power within the party in 1862 to force a change of course.

85. Neely, *Union Divided*, 195–96.

86. Weber, *Copperheads*, 187–88.

87. "Response to a serenade," 10 November 1864, in *CWAL*, Basler, 8: 100–101. Lincoln's reflections on the "necessity" of the election were uttered after the election was over, once the danger of Democratic victory had passed. Neely, *Union Divided*, 3.

88. Significant limitations on the reach of federal power, discussed in Chapter 6, became apparent after the war as resistance mounted in the South to Republican Reconstruction policies.

89. Abraham Lincoln, Message to Congress, 4 July 1861, in *CWAL*, Basler, 4: 439.

Chapter 6. Redrawing the Limits of Legitimate Party Opposition

1. See James McPherson, "Abraham Lincoln and the Second American Revolution," in Thomas, *Abraham Lincoln and the American Political Tradition*, 142–60;
Greenstone, *Lincoln Persuasion*.

2. See Leonard P. Curry, *Blueprint for Modern America: Nonmilitary Legislation of
the First Civil War Congress* (Nashville: Vanderbilt University Press, 1968); Heather
Cox Richardson, *The Greatest Nation of the Earth: Republican Economic Policies During the Civil War* (Cambridge, Mass.: Harvard University Press, 1997); Bensel, *Yankee
Leviathan*, 10–11, 402; Richard Franklin Bensel, *Political Economy of American Industrialization* (Cambridge: Cambridge University Press, 2000).

3. See Gregory Downs's insightful critique of this scholarly inclination to read
stability into postbellum American politics. "The Mexicanization of American Politics: The United States' Transnational Path from Civil War to Stabilization," *American
Historical Review* 117 (April 2012): 387–409.

4. Madison to Robert Walsh, 27 November 1819, *Writings of James Madison*, Hunt,
9: 12.

5. For an analysis of these conventions, see Eric Foner, *Reconstruction: America's
Unfinished Revolution, 1863–1877* (New York: Perennial Classics, 2002), 316–33.

6. The literature examining the limitations of Reconstruction policy is too ex-
tensive to survey here. For a useful discussion of the relevant historiography, see Xi
Wang, *The Trial of Democracy: Black Suffrage and Northern Republicans, 1860–1910*
(Athens: University of Georgia Press, 1997), xix–xxii.

7. For a detailed account of the framing and passage of this act, see Lawanda Cox,
"Promise of Land for the Freedmen," *Mississippi Valley Historical Review* 45 (December 1958): 413–40.

8. Richard M. Valelly, *The Two Reconstructions: The Struggle for Black Enfran-
chisement* (Chicago: University of Chicago Press, 2004), 25–27, 83. For an illuminat-
ing look at the role Johnson played in subverting Radical Republican policy aims, see
Nicole Mellow and Jeffrey K. Tulis, "Andrew Johnson and the Politics of Failure," in
Formative Acts: American Politics in the Making, ed. Stephen Skowronek and Matthew
Glassman (Philadelphia: University of Pennsylvania Press, 2007), 153–70.

9. Foner, *Reconstruction*, 199–201, 208–9; William Cohen, "Negro Involuntary
Servitude in the South, 1865–1940: A Preliminary Analysis," *Journal of Southern History* 42 (February 1976): 35–50.

10. On the link between electoral support for the Republican party and the presence of federal forces, see Bensel, *Yankee Leviathan*, 390–95; Valelly, *Two Reconstructions*, 91–96; Stephen Cresswell, "Enforcing the Enforcement Acts: The Department of
Justice in Northern Mississippi, 1870–1890," *Journal of Southern History* 53 (August
1987): 421–40. On the threat posed by the White Leagues, see William Gillette, *Retreat from Reconstruction, 1869–1879* (Baton Rouge: Louisiana State University, 1979),

229; George C. Rable, *But There Was No Peace: The Role of Violence in the Politics of Reconstruction* (Athens: University of Georgia Press, 1984), 132–42.

11. See the state-by-state analysis in Allen Trelease, *White Terror: The Ku Klux Klan Conspiracy and Southern Reconstruction* (Baton Rouge: Louisiana State University Press, 1971). Also see Richard M. Valelly, "Party, Coercion, and Inclusion: The Two Reconstructions of the South's Electoral Politics," *Politics and Society* 21 (1993): 47–51; Rable, *But There Was No Peace*.

12. Bensel, *Yankee Leviathan*, 380, 398–400.

13. Wang, *Trial of Democracy*, 100–102.

14. Ibid.

15. Valelly, *Two Reconstructions*, 92–93.

16. It is important to note that Republicans began to incur significant electoral losses *before* the economic crisis produced by the Panic of 1873 dislocated millions of Americans. See Paul Frymer, *Uneasy Alliances: Race and Party Competition in America* (Princeton, N.J.: Princeton University Press, 2012), 56–57; Michael Les Benedict, "The Rout of Radicalism: Republicans and the Elections of 1867," *Civil War History* 18 (December 1972): 342–44.

17. Valelly, *Two Reconstructions*, 15–21.

18. Ibid., 113–18.

19. Bradley supported the majority because he believed that the U.S. attorney incorrectly drafted the indictment. Public appearances aside, Justice Bradley's circuit court opinion in the Cruikshank case did not represent an abandonment of blacks; rather, it articulated a coherent approach to the defense of civil rights that, as Pamela Brandwein explains, has gone unrecognized by legal historians. It maintained that the federal government possessed the authority in Article 1, Section 4 of the Constitution (the "times, places, and manner" clause) to punish private and public actors who interfere with federal elections. It also found federal authority under the Thirteenth, Fourteenth, and Fifteenth Amendments to prohibit and prosecute racially discriminatory private (nonstate) violence if this violence interferes with civil rights or the right to vote in national elections. Pamela Brandwein, *Rethinking the Judicial Settlement of Reconstruction* (Cambridge: Cambridge University Press, 2011), 93–108.

20. Brandwein, *Rethinking the Judicial Settlement of Reconstruction*, 11. *United States v. Harris* and the *Civil Rights Cases*, both handed down by the Supreme Court in 1883, struck down a section of the Ku Klux Klan Act of 1871 and two sections of the Civil Rights Act of 1875, respectively. Ibid., 11 n. 49.

21. Valelly, *Two Reconstructions*, 115.

22. This setback notwithstanding, the abandonment of southern freedmen by the Republican party is more precisely dated to the 1890s rather than the Compromise of 1877 (to be discussed below). Brandwein identifies the failure of the Lodge Elections Bill of 1890–91 as the "definitive *political* abandonment" of southern blacks. She dates the *judicial* abandonment of civil rights to the *Hodges v. United States* (1906) decision, which gutted the Civil Rights Act of 1866. *Rethinking the Judicial Settlement of Recon-*

struction, 7, 10, 18 emphasis added. For a helpful survey of the Reconstruction literature that posits 1877 as the crucial turning point, see ibid., 5–7.

23. Frymer, *Uneasy Alliances*, 65–72.

24. Bensel, *Yankee Leviathan*, 405–6.

25. On the competition for distributive resources within the Republican party, see Terry L. Seip, *The South Returns to Congress: Men, Economic Measures, and Intersectional Relationships, 1868–1879* ((Baton Rouge: Louisiana State University Press, 1983), 275–80; Richard H. Abbott, *The Republican Party and the South, 1855–1877: The First Southern Strategy* (Chapel Hill: University of North Carolina Press, 1986), 178–81, 222–27; Michael Perman, *The Road to Redemption: Southern Politics, 1869–1879* (Chapel Hill: University of North Carolina Press, 1984), 265–70. On the decline of prewar Whiggery in the South and the emergence of "Republican" as a negative reference point, see Kleppner, *The Third Electoral System, 1853–1892* (Chapel Hill: University of North Carolina Press, 1979), 103.

26. Data from the post-Reconstruction period (beginning in 1879) shows that the new lines of opposition produced a level of polarization in Congress surpassed only by the congresses of the 1990s and the 2000s. See voteview.com/political_polarization; accessed 23 March 2014. For a discussion of this data, see Keith T. Poole and Howard Rosenthal, *Ideology and Congress* (New Brunswick, N.J.: Transaction Books, 2007), 104–10.

27. Bensel, *Yankee Leviathan*, 382.

28. Valelly, *Two Reconstructions*, 134–39, emphasis in original. On the belief that emerged in Republican ranks that the party could win national elections without the South, see Frymer, *Uneasy Alliances*, 52–53.

29. Valelly, *Two Reconstructions*, ch. 3.

30. For a definitive account of the political economic program of the Republican party in the late nineteenth century, see Richard F. Bensel, *Political Economy of American Industrialization*.

31. Protectionist trade policies that redistributed wealth from south to north made the Republican coalition—a coalition that united capital together with a significant proportion of labor—politically possible. Richard Franklin Bensel, *Sectionalism and American Political Development: 1880–1980* (Madison: University of Wisconsin Press, 1984), 62–63; Bensel, *Yankee Leviathan*, 12, 424–31.

32. For a comprehensive assessment of the election of 1876, see Michael F. Holt, *By One Vote: The Disputed Presidential Election of 1876* (Lawrence: University of Kansas Press, 2008). Also see Roy Morris Jr., *Fraud of the Century: Rutherford B. Hayes, Samuel Tilden, and the Stolen Election of 1876* (New York: Simon and Schuster, 2003), and Michael Les Benedict, "Southern Democrats in the Crisis of 1876–1877: A Reconsideration of *Reunion and Reaction*," *Journal of Southern History* 46 (November 1980): 489–524.

33. See Gregory Downs's survey of public sentiment in "Mexicanization," 399–402.

34. Downs, "Mexicanization," 400–402.

35. Morris, *Fraud of the Century*, 173–74.

36. The suggestion that Reconstruction "ended" at this point should not be taken to imply that Republicans discontinued their efforts to enforce civil and political rights in the South. Indeed, as Xi Wang demonstrates, the number of cases brought under the Enforcement Acts peaked in 1873 and declined thereafter, but they did not decline continuously: the number of cases brought under the acts declined in the mid- to late 1870s but then increased in the early 1880s, only to decline again by the mid-1880s. In fact, the number of cases brought in the North from 1885 to 1894 exceeded the number brought from the South. See *Trial of Democracy*, appendix 7. Also see Gillette, *Retreat from Reconstruction*, ch. 2.

37. The general in charge of his office, in fact, complained that McClellan and his supporters lacked the means to resist a Republican usurpation of power: "To do a thing of this kind without money is quite absurd." William F. Smith to McClellan, 30 December 1876, quoted in Downs, "Mexicanization," 402.

38. Benedict, "Southern Democrats in the Crisis of 1876–1877," 512.

39. On the influx of new immigrants and nativist reactions, see Kraut, *The Huddled Masses: The Immigrant in American Society, 1880–1921* (Wheeling, Ill.: Harlan Davidson, 1982), and Gwendolyn Mink, *Old Labor and New Immigrants in American Political Development: Union, Party, and State, 1875–1920* (Ithaca, N.Y.: Cornell University Press, 1986), ch. 2. On turn-of-the-century labor activism and violence, see Nell Irvin Painter, *Standing at Armageddon: The United States, 1877–1919* (New York: W. W. Norton, 2008), 117–23; Bensel, *Political Economy of American Industrialization*, 207–17, 247–53, 269–72.

40. A breed of publications equally committed to these causes also appeared on the political scene in the postwar years. These included such notables as the *Atlantic Monthly*, *Century*, *Forum*, *Harper's Weekly*, the *Nation*, and the *North American Review*. See Morton Keller, *Affairs of State: Public Life in Late Nineteenth Century America* (Cambridge, Mass.: Belknap Press of Harvard University Press, 1977), 290; Skowronek, *Building a New American State*, 43.

41. Rosenblum, *On the Side of the Angels*, 166–67.

42. James Sundquist, *Dynamics of the Party System* (Washington, D.C.: Brookings Institution Press, 1983), 154.

43. Daniel Bell, *Marxian Socialism in the United States* (Ithaca, N.Y.: Cornell University Press, 1996), 55; McCormick, *Party Period and Public Policy*, 174–78.

44. See Allen F. Davis, *Spearheads for Reform: The Social Settlements and the Progressive Movement, 1890–1914* (New York: Oxford University Press, 1967), 154–57, 197–201; Kraut, *Huddled Masses: The Immigrant in American Society, 1880–1921*, 143.

45. See John G. Sproat, *"The Best Men": Liberal Reformers in the Gilded Age* (New York: Oxford University Press, 1968), 50–55.

46. Michael Schudson, *Discovering the News: A Social History of American Newspapers* (New York: Basic Books, 1978), ch. 2.

47. The inclination to reform rather than shun or abolish parties was commonplace among liberal reformers. See Sproat, *"Best Men,"* 60–66. La Follette and Roosevelt, to be sure, were at odds over the requisites of party reform. La Follette embraced a Wilsonian vision of executive leadership (discussed in greater detail below), though he did not necessarily agree with Wilson's critique of the separation of powers. Roosevelt, for his part, distanced himself from Wilson's Anglophile preference for parliamentary government. On Roosevelt's repudiation of Wilson's notion of responsible party government, see Jean M. Yarbrough, *Theodore Roosevelt and the American Political Tradition* (Lawrence: University of Kansas Press, 2012), 97–104. For a discussion of La Follette's views on executive-centered reform, see Saladin M. Ambar, *How Governors Built the Modern American Presidency* (Philadelphia: University of Pennsylvania Press, 2012), 39–43.

48. *The Political Philosophy of Robert M. La Follette, as Revealed in His Speeches and Writings*, ed. Ellen Torelle (Madison, Wis.,: Robert M. La Follette, 1920), 53–54.

49. See ibid., 21–25, 45–47, 53–55.

50. "Peril in the Machine," in *The Gilded Age and the Progressive Era: A Documentary Reader*, ed. William A. Link and Susannah J. Link (Malden, Mass: John Wiley and Sons, 2012), 271, emphasis added.

51. Ibid., 270–71.

52. Perceptions, of course, are not the same as reality: party politicians were responsive when the public was able to credibly threaten legislators who opposed highly salient and popular reforms. See Sean M. Theriault, "Patronage, the Pendleton Act, and the Power of the People," *Journal of Politics* 65 (February 2003): 50–68.

53. There were, to be sure, some voices of reform who hoped to abolish the parties— at least at the state and municipal levels of government. For a discussion of Albert Stickney, Charles C. P. Clark, Samuel E. Moffett, and James S. Brown, critics who called for the abolition of parties, see McCormick, *Party Period and Public Policy*, 228–59. McCormick acknowledges that these figures, who are not well known today, were not widely recognized even in their own day, ibid., 230.

54. Shefter, *Political Parties and the State*, 77. For an insightful analysis of the Progressives' reformist outlook and the difficulties reformers confronted as they sought to institutionalize new modes of governance, see James Morone, *Democratic Wish*, 97–128. Also see Milkis, *Political Parties and Constitutional Government*, ch. 3, and Richard Hofstadter, *The Age of Reform: From Bryan to F.D.R.* (New York: Vintage, 1955), 174–214.

55. For a survey of the new generation of issues that cropped up in the late nineteenth century, see Robert H. Wiebe, *The Search for Order, 1877–1920* (New York: Hill and Wang, 1967), ch. 7.

56. On the timing and impact of the professionalization of social science in the United States, see Robert Adcock, *Liberalism and the Emergence of American Political Science: A Transatlantic Tale* (Oxford: Oxford University Press, 2014); Thomas Haskell, *The Emergence of Professional Social Science: The American Social Science*

Association and the Nineteenth-Century Crisis of Authority (Urbana: University of Illinois Press, 1977); Dorothy Ross, *The Origins of American Social Science* (Cambridge: Cambridge University Press, 1991).

57. Wilson, *Constitutional Government in the United States* (New York: Columbia University Press, 1908), 217. For a helpful discussion of the approach adopted toward parties by the first generation of political scientists, see Epstein, *Parties in the American Mold*, 24–28.

58. James Bryce, *Modern Democracies* (New York: Macmillan, 1921), 2: 43.

59. Henry Jones Ford, *The Rise and Growth of American Politics: A Sketch of Constitutional Development* (New York: Macmillan, 1898), 306.

60. Ford, *Rise and Growth of American Politics*, 215.

61. Quoted in Ford, *Rise and Growth of American Politics*, 303.

62. Ibid. That parties could inflame sectional divisions, a fact he clearly acknowledged in this passage, did not appear to qualify his view that parties were fundamentally harmless.

63. Ibid., 304.

64. Bryce, *Modern Democracies*, 2: 44.

65. Ford, *Rise and Growth of American Politics*, 302.

66. Herbert Croly, *Progressive Democracy* (New York: Macmillan, 1914), 79; see also Croly, *The Promise of American Life* (1909; New York: Macmillan, 1910), 323.

67. James Bryce, *The American Commonwealth* (1893; New York: Macmillan, 1919), 2: 21–22; A. Lawrence Lowell, *Public Opinion and Popular Government* (New York: Longmans, Green, 1913), 78–79, 118–20. The contrast between the American system of separated powers and the British system of parliamentary government is an organizing theme of Wilson's *Congressional Government* (1885; Boston: Houghton, Mifflin, 1887).

68. Herbert Agar, *The Price of Union* (Boston: Houghton Mifflin, 1950), 689. Also see Edward C. Banfield, "In Defense of the American Party System," in *Political Parties, U.S.A.*, ed. Robert A. Goldwin (Rand McNally, 1961), 21–39. For assessments of the integrative role that parties have played in the American political system, see Theodore J. Lowi, "Party, Policy, and Constitution in America," 238–76; Skowronek, *Building a New American State*, 26.

69. Quoted in Keller, *Affairs of State*, 271. See also Bryce, *Modern Democracies*, 2: 38.

70. Wilson, *Constitutional Government*, 214.

71. Ibid., 46.

72. Ibid., 221.

73. The work that best reflects Wilson's early thought on the role of party in American government is *Congressional Government*.

74. Wilson, *Congressional Government*, 92.

75. Ibid., 324.

76. Ibid., 92.

77. Ibid., 79, 81.

78. For a similar point applied instead to state and local bosses, see Croly, *Promise of American Life*, 125.

79. Wilson, *Congressional Government*, 284, emphasis in original.

80. Austin Ranney, *The Doctrine of Responsible Party Government: Its Origins and Present State* (Westport, Conn.: Greenwood, 1982), 29–30.

81. Woodrow Wilson, *Constitutional Government*, 220.

82. Jeffrey K. Tulis, *The Rhetorical Presidency* (Princeton, N.J.: Princeton University Press, 1987), 128–34. *Constitutional Government* was, in fact, the first major academic work to construct what Terri Bimes and Stephen Skowronek term the "bifurcated developmental frame" of presidential history, a periodization scheme that distinguished between the original and constitutional leadership of the nineteenth century and the modern opinion leadership of the twentieth. This distinction is the hallmark of the conventional wisdom concerning Wilson's understanding of presidential history. Bimes and Skowronek use the two histories Wilson authored, *Division and Reunion, 1829–1889* (Longmans, Green, 1893) and a five-volume series entitled *A History of the American People* (New York: Harper and Brothers, 1902), to argue that Wilson distanced himself from the traditional-modern distinction once he undertook a serious investigation of American presidential history. As Wilson confessed, "I wrote the history of the United States in order to learn it." Terri Bimes and Stephen Skowronek, "Woodrow Wilson's Critique of Popular Leadership: Reassessing the Modern-Traditional Divide in Presidential History," *Polity* 29 (1996): 32–33, 35, 40. For a thoughtful analysis that challenges scholarly assumptions about what it means for a president to be "modern," see Daniel P. Klinghard, "Grover Cleveland, William McKinley, and the Emergence of the President as Party Leader," *Presidential Studies Quarterly* 35 (December 2005): 736–60. For an analysis of Wilson's attempt as president to institutionalize the notion of party government he contemplated as a scholar, see Daniel D. Stid, *The President as Statesman: Woodrow Wilson and the Constitution* (Lawrence: University of Kansas Press, 1998), ch. 6.

83. Woodrow Wilson, *Constitutional Government*, 59.

84. Ibid., 75.

85. Tulis, *Rhetorical Presidency*; also see Tulis, "The Two Constitutional Presidencies," in *The Presidency and the Political System*, ed. Michael Nelson (Washington, D.C.: Congressional Quarterly, 1990), 85–115.

86. Quoted in Ceaser, *Presidential Selection*, 190, emphasis in original.

87. As Ceaser noted, party, for Wilson, was secondary to leadership: "Wilson molded his view of parties to fit his view of political leadership; the party system was the means and leadership the end." *Presidential Selection*, 197.

88. Ibid., 191.

89. Wilson, *Constitutional Government*, 38. He repeated this same view as late as 1915, after World War I broke out in Europe (see below).

90. Wilson, *Constitutional Government*, 38.

91. *Gitlow v. New York*, 268 U.S. 673 (1925).

92. Bimes and Skowronek argue that Wilson's concept of interpretation was less of a methodology to guide the expression of the public's will and more of a pretext for infusing the patrician, elitist values of the educated class into public discourse. "Woodrow Wilson's Critique of Popular Leadership," 48. Ceaser points out, however, that his notion of statesmanship—"popular statesmanship"—as Wilson called it, was very democratic for his time. *Presidential Selection*, 182.

93. Wilson, *Constitutional Government*, 220.

94. Ford, *Rise and Growth of American Politics*, 327.

95. A. Lawrence Lowell, *Essays on Government* (Boston: Houghton, Mifflin, 1889), 5. For an extended critique of Wilson's *Congressional Government*, see Lowell, *Essays on Government*, 46–59.

96. Ibid., 107–8.

97. Bryce, *Modern Democracies*, 2: 114–15. Lowell used the distinction between "horizontal" and "vertical" partisan cleavages in the opposite way, equating horizontal distinctions with class divisions. His meaning, however, was the same: "So long . . . as party lines are vertical, popular government is on a sound basis. But if all the rich men, or all the educated men, are grouped together, the state is in peril; and if the party lines become really horizontal, democracy is on the high road to class tyranny, which leads, as history proves, to a dictatorship." A. Lawrence Lowell, *Governments and Parties in Continental Europe* (Boston: Houghton, Mifflin, 1896) 2: 66.

98. S. K. Stevens, "The Election of 1896 in Pennsylvania," *Pennsylvania History* 4 (1937): 67. Stevens quoted in Elizabeth Sanders, *Roots of Reform: Farmers, Workers, and the American State, 1877–1917* (Chicago: University of Chicago Press, 1999), 139.

99. See Sundquist, *Dynamics*, 155–57.

100. Quoted in C. Vann Woodward, "The Populist Heritage and the Intellectual," *American Scholar* 29 (Winter 1959–60): 68–69.

101. Ibid., 69.

102. Quoted in Walter Dean Burnham, "The System of 1896: An Analysis," in Kleppner et al., *Evolution of American Electoral Systems*, 162. On the panic that overtook conservative elites, see Sproat, *"Best Men,"* ch. 8; Wiebe, *Search for Order*, 103–4.

103. For helpful analyses of the election, see Sanders, *Roots of Reform*, 138–47; Sundquist, *Dynamics*, 155–59, 162–65; Samuel T. McSeveney, *The Politics of Depression: Political Behavior in the Northeast, 1893–1896* (New York: Oxford University Press, 1972), 163–221.

104. Sundquist, *Dynamics*, 157.

105. See, for example, Sundquist, *Dynamics*, ch. 7; Walter Dean Burnham, "Periodization Schemes and 'Party Systems': The 'System of 1896' as a Case in Point," *Social Science History* 10 (1986): 263–313; Joel H. Silbey, "Beyond Realignment and Realignment Theory: American Political Eras, 1789–1989," in *The End of Realignment? Interpreting American Electoral Eras*, ed. Byron E. Shafer (Madison: University of Wisconsin Press, 1991), ch. 1. For an insightful critique of the realignment literature,

see David Mayhew, *Electoral Realignments: A Critique of An American Genre* (New Haven, Conn.: Yale University Press, 2002).

106. Sundquist, *Dynamics*, 155.

107. On the Populists' antistatism, see Sanders, *Roots of Reform*.

108. Croly, *Progressive Democracy*, 3.

109. Wilson, *Congressional Government*, 282–83. Also see Wilson, *Constitutional Government*, 199–200.

110. See John Milton Cooper, *The Vanity of Power: American Isolationism and the First World War, 1914–1917* (Westport, Conn.: Greenwood, 1969), 98, 220–29; Paul L. Murphy, *World War I and the Origin of Civil Liberties in the United States* (New York: Norton, 1979), 53; C. Roland Marchand, *The American Peace Movement and Social Reform, 1898–1918* (Princeton, N.J.: Princeton University Press, 1973), 97–98, 177.

111. A hyphenate was an immigrant or a descendant of an immigrant who linked his or her American identity with the nationality of the native homeland. This expression took on a pejorative connotation in this period, especially as applied to German Americans and Irish Americans. Murphy, *World War I and the Origin of Civil Liberties*, 29 n. 39.

112. Third Annual Message to Congress, 7 December 1915, in *The Public Papers of Woodrow Wilson*, ed. Ray Stannard Baker and William E. Dodd (New York: Harper and Brothers, 1925) 3: 423–24. On his view that the "hyphenates" had come under the influence of German war propaganda, see Flag Day Address, 14 June 1917, ibid., 5: 65–66. Wilson went to great lengths to ensure that the Democratic party, his party, was unwaveringly committed to the national interest above any ethnic bonds some Democratic party members may have to the combatants. In this spirit, he pushed strongly in 1916 for a plank on "Americanism" in the national party platform. This provision announced, "We . . . condemn as subversive to this Nation's unity and integrity, and as destructive of its welfare, the activities and designs of every group or organization, political or otherwise, that has for its object the advancement of the interest of a foreign power, whether such object is promoted by intimidating the government, a political party, or representatives of the people, or which is calculated and tends to divide our people into antagonistic groups and thus to destroy that complete agreement and solidarity of the people and that unity of sentiment and purpose so essential to the perpetuity of the Nation and its free institutions." *National Party Platforms*, ed. Donald Bruce Johnson (Urbana: University of Illinois Press, 1978), 195.

113. Address to the Daughters of the American Revolution, 11 October 1915, in *Public Papers of Woodrow Wilson*, Baker and Dodd, 3: 380.

114. Address to the American Electric Railway Association, 29 January 1915, in *Public Papers of Woodrow Wilson*, Baker and Dodd, 3: 265–66.

115. The CPI was created on 14 April 1917. Harry N. Scheiber, *The Wilson Administration and Civil Liberties, 1917–1921* (Ithaca, N.Y.: Cornell University Press, 1960), 15–16, 21. For a helpful discussion of the climate of political repression during World

War I, see Seymour Martin Lipset and Gary Marks, *It Didn't Happen Here: Why Socialism Failed in the United States* (New York: W. W. Norton, 2000), ch. 7.

116. Title I, sec. 3, U.S. *Statutes at Large* 40 (1917): 219.

117. Title XII, sec. 2, U.S. *Statutes at Large* 40 (1917): 230.

118. For a discussion of the regulation of the mail, see Scheiber, *Wilson Administration*, ch. 3.

119. U.S. *Statutes at Large* 40 (1918): 553.

120. 56 *Cong. Rec.* 4783 (1918). Quoted in Stone, *Perilous Times*, 186.

121. Quoted in Scheiber, *Wilson Administration*, 24.

122. U.S. *Statutes at Large* 40 (1918): 1012.

123. Quoted in Scheiber, *Wilson Administration*, 53, 55.

124. Ibid., 57.

125. Quoted in Cooper, *Warrior and the Priest*, 264.

126. The inclination to avert one's eyes from the struggle for civil rights was even rationalized as a patriotic good. The restoration of states' rights—the institutional prerequisite for white supremacist violence—was taken by many to be a signal of a long overdue sectional reconciliation, one that would lay the groundwork for a new spirit of national community. See Rogan Kersh, *Dreams of a More Perfect Union*, 224–27, 240–41.

127. See A. Lawrence Lowell, *Public Opinion and Popular Government* (London: Longmans, Green, 1913), 37, 39.

Epilogue. Party Legitimacy, Then and Now

1. William Preston Jr., *Aliens and Dissenters: Federal Suppression of Radicals, 1903–1933* (Cambridge, Mass.: Harvard University Press, 1963); Lipset and Marks, *It Didn't Happen Here*, ch. 7.

2. Steven J. Rosenstone, Roy L. Behr, and Edward H. Lazarus, *Third Parties in America* (Princeton, N.J.: Princeton University Press, 1996), ch. 3; J. David Gillespie, *Politics at the Periphery: Third Parties in Two-Party America* (Columbia: University of South Carolina Press, 1993), ch. 2. On the nineteenth-century conception of third parties as "antiparties," more akin to social movements than to traditional major party organizations, see Mark Voss-Hubbard, "The 'Third-Party Tradition' Reconsidered: Third Parties and American Public Life, 1830–1900," *Journal of American History* 86 (June 1999): 124, 121–50.

3. Richard Bensel, "The American Ballot Box: Law, Identity, and the Polling Place in the Mid-Nineteenth Century," *Studies in American Political Development* 17 (Spring 2003): 7–9.

4. Alternatively, a major party could opt to nominate a minor party candidate or set of candidates. One need not even think of candidates as belonging to one party or the other: if they chose to do so, multiple parties could convene and decide on mutually agreeable candidates.

5. Republicans, as a result, were particularly hostile to fusion laws. Peter H. Argersinger, "'A Place on the Ballot': Fusion Politics and Antifusion Laws," *American Historical Review* 85 (April 1980): 287–306.

6. The Australian ballot created a unique opportunity for the two major parties that prevailed at the time—the Democrats and the Republicans—to entrench their positions in the electoral arena. Lisa Disch aptly likens this episode to a power play in hockey: in her description, the introduction of the Australian ballot represented an opportunity within the terms of the political game to change the rules of the political game itself. Disch, *Tyranny*, 46–48. Whether or not the new ballot system was put in place to shift the balance of power between the major and minor parties is unclear. The dominant motive, no doubt, was to clean up the rampant corruption that prevailed at polling places across the country. For a debate over whether this reform was also intended to shift the balance of electoral power among the two major parties in favor of the Republicans, see Walter Dean Burnham, "The Changing Shape of the American Political Universe," *American Political Science Review* 59 (1965): 7–28; Jerrold G. Rusk, "Comment: The American Electoral Universe: Speculation and Evidence," *American Political Science Review* 68 (1974): 1028–49; Walter Dean Burnham, "Rejoinder to 'Comments' by Philip Converse and Jerrold Rusk," *American Political Science Review* 68 (September 1974): 1050–57. Setting aside the matter of what advocates of the Australian ballot intended to accomplish, Peter Argersinger persuasively demonstrates that antifusion laws were deliberately supported by Republicans to marginalize third-party challengers. Gilded Age Republicans, eager to prevent Democrats and minor parties from cooperating at the polls, were largely responsible for the proliferation of antifusion laws in states across the country. Argersinger, "'Place on the Ballot.'"

7. Howard A. Scarrow, "Duverger's Law, Fusion and the Decline of American 'Third' Parties," *Western Political Quarterly* 39 (1986): 638–39; Argersinger, "'Place on the Ballot'" 287–306. On the proliferation of ballot access rules in the 1890s and thereafter, see Rosenstone et al., *Third Parties in America*, 19–25. On the courts' treatment of ballot access and antifusion laws in the 1980s and 1990s, see Richard L. Hasen, "Entrenching the Duopoly: Why the Supreme Court Should Not Allow the States to Protect the Democrats and Republicans from Political Competition," *Supreme Court Review* 1997 (1997): 331–71.

8. It was fairly common, for example, for states to adopt rules that automatically allocated lines on the ballot to (major) parties that received a specified percentage of the vote in the past election cycle. Those parties that failed to achieve this threshold had to expend often limited resources to petition for a line on the ballot. It was also common for states to demand expensive fees to process these petitions. For a helpful survey of ballot access restrictions in place in the early 1940s, see American Civil Liberties Union, *Minority Parties on the Ballot: A Survey of Restrictions on Minority Parties, Together with Recommended Legislation* (New York: American Civil Liberties Union, 1943). These restrictions are still quite common. See Rosenstone et al., *Third Parties in America*, 19–25.

9. Disch, *Tyranny*, 8–11; Sundquist, *Dynamics*, 155.

10. E. Pendleton Herring, *The Politics of Democracy: American Parties in Action* (New York: Rinehart, 1940), 181–82; Disch, *Tyranny*, 169 n. 97. The proposition that pragmatic governing responsibility is most effectively promoted by two-party competition is advanced, most prominently, in the American Political Science Association report on political parties. Committee on Political Parties, American Political Science Association, "Toward a More Responsible Two-Party System," *American Political Science Review* 1 (1950): 44.

11. Perhaps the most noteworthy essay advancing the notion that American parties have, since the Jacksonian era, been fundamentally conservative and establishmentarian in their orientation is Lowi's "Party, Policy, and Constitution in America," 238–76. Also see Theodore J. Lowi, "Toward a Responsible Three-Party System: Plan or Obituary?" in *The State of the Parties: The Changing Role of Contemporary American Parties*, ed. John C. Green and Daniel M. Shea (Lanham, Md.: Rowman and Littlefield, 1999), 171–89. For a more polemical critique of the American party system from the Left, see the commentary of New Deal–era Socialist party leader Norman Thomas, *Socialism Re-Examined* (New York: W. W. Norton, 1963), ch. 8. A more recent and theoretically sophisticated view from the Left is advanced by Disch in *Tyranny*.

12. Committee on Political Parties, "Toward a More Responsible Two-Party System," 16, emphasis in original.

13. Ibid., 96, emphasis in original.

14. Disch, *Tyranny*, especially 67–73 and 97–106.

15. The view that two-partyism was strategically essential when confronted with a totalitarian enemy was of apiece with the Cold War consensus inclination to minimize partisan "extremes." See, for example, Walter Berns, "Reform of the American Party System," in *Political Parties, U.S.A.*, ed. Robert A. Goldwin (Chicago: Rand McNally, 1961), 41, 54–55; Banfield, "In Defense of the American Party System," in Goldwin, *Political Parties, U.S.A.*, 23. The authors of the APSA report were also quite wary of partisan extremes and situated their concerns in the context of Cold War policy challenges. See Committee on Political Parties, "Toward a More Responsible Two-Party System," 92–93, 95–96. Of the Western European democracies with "irresponsible" or "unstable" multiparty systems, postwar Italy and France defined the type. See Giovanni Sartori, "European Political Parties: The Case of Polarized Pluralism," in *Political Parties and Political Development*, ed. Joseph LaPalombara and Myron Weiner (Princeton, N.J.: Princeton University Press, 1966), 137–76.

16. This interpretation is adapted from Lisa Jane Disch's incisive study of the political scientific ideas that underwrote the discipline's faith in the two-party system. See Disch, *Tyranny*, ch. 4.

17. Committee on Political Parties, "Toward a More Responsible Two-Party System," 18, emphasis in original.

18. To be sure, much depends on how one chooses to evaluate partisan diversity. Though a full vetting goes beyond the scope of this study, one may well argue that, thanks to the institution of the direct primary, the American party system provides voters with a very wide range of choices. On the institutional development of the direct primary system, see Ware, *American Direct Primary*. For an analysis of the presidential primary system and an argument that party insiders wield an outsized influence on the nomination process, see Marty Cohen, David Karol, Hans Noel, and John Zaller, *The Party Decides: Presidential Nominations Before and After Reform* (Chicago: University of Chicago Press, 2008).

19. For a sample of some of the more thoughtful commentary on the subject, see Peter Orszag, "Too Much of a Good Thing," *New Republic*, 6 October 2011; Francis Fukuyama, "American Power Is Waning Because Washington Won't Stop Quarreling," Newrepublic.com, 10 March 2014, accessed 8 May 2014; Mann and Ornstein, *It's Even Worse Than It Looks*.

20. On the impact of polarization on Congress's productivity, see Sara A. Binder, "The Dynamics of Legislative Gridlock, 1947–96," *American Political Science Review* 93 (1999): 519–34; Sarah A. Binder, *Stalemate: Causes and Consequences of Legislative Gridlock* (Washington, D.C.: Brookings Institution Press, 2003); Lawrence C. Dodd and Scot Schraufnagel, "Party Polarization and Policy Productivity in Congress: From Harding to Obama," in *Congress Reconsidered*, 10th ed., ed. Lawrence C. Dodd and Bruce I. Oppenheimer (Los Angeles: Sage, 2013), 437–63. On policy stalemate and polarization as a source of the American public's frustration with the political process, see John R. Hibbing and Elizabeth Theiss-Morse, *Stealth Democracy: Americans' Beliefs About How Government Should Work* (Cambridge: Cambridge University Press, 2002).

21. Chris McGreal, "War Breaks Out Between Fox News and the Obama Administration," *Theguardian.com*, 13 October 2009, accessed 21 April 2014.

22. Jonathan Weisman, "Issa Hands Democrats Weapon to Use on Him," *New York Times*, 7 March 2014, A13.

23. See Nicholas Toloudis, "The Golden Dawn: The Financial Crisis and Greek Fascism's New Day," *New Labor Forum* 23 (2014): 38–43; Antonis A. Ellinas, "The Rise of Golden Dawn: The New Face of the Far Right in Greece," *South European Society and Politics* 18 (2013): 1–22. For a helpful discussion of the concept of an "anti-system party," see Giovanni Capoccia, "Anti-System Parties: A Conceptual Reassessment," *Journal of Theoretical Politics* 14 (2002): 9–35.

24. See Kristen Ghodsee, "Left Wing, Right Wing, Everything: Xenophobia, Neo-Totalitarianism, and Populist Politics in Bulgaria," *Problems of Post-Communism* 55 (May–June 2008): 26–39; Gergely Karácsony and Dániel Róna "The Secret of Jobbik: Reasons Behind the Rise of the Hungarian Radical Right," *Journal of East European and Asian Studies* 2 (2011): 61–92 and Andras Biro Nagy, Tamas Boros, and Zoltan Vasali, "More Radical than the Radicals: The Jobbik Party in International Comparison,"

in *Right-wing Extremism in Europe: Country Analyses, Counter-Strategies, and Labor-Market Oriented Exit Strategies*, ed. Ralf Melzer and Sebastian Serafin (Berlin: Friedrich Ebert Stiftung, 2013), 229–253.

25. Mark Landler, "Social Democrats Defeat Governing Party in Austria," *New York Times*, 2 October 2006; Joshua Tucker, "The 2013 Austrian Elections: Standing Still Despite Change?" *Washington Post*, 30 September 2013.

26. Ian Traynor, "Front National Wins European Parliamentary Elections in France," *Theguardian.com*, 25 May 2014, accessed 21 June 2014. To be clear, by calling attention to the incidence of extremism in a selection of European multiparty systems, I do not mean to suggest that multiparty systems are incapable of moderating or containing political radicalism. There are, in fact, ways in which multiparty governing arrangements may moderate or at least contain the kind of radicalism described above. Sartori addresses this problem with his distinction between cases of moderate pluralist and polarized pluralist multiparty systems. Sartori, "European Political Parties: The Case of Polarized Pluralism."

27. See Stephan Sonnenberg, "When Justice Becomes the Victim: The Quest for Justice After the 2002 Violence in Gujarat," International Human Rights and Conflict Resolution Clinic, Stanford Law School, Stanford, Calif., May 2014. Available at http://humanrightsclinic.law.stanford.edu/project/the-quest-for-justice/; accessed 24 March 2015.

28. In the United States, nativist, ethno-racial appeals are relatively commonplace in Republican party primary elections that take place in "red" or "purple" states. When addressing a small subset of the population, some nativist American politicians use rhetoric that is comparable to that wielded by their nativist counterparts in Europe and elsewhere. Yet when addressing a wider audience—as American politicians must in order to win in general elections—candidates who traded in ethno-racial appeals are pressed to mute this divisive rhetoric and sound more inclusive themes. Though this matter reaches beyond the scope of the present study, one might conjecture that American electoral institutions discourage the kind of crass, openly discriminatory rhetoric that is publicly displayed during general elections in other polities.

29. See, for example, Evan Bayh, "Why I'm Leaving the Senate," *New York Times*, 21 February 2010, WK9; Lea Berman, "Fewer Dinners Mean Meaner Politics," *Washington Post*, 5 August 2011. Scholars tend to be less nostalgic. Amy Gutmann and Dennis Thompson, for example, link the emergence of an "uncompromising mindset" with the rise of what political scientists have called the "permanent campaign." Amy Gutmann and Dennis Thompson, *The Spirit of Compromise: Why Governing Demands It and Campaigning Undermines It* (Princeton, N.J.: Princeton University Press, 2012), 1–24. On the idea of the permanent campaign, see Norman Ornstein and Thomas Mann, eds., *The Permanent Campaign and Its Future* (Washington, D.C.: American Enterprise Institute, 2000). Mann and Ornstein, in their recent work *It's Even Worse Than It Looks*, feature a very different sort of nostalgia: it is a longing for a more ideologically moderate Republican party. They argue that dysfunction in Con-

gress should be attributed, not to polarization per se, but to "asymmetric polarization," that has seen the Republican party shift its ideological and policy position significantly to the right (while the Democratic party has remained relatively stable). Mann and Ornstein, *It's Even Worse Than It Looks*, 51–58. For additional evidence and analysis supporting the asymmetric polarization claim, see Matt Grossmann and David A. Hopkins, "Ideological Republicans and Group Interest Democrats: The Asymmetry of American Party Politics," *Perspectives on Politics* 13 (March 2015): 119–139 and Michael Barber and Nolan McCarty, "Causes and Consequences of Polarization," in *Negotiating Agreement in Politics: Report of the Task Force on Negotiating Agreement in Politics*, ed. Jane Mansbridge and Cathie Jo Martin (Washington, D.C.: American Political Science Association, 2013), 19–53. For an illuminating discussion of the historical antecedents and behavioral dynamics that gave rise to today's polarized and evenly divided two-party system, see John Aldrich, "Did Hamilton, Jefferson, and Madison 'Cause' the U.S. Government Shutdown? The Institutional Path from an Eighteenth Century Republic to a Twenty-First Century Democracy," *Perspectives on Politics* 13 (March 2015): 7–23.

30. For an insightful summary analysis of this fraught period, see Fredrik Logevall, "The Vietnam War," in *The American Congress*, ed. Julian E. Zelizer (Boston: Houghton Mifflin, 2004), 584–600.

31. See David B. Filvaroff and Raymond E. Wolfinger, "The Origin and Enactment of the Civil Rights Act of 1964," in *Legacies of the 1964 Civil Rights Act*, ed. Bernard Grofman (Charlottesville: University of Virginia Press, 2000), 9–32; Charles Whalen and Barbara Whalen, *The Longest Debate: A Legislative History of the 1964 Civil Rights Act* (Washington, D.C.: Seven Locks, 1985).

32. This price is not acknowledged in Gutmann and Thompson's otherwise insightful book *The Spirit of Compromise*. To their credit, they explain that "our defense of compromise in democratic governance is consistent with—indeed requires—a vigorous and often contentious politics in which citizens press strongly held principles and mobilize in support of boldly proclaimed causes." *Spirit of Compromise*, 4. Yet the cases they select to illustrate their argument about the attributes of the "uncompromising mindset" and the role the permanent campaign played in the development of this frame of mind tells a different story. They focus their analysis on a comparison of the Tax Reform Act of 1986 and the Affordable Care Act of 2010. The comparison might have looked very different, however, had they looked, for example, at the Civil Rights Act of 1964, or, for that matter, at past attempts to put in place a system of universal (or near universal) health care. The ethos of compromise broke down when these policy questions (civil rights and national health care) were placed on the national agenda; these episodes, moreover, took place well before the emergence of the permanent campaign. On past efforts to institutionalize universal health care in the United States, see Jacob Hacker, *The Divided Welfare State: The Battle over Public and Private Social Benefits in the United States* (Cambridge: Cambridge University Press, 2002), chs. 4 and 5.

33. Suspicion of this sort was taken for granted by a prior cohort of political scientists whose explanatory focus was not on politics per se, but on the absence of politics. See, for example, Matthew A. Crenson, *The Un-Politics of Air Pollution: A Study of Non-Decision-Making in the Cities* (Baltimore: Johns Hopkins University Press, 1971); John Gaventa, *Power and Powerlessness: Quiescence and Rebellion in an Appalachian Valley* (Urbana: University of Illinois Press, 1980).

34. See Robin Einhorn, "Slavery and the Politics of Taxation in the Early United States," *Studies in American Political Development* 14 (Fall 2000): 159.

35. See, for example, the discourse in Congress surrounding Henry Cabot Lodge's Elections Bill in 1890. Richard F. Bensel, *Sectionalism and American Political Development: 1880–1980* (Madison: University of Wisconsin Press, 1984), 75–88.

36. Joanne Freeman, "Dirty Nasty Politics in Early America," Santagata Lecture, Bowdoin College, Brunswick, Maine, 24 October 2012; for an analysis of the rituals of violence in Congress during the early national period, see Freeman's *Affairs of Honor: National Politics in the New Republic* (New Haven, Conn.: Yale University Press, 2001). See more generally Donald C. Bacon, "Violence in Congress," in *The Encyclopedia of the United States Congress*, ed. Donald C. Bacon, Roger H. Davidson, and Morton Keller (New York: Simon and Schuster, 1995), 4: 2062–66.

37. To be clear, my purpose here is to describe the ways in which public expectations concerning the process of public deliberation have changed. One can make this case without condoning (in Congressman Joe Wilson's case) the act of shouting "liar" or any other term of abuse during a State of the Union address.

38. Both parties are heavily dependent on a wide range of private business interests for support. For a survey of the sources of campaign finance support enjoyed by the two parties broken down by industry sector, see *Opensecrets.org/industries*, accessed 24 June 2014. On the rightward drift of both parties in the post–World War II era on trade policy (favoring trade liberalization) and fiscal policy (toward fiscal conservatism for the Democrats and supply-side economics for the Republicans), see David Karol, *Party Position Change in American Politics: Coalition Management* (Cambridge: Cambridge University Press, 2009), chs. 2 and 5. For a similar interpretation of the parties' shifting positions on fiscal policy, see Catherine E. Rudder, "The Politics of Taxing and Spending in Congress: Ideas, Strategy, and Policy," in *Congress Reconsidered*, ed. Lawrence C. Dodd and Bruce I. Oppenheimer (Washington, D.C.: Congressional Quarterly Press, 2005), 319–42.

39. To be clear, they stand at opposing ends of this continuum. According to the metrics commonly employed by political scientists, the parties in government are more ideologically divided today than they have been in generations. Poole and Rosenthal, *Ideology and Congress*, 104–10.

40. The American president is not wanting for authority to act in times of emergency. His authority to act on his own in various realms of policy—not just in the arenas of foreign policy and national security—has expanded significantly over the course of American political history. See Andrew Rudalevige, *The New Imperial Pres-*

idency: Renewing Presidential Power After Watergate (Ann Arbor: University of Michigan Press, 2005).

41. James Q. Wilson, "How Divided Are We?" Commentarymagazine.com, 1 February 2006, accessed 24 June 2014. A similar point was stated less delicately by reactionary figures in government and in the media. See, for example, Dinesh D' Souza, *The Enemy at Home: The Cultural Left and Its Responsibility for 9/11* (New York: Broadway Books, 2007).

42. To be sure, the impact that partisan division in the United States had on the perceptions of America's enemies and allies is itself open to debate. On the strategic challenges that democracies face when they are engaged in small wars against determined insurgencies, see Gil Merom, *How Democracies Lose Small Wars* (Cambridge: Cambridge University Press, 2003).

43. On the implications of image making as a U.S. foreign policy goal, see Hannah Arendt, "Lying in Politics: Reflections on the Pentagon Papers," in *Crises of the Republic* (San Diego: Harcourt Brace, 1972), 1–47.

44. Madison to Thomas Jefferson, 13 May 1798, in *Letters and Other Writings of James Madison*, 2: 141.

INDEX

ACKNOWLEDGMENTS

This book has taken some time to gestate, and I have incurred a number of debts along the way. At Cornell University, Richard Bensel, Jason Frank, Isaac Kramnick, Jeremy Rabkin (now at George Mason University School of Law), Elizabeth Sanders, and Martin Shefter provided invaluable guidance and encouraged me to pursue my subject on my own terms. I am especially grateful to Ted Lowi for his steadfast support and for the example he set for me both as a teacher and as a scholar.

Bowdoin College and the Department of Government and Legal Studies provided vital institutional assistance as I began my career. As a group, the department faculty model an authentic spirit of academic pluralism; I owe them a debt of gratitude for supporting me as I followed my own intellectual path. Lynne Atkinson, the department's "listener in chief," has helped me with challenges both great and small. Ginny Hopcroft and Barbara Levergood at Hawthorne-Longfellow Library have helped me navigate the tangled web of documents published by the Government Printing Office. Charlie Allen, Nora Biette-Timmons, and Stephanie (Stevie) Lane offered valuable research assistance.

A number of colleagues at Bowdoin and beyond have read my work at various stages and generously offered their time and insight. They include Robert Adcock, Steve Engel, Mike Franz, David Hecht, Matt Klingle, Janet Martin, Steve Meardon, Stephen Mihm, Bruce Miroff, Chris Potholm, Brian Purnell, Patrick Rael, Meghan Roberts, Strother Roberts, Andy Rudalevige, Stephen Skowronek, and Dan Tichenor. Two close friends went well beyond the call of duty. Jason Opal and Nick Toloudis read the manuscript from beginning to end (and parts of it multiple times); they provided invaluable guidance from their own areas of expertise, early American history and comparative politics, respectively. Paul Hoffman, Belinda Kong, Rachel Sturman, and Hilary Thompson all read portions of the book and provided a constructive space for me to vent my frustrations with the writing process.

And a number of people at the University of Pennsylvania Press offered valuable assistance as I completed the project. Among them, Peter Agree and Rick Valelly deserve special praise: they insisted that they wanted me to "write the book that I wanted to write"—and they meant what they said. They also deserve thanks for finding two conscientious and knowledgeable readers who caught a number of argumentative ambiguities and helped me place this book on firmer footing.

Research for the book was generously supported by a fellowship from the American Council of Learned Societies (ACLS) and by funding from the Eisenhower Institute and the Center for the Study of the Presidency and Congress. The Academy of Political Science and the Center for the Study of the Presidency and Congress permitted me to use portions of work published in their journals. These are, respectively, "Rethinking the Development of Legitimate Party Opposition in the United States, 1793–1828," *Political Science Quarterly* 127 (Summer 2012): 263–87, and "Making Sense of Presidential Restraint: Foundational Arrangements and Executive Decision-Making Before the Civil War," *Presidential Studies Quarterly* 44 (March 2014): 27–49.

My family has been my most consistent source of support as this project has advanced. Debbie and Seth, Doug and Rosie provided vital emotional sustenance and moral support. Radha, Balaji, and Badri encouraged me from afar, sending their best wishes from different time zones.

My children, Anjali (now ten years old) and Isaac (now seven), grew up with this project. Both love to read and write books. I don't know if they'll enjoy this one, but they might. There are no preteen "Goddess Girl" characters with supernatural powers—but there is one "Little Magician" (one of Martin Van Buren's nicknames). Nor are there any descriptions of dinosaurs and their eating habits—though one might say that if *Tyrannosaurus rex* had ever taken a human form, it would closely approximate a character who appears in Chapter 4—Andrew Jackson.

No one has done more than Jayanthi to see this book to fruition. I am indebted to her for all the time she dedicated to the kids when she had her own writing to do and for the unconditional love she's given to me and to our children. This book is dedicated to my parents, Barbara and Carl Selinger, two people who have given me so much, and ask for so little in return.

LITTLE
DoLPHiN
RESCUE

tiger tales

5 River Road, Suite 128, Wilton, CT 06897
Published in the United States 2021
Originally published in Great Britain 2019
by the Little Tiger Group
Text copyright © 2019 Rachel Delahaye
Inside illustrations copyright © 2019 Jo Anne Davies at Artful Doodlers
Cover illustration copyright © 2019 Suzie Mason
ISBN-13: 978-1-68010-463-9
ISBN-10: 1-68010-463-2
Printed in the USA
STP/4800/0421/0721
All rights reserved
10 9 8 7 6 5 4 3 2

For more insight and activities, visit us at www.tigertalesbooks.com

LITTLE
DOLPHIN
RESCUE

by Rachel Delahaye

For Grace, who can't choose a favorite animal
but thinks it might be a dolphin
—Rachel

CONTENTS

Splash!

"Look! There's a sea monster in the swimming pool," said Emma.

"Nice try," laughed Callie. "But I don't believe you."

"You never fall for my pranks anymore," moaned Emma.

Callie and Emma were sitting on the edge of the pool, waiting for their swimming lesson. They dangled their legs in the water, swishing them backward and forward.

"Do you see that bug?" Emma said suddenly. "Over there. It's drowning!"

"There's no bug." Callie shook her head.

"This time I mean it, Callie! There is, honestly."

Callie sighed. Emma knew her so well—she knew that Callie would have to look, just in case it was true. Because if there was a bug and she let it drown, she would be upset. Callie loved all animals and wanted to be a vet when she grew up.

"Where is it, then?" Callie leaned forward. "Show me."

Emma put her hand in the pool, but instead of pointing out the beetle, she cupped up some water and threw it in Callie's face.

"Got you!" she shouted happily.

Callie shrieked. She was about to splash Emma back when their teacher blew his whistle. It was time for their lesson to begin. "I'll get you later!" she said with a giggle.

The girls lined up by the pool with the rest of the swimming class—

including their friends Maya, Ben, Denny, and Kevin—and Mr. Luck clapped his hands for attention. "Hello, everyone," he said.

"Hello, Mr. Luck!" The greeting echoed around the room.

"I'm sorry you haven't had a lesson for three weeks. It took longer than we thought to redecorate! But what do you think of the newly painted rec center?"

"That's awesome!" said Maya, pointing to a beach scene painted on the walls.

"Just wait until you see what's underwater at the deep end," Mr. Luck said with a wink. "Now, I have an announcement. We are starting an under-12 swim team, and we need a name. Give me your best ideas at the end of the lesson, and I'll choose a winner."

"What do we win?" asked Maya.

"Is it a tropical island vacation?" Emma squeezed Callie's arm and jumped up and down.

Mr. Luck laughed. "You'll have to wait and see!"

"Definitely a tropical vacation," Emma whispered in Callie's ear.

"As a special treat, it's a free-play lesson today. Help yourselves to inflatables, but don't forget to go for a swim in the deep end. I think you're going to like what you see!"

The children jumped into the pool. By the time Callie had adjusted the straps on her goggles, the entire shallow end was churned up with splashing. Emma had

found a giant doughnut and was floating
in the middle of the pool, as Ben and his
friends tried to flip her over.

"Help me, Callie!" Emma called,
kicking water in their faces.

Callie was tempted to join in with
Ben to pay Emma back for her trick,
but she wanted to check out Mr. Luck's
underwater surprise while the deep end
was quiet.

Callie was nervous about being out
of her depth, so she stayed close to the
side of the pool where she could grip
the edge if she needed to. When her feet
could no longer touch the bottom, she
put her face in the water....

Wow!

The walls of the deep end were
painted to look like a tropical reef.

There was coral, seaweed, and marine life like fish, octopuses, sea stars, and sharks. And it wasn't cartoony, like a lot of murals. In fact, with all the detail, it was easy to imagine that a real-life reef shark might suddenly appear....

Just then, a dark shape passed beneath her. Callie caught her breath and grabbed the edge of the pool. But when she looked down, she saw it wasn't a sea monster—it was Denny! What was he doing?

Denny was gliding along the bottom of the pool with his arms by his side and his legs together. He kicked them at the same time, as if he were flipping a tail! He looked very much at home against the backdrop of the reef. Callie kept holding the edge of the pool and waited for him to come up for air.

"Hey, Denny, can you teach me how to do that swimming stroke?"

"The dolphin kick? Sure, it's easy! Just keep your arms by your sides and your legs together. Roll your body from head to toe, and kick your feet together last. Oh, and don't forget to hold your breath!"

Denny disappeared back down to the bottom of the pool, and Callie took a moment to clean her goggles and think.

The water was deep and that scared
her, but if she stayed close to the side
of the pool, she'd be okay. She let
herself sink a little below the surface
and tried Denny's dolphin kick. But
although she thought she had followed
Denny's instructions, it was more of a
going-nowhere thrash than an elegant
dolphin swim!

"What am I doing wrong?" she asked
when Denny came up again.

"It works better if you go deeper."
Callie look worried, so Denny added,
"Follow me and you'll be fine. One,
two, three...."

They both took a deep breath and
swam down, using their arms to go
lower and lower. Once they were at
the bottom of the pool, Denny began

to roll his body, propelling himself
through the water with a final kick.
Callie soon got the hang of it, too.
Roll and kick, roll and kick! She even
started to feel at home in the water, as
if she were a sea creature herself.

Callie reached the back wall of the pool and came up for air, grinning. She had swum underwater for at least fifteen feet without panicking!

Denny popped up next to her. "You're a natural," he said.

"I am?" said Callie, unable to hide her pride.

"Yep. A pod of dolphins would be happy to hang out with you!"

"Callie!" shrieked Emma as Ben spun the doughnut around and around. "Come and get dizzy! It's fuuuuuun!"

Not as fun as swimming like a dolphin, Callie thought. She laughed at Emma, then ducked back underwater. With her feet flat against the wall, she pushed herself back down into the deep water, and Denny followed.

Rays from the ceiling lights pierced the water and sent reflections rippling across the mural. Callie imagined that it was all real—the eel in the coral, the sea stars on the rock, the shoal of blue and yellow fish. The more she thought, the clearer the pictures seemed, and the brighter they became. And then Callie stopped kicking. Was that shoal of fish actually moving? *Of course not*, she thought. It was just a trick of the light.

Then something swam alongside her. Denny? It glided by her with a flap of its enormous wings.

No, it wasn't Denny.

A Trip to Paradise

There was a manta ray in the swimming pool! Callie had to tell someone immediately. Surely *that* wasn't part of Mr. Luck's underwater surprise.

She put her feet on the bottom and realized she could stand up—she was no longer out of her depth. Had she swum all the way to the shallow end? Why was there sand beneath her feet? Callie was confused, especially as her goggles had misted up, and she couldn't see a thing.

"Mr. Luck?" she called, taking off her goggles and rubbing her eyes. As she said his name, she noticed something strange. Just a minute ago, the pool had sounded like a baboon party, and now it was silent. Did everyone leave?

When she could finally see, Callie couldn't believe her eyes. Yes, everyone *was* gone. Denny, Emma, Ben, Mr. Luck—the entire class! Even the pool was gone. Callie was now standing up to her waist in turquoise seawater by a white sandy beach.

"A tropical island?" Callie laughed. It was like a picture postcard, a place you only saw in expensive vacation brochures.... But what was she doing here? And how was she going to get back? Mr. Luck always did a head count at the end of the lesson, and he would be worried if she was missing.

Callie knelt down so she was completely underwater. There was nothing but crystal-clear water and shoals of fish in all different shapes and colors and patterns! Maybe she could spend a little more time here before trying to find her way back home....

The sun sparkles danced on the water, and Callie shielded her eyes so she could look around. There was no one on the beach, but there was a small building not far away. The owner would be able to tell her where she was.

Callie watched the pretty fish dart away to safety as she waded through the water. But they weren't the only pretty things at her feet. Scattered across the seabed were shells. They were so shiny and beautiful that they looked like jewels. Callie wanted to run her hands through them, like a pirate enjoying her treasure! As she reached down, her hand brushed against a large brown disc. It floated upward and then sank back down, landing on its other side.

The shell was as big as her hand and

looked like mother-of-pearl—silvery, with dashes of purple, green, and blue. The colors swirled together like a liquid rainbow. It was mesmerizing. As she walked toward the beach, she gazed at the seashell in her hand.

OUCH!

Callie's foot began to sting and throb. She must have cut it on something! Clutching her beautiful shell, she hobbled along the beach to the building she had seen, hoping there would be someone there who could help.

Izad's Fruit Shack was a tiny juice bar. It had a couple of tables and chairs on the sand and a hatch in the wall. Callie hopped forward and peered through the hatch.

"Hello? Is anyone there?"

A tall man rose from behind the counter with a sleepy smile. He wore a little straw hat, and around his neck hung a bunch of necklaces, some plain, some with painted beads.

"Izad at your service. Mango juice, coconut water, what would you like?"

"Hello, Izad. My name is Callie. I cut my foot in the water, and I was hoping you could help me."

Izad looked concerned. "Take a seat, and I'll be right there."

Callie sat, and Izad appeared with a medical bag and a bottle of water, which he poured over the cut to clean out the sand.

"Looks like a shell cut," he said. "Broken shells can be very nasty. But this isn't too deep." Callie winced as

18

Izad dabbed on some antiseptic. Then
he took out a bandage and stuck it on
top. "You'll be fine in no time," he said
with a huge smile.

"Thank you!" said Callie, and then
she remembered the beautiful shell.
"Oh, and could you tell me what kind
of shell this is?" she asked, showing him
her find.

"That's an abalone."

"*Ah-bah-lone-ee.*" Callie sounded it out.

"You're not going to keep it, are you?" Izad asked. Callie's face must have fallen because he wagged his finger. "What belongs to the sea must be returned to the sea. But you can take care of it while you're here. Have this."

Izad took off one of his plain string necklaces. He threaded it through a hole in the shell and then tied it around Callie's neck.

"You look like a proper tropical island girl now."

"Thank you, Izad," said Callie. "I promise I'll give it back to the sea when I leave."

"Thank *you*, Callie." Izad smiled. "Here on Payocos we take care of our precious

20

environment.
We live as part
of the island.
We don't
own it."

"I think your
island is the most
beautiful place I've
ever seen!"

"You haven't seen half of it yet!" said
Izad. He pointed out to sea. "Payocos
is surrounded by a ring of shallow coral
reef. It goes all the way from here to
Coral Point, over in the distance. We
call it the Blue Halo. Explore it, and
you'll see why we are so protective of it.
Now, wait here."

Izad disappeared and returned a
minute later with a yellow drink, a

snorkeling mask, and two small socks.

"Coconut and pineapple," he said as he handed her the drink. "A taste of Payocos just for you."

Callie took a sip and sighed. It was totally yummy!

"And here is a mask so you can see the reef better."

"Thank you! Those are funny flippers," said Callie, pointing at the socks.

"Not flippers. Flippers damage coral. These are reef slippers," Izad replied.

"Do they protect the coral from human germs?" asked Callie.

Izad tipped back his head and let out a deep laugh that made Callie want to laugh, too. "No. They're to keep your bandage from falling off!"

The Underwater Playground

Callie waded into the water with her new slippers and mask and looked back at Izad. He was standing on the beach with his hands on his hips and a big, friendly smile.

"You're going to love it!" he said, full of pride. "Payocos is very special. You'll see."

"Is it safe to swim?" asked Callie. She was worried that if she got out of her depth, there would be nothing to hang on to. She wasn't in a pool now.

"Inside the ring of coral, the water never gets too deep, so it's safe to swim there. On the other side of the reef—outside the Blue Halo where the water gets dark—that's deep. It's not dangerous, but if you're nervous, you should stay inside the reef."

Callie stepped farther into the crystal waters, feeling reassured by Izad's answer.

"Watch out for lions, zebras, and parrots!" Izad shouted.

What? Callie spun around.

Izad took one look at her face and burst out laughing. "They're types of fish!" he hooted, slapping his thigh. Then he wandered back to his juice bar, and Callie could still hear him laughing as she swam out into the Blue Halo.

24

Wearing Izad's mask, Callie put her head underwater. Wow! She could see everything so clearly—even groups of playful fish much farther out. Below her, hermit crabs scuttled across the sandy seabed, dragging their brightly colored houses behind them.

The farther Callie went out, the more the underwater landscape changed. There were rocks and different types of coral—some spread out like fans, and others clustered together like cauliflower. Bigger fish appeared with pouty lips and large eyes. Some had funny markings, and Callie laughed when she saw a group that looked as if they had angry eyebrows.

It was an underwater paradise, and this was only a small piece of it. The Blue Halo reef was vast. Callie continued swimming away from the island, spotting eels snooping in the rocks and sea stars the size of dinner plates. She even saw a puffer fish that had blown up like a balloon and was bobbing around like a spiky melon.

Just as Izad said—the reef was shallow

and safe. Even if Callie had a reason to be nervous, she was too distracted to worry. The colors and the creatures were breathtaking. Even the sounds were amazing—the gentle lapping of the water, the crackling as fish sucked up and spat out stones, the popping of air bubbles coming from holes in the rocks. And the clicking.

What *was* the clicking?

The water was getting a little deeper now, and the walls of coral were thicker, brighter, and teeming with life. The funny clicking noise was getting louder. Callie swam down a channel between the coral, just as something large was swimming up it. The thing was heading right toward her....

A shark? Callie's breath caught in her throat. There was nowhere to go, nothing to do except keep her face in the water so she could see what was coming. But then she recognized the swimming stroke.... Roll and kick, roll and kick. A dolphin!

It was only a little one—no bigger than a dog—with pretty stripes of black, gray, and white along the length of its body. When the dolphin got closer,

Callie reached out to touch it, but it dodged her hand, shot past her, and vanished into the coral. It emerged from another clump of coral and made its way toward her again. Then it rushed past her, vanished, and reappeared, over and over, clicking and squealing all the time. It reminded Callie of an excited child, and judging by the size of it, it had to be a baby.

When the dolphin swam past her
on its side, revealing the smile-shaped
curve of its mouth, Callie clapped. At
the sound, the dolphin slowed down.
It swam up to her. It looked curious.
Callie clapped her hands again, and the
dolphin bobbed its head.

You like that, don't you? Callie
thought. *Well, how about if I sing?*

Callie hummed a tune. It sounded
funny underwater, but the dolphin
seemed to like it. Now it came so
close that Callie could have touched it
if she wanted to, but she didn't. Instead,
she made more sounds, and the dolphin
began to inspect her—it looked right
into her mask! Then a sudden noise
caused it to back away. Callie heard
it, too. A chorus of whistles, so high-

pitched they almost hurt her ears. The dolphin nodded. Then it was gone, "dolphin kicking" back down the watery channel and out of sight.

Callie raised her head above the water. She was close to the outside edge of the Blue Halo. Over the next boundary of pale coral was the dark blue sea. And bursting out of it, spinning once, twice, three times before crashing back down, was the little dolphin. It did it again— spinning as if it were in a gymnastics show, falling with a splash back into the water.

It was putting on a display for her! As it leaped high once again, Callie spotted a single groove on the dolphin's underside. She knew, from her *World of Dolphins* book, that females had two slits, side by side. This was definitely a boy.

"Great job, Spinner!" she called. The name came to her instantly. Yes, Spinner was the perfect name for the little dolphin.

Spinner then performed a single jump, a perfect arc. The sea spray caught the sun, and a colorful rainbow curved above her head.

"You're a very special dolphin, aren't you, Spinner?" Callie said.

But Spinner was gone.

4

The Catch

Callie swam along the edge of the reef, looking for a gap into the deep sea. Spinner must have made it through somewhere! But all she could see was a thick boundary of coral and thousands of dazzling fish.

She found a rocky boulder and climbed onto it carefully, so as not to crush the sea snails that clung to it. It was the perfect lookout because when she stood up—wow!—she felt as if she were standing on the water, right in the middle of the ocean. On one side was the turquoise water full of bright fish and coral, and on the other, the dark blue sea. What that was full of, she didn't know—she was only interested in finding Spinner.

Spinner didn't appear, but Callie did see a group of boats heading her way. As they got closer, Callie could see that the boats were named—*Fortune, Amour,* and *Belle*. They towed small, brightly colored wooden boats behind them, like a shoal of tropical fish.

Callie wondered if, like Spinner, they knew about a secret gap to get through the Blue Halo. But the boats slowed down before they reached the reef and dropped their anchors, and groups of men and women appeared on their decks.

"Hi!" A woman dressed in shorts and a vest top waved at Callie.

"Hello!" Callie waved back. "What are you doing?"

"Do you want to come and see?"

Callie hesitated. It was only a short swim over to the boats, but it would mean crossing the deep blue water.

"I'll swim with you, if you'd like," the woman said. "I need to cool off. I'm Sandy, by the way!"

Then—splash!—she jumped overboard and swam toward Callie. She bobbed in the dark water between the boats and the reef. With an adult around, Callie felt more confident, and she jumped right in.

The Catch

Callie swam alongside Sandy. She couldn't believe it! She was swimming in deep water! Just a few more strokes, and she was at the boat named *Belle*. She climbed the ladder, and everyone on board gave her a welcome cheer. Along with all the people on the deck there was a huge net, wriggling with fish.

"Our haul for the market!" Sandy explained, pointing to the net.

"But why did you stop here?" Callie asked. "Why don't you take the boats to the shore?"

"The reef is too shallow, and we don't want to damage the coral. We'll sort through the fish here on board and take our catch to the island on the *pirogues*." She pointed to the pretty wooden boats tied up behind.

"Can I help you sort the fish?"

"Absolutely!" Sandy beamed. "But it's not just fish you have to handle. A whole range of creatures get caught in our nets. This morning, a huge sea turtle got trapped."

"Is it still here?" asked Callie, peering into the net.

"No, we jumped in and cut it free. We lost a piece of the net, though—we're alerting all of Payocos's boats to look out for it. We don't want it hurting the wildlife. But usually we pull up squid, octopuses, and eels. Do you think you'll be okay handling them?"

"I'm not sure," Callie said, honestly. "But when I grow up, I want to be a vet, so it's good experience."

Sandy gave a thumbs up. "That's a great attitude. I think you have exactly what it takes to be a vet. Bravery!"

One of Sandy's fishing crew unhooked a piece of the net and it slid open, releasing the catch. Fish of all sizes flipped and flapped on the deck, and octopuses oozed over the top of them, looking for an escape. Shark-like creatures jerked angrily from side to side.

"Sharks!" Callie said, alarmed.

"Yes, sharks! Tourists always worry about sharks," Sandy laughed. "Did you know that we've never had a shark attack in Payocos? There are many shark species out there," she said, pointing out to sea, "but they've never bothered us. If a shark ever does come near, just bop it on the nose."

Callie smiled with relief. It was good to know that sharks weren't a problem.

"Should I start by picking up the octopuses?"

"They can find their own way back to the ocean—they slither overboard!" said Sandy. "And actually, octopuses have a sharp beak and can give you a nasty bite. It's better if you start by throwing back the little fish and rays. The baby sharks, too. Hold them up by the tail and tummy and give them a good heave overboard."

Before she could talk herself out it, Callie reached into the pile of slithering fish. As her hand touched the cold slime, she reminded herself that one day she might have to help a calf being born or perform an operation on a sick pet.

Getting gooey was good practice!

Callie quickly became used to the slime and worked happily alongside her new friends, who sang enchanting songs about the ocean. When the unwanted sea creatures had been thrown back, they passed buckets of good-sized fish to people on the *pirogues* to be paddled across the shallow water to Payocos.

"You did a great job, Callie," Sandy said. "Do you want a lift to shore?"

"I think I'd like to spend more time on the reef," Callie said. The hard work had made her hot and sweaty, and the bright blue water looked inviting.

"I can swim you back if you'd like," Sandy smiled.

Callie looked at the dark water. She could do it now. It wasn't about ability;

it was about bravery. Just like sticking her hand in with the slimy fish, she had to get on with it.

"Thanks, Sandy, but I think I can manage on my own," said Callie before leaping overboard and into the water.

In a few short strokes, Callie made it back to the reef. She watched as her fishing friends abandoned the *Belle,* the *Amour,* and the *Fortune* and set off on the pretty *pirogues* with their fresh catch.

Callie put on her mask and immersed herself once more in the beautiful underwater world. It was a world she could never get bored of. But as she swam through the channels of coral, the thought returned—*why was she here?*

The Big Blue

"Why am I here?" Callie asked aloud, hoping the reef would give her a sign. A sunken treasure chest jutting out of the sand or a message in a bottle would be useful. But there was only the continuous bustling life of the rainbow reef.

Callie decided there was no point in worrying about it. And just in case she suddenly found herself back in the pool being splashed by Ben and Emma, she was determined to make the most of her extraordinary visit to Payocos. She paid attention to everything around her. Watching animals go about their lives was her favorite hobby.

Large crabs fed themselves busily, shoveling bits and pieces from the seabed into their mouths. Blue-and-yellow sea slugs with funny horns and rippling skirts slid over rocks. Sea anemones waved with long tentacles that looked like clay. All around, the water fizzed and crackled with activity—the sound of endless air bubbles and a million creatures pecking at particles on the reef.

And then she heard a squeal. Was it air escaping from a giant clam? Or the pressure of the water on the coral and sponges?

There was another one. It was high-pitched—a sound that wasn't in harmony with the reef. Over and over again it came. It sounded urgent. A cry for help. Then she heard the clicking—clicking and squealing, clicking and squealing— and Callie knew. It was a dolphin in trouble.

Maybe a dolphin had entered the reef and was stuck in the shallow water. Callie swam through the channels of the reef, searching for the lost dolphin, trying to follow its cries. They were so desperate, and Callie felt helpless. How was she going to find it? Not by swimming around and around in circles. She needed a better viewpoint so she could see a large shape quickly and easily, just as she'd seen Denny gliding below her at the bottom of the pool. Of course! She needed to look down!

Callie found a large rock to stand on. It raised her above the reef, and she looked out over the water, but the only dark shapes she could see were clumps of coral.

Maybe the sound hadn't come from the reef at all.

Callie looked behind her at the deep sea. *Belle*, *Amour*, and *Fortune* were still there, anchored until the next fishing trip. They were only a few feet from the edge of the reef. Not even as far as a length of the swimming pool. She could swim that easily. She already had! She could look

through her mask on the short journey
across to see if a dolphin was there. She
just had to be brave.

"Remember the vet's oath," Callie
reminded herself. "I must do everything in
my power to help animals in need." She
took another look at the deep water. "I can
do it, I can do it, I can do it!"

And before she could change her mind,
she leaped in.

The moment her head went under, she heard the call. It was louder than before. The clicks were like bursting popcorn kernels, and the squeals were sharp as knives. Callie headed toward the boats, searching the water as she swam.

Behind her, she saw the pale wall of the coral reef, bright with fish, before the seabed dipped down into unknown depths. Looking forward, there was just the odd sea jelly bobbing along, or a slow-trailing shoal of fish. Except for that, there was nothing. Nothing *she* could see, anyway. But that didn't mean there was nothing there in the great big blue....

Panic caught up with her bravery, and Callie's heart began thumping in her chest. The undersides of the boats ahead of her looked like floating icebergs, and she swam toward them as fast as she could.

Then something touched her feet. Callie squealed, drawing her legs up to her chest, and looked down, fearing sea jellies or something worse. It was bubbles. A stream of large bubbles was rising from the deep. Totally spooked, Callie swam quickly to the boat. Once she was safely on the ladder, she caught her breath and began to think about the bubbles. Small bubbles escaped from plants and rocks all the time, but these were big. Something big was down there. Something that needed air. Sharks didn't need air. In fact, she'd read in *Nature Magazine* that they were scared of bubbles. But dolphins....

Callie let go of the ladder. Leaving her fear at the surface, she swam as fast as she could, heading down into the depths, following the column of bubbles. Then she saw it. A little dolphin, twisting and turning, its flippers caught in a torn piece of orange net. The piece the fishing boat had lost!

The dolphin had black, gray, and white markings and was small. As she swam closer, the dolphin saw her. It stopped twisting and nodded—its whole body bowing to her—and then it started to struggle again, bubbles escaping from the blowhole on top of its head as it struggled.

"Oh, Spinner!" Callie's words came out in a strange squeak of her own. She put her face close to the little dolphin and rubbed his nose.

I'm going up for air, but I'll be back. I won't leave you, Spinner. I promise.

Callie hoped he would understand. She kicked as hard as she could back to the surface and took a huge gulp of air. That's when she noticed a group of dorsal fins cutting through the water. They were moving fast and heading in her direction. Then they dipped under the water and vanished, and Callie felt herself turn cold with fear.

Danger!

Callie ducked her head underwater. Dolphins!

She wanted to cry with relief, although she still felt nervous. A huge pod of dolphins was an intimidating sight. But they weren't interested in her—they were heading toward Spinner. They must be Spinner's family. They'd know what to do!

Callie didn't want to miss a minute. She took another deep breath and went down, hoping they wouldn't see her as a threat. She had to see Spinner released from his fishing-net prison. She wanted to see him spin in the air again, happy and free.

The big dolphins circled the baby one. Some nudged his body, others pushed at the net wrapped around his flippers. But the net was wound so many times and so tightly, it wouldn't move. There were panicked squeals, and Callie could sense the despair of the pod. And poor Spinner.... He was running out of air.

"Spinner!" Callie called underwater. He saw her and lifted his head.

"I'm here! I'm not going to leave you."

The pod of dolphins stopped what

they were doing and turned to look
at her. There in the deep blue water,
Callie wondered if this was a dream—
who didn't dream of being smiled at
by a pod of dolphins? But Callie knew
that this was the wild, and if they
felt they were in danger, the dolphins
might become aggressive. Especially
if they thought she was going to hurt
their baby.

A few of the dolphins suddenly
broke away from the pod and sped
toward her—their bodies weaving
through the water with speed and
purpose. Was this an attack? Were they
angry with her? Did they think she'd
trapped Spinner? Callie started to swim
upward, and before she knew it, she
was surrounded.

The dolphins didn't touch her,
though. Instead, they swam around her,
looking into her mask and nodding,
just like Spinner had done. Then they
backed away. They weren't trying to
scare her off—they were asking her for
help! Callie nodded. She wanted to be
a vet. It was her dream to help animals.

But first she needed air.

The dolphins swam with her to the surface, as if they were making sure she wouldn't leave them. They nudged her softly with their noses.

"I'm only human!" she said, gasping for air. "But I'll do my best."

With as much fresh air as her lungs could take, she swam with the pod back to Spinner and inspected the net. It was too tight, too tough. She tore at it with her nails until they ached, but the twine was too thick. Spinner was twisting and turning, but slowly now. He was tiring. And with all the effort she'd used in trying to release the net, she was quickly running out of breath.

She nodded to Spinner. *I'll be back.*

Callie gulped the air, but as she was

about to go back under, she heard an almighty roar—the growl of engines. Three personal watercrafts were zooming in her direction. They skimmed across the sea, whisking the surface into a froth of bubbles. In just a few seconds, they'd be right above the dolphins, and rescuing Spinner would become dangerous. Maybe even impossible.

"Stop it! Stop it!" Callie yelled, but her voice couldn't be heard above the noise.

She ducked back underwater to check on Spinner. He was still in the net, rolling from side to side. His family had stopped nudging and pushing. Instead, they hung in the water all around him. It was as if they had lost hope.

And then the watercrafts were there. They made the water crackle and hiss.

The dolphins broke out of their sad trance and swam frantically around Spinner again as if it was their last chance to free him. Callie was finding it harder to stay underwater, and the watercrafts were making things worse. She needed to find a way to make them go away.

As Callie swam up to the surface, she heard Spinner's faint squeal. She turned, clapped her hands, and nodded to tell him she'd be back. She just hoped it wouldn't be too late.

On the surface, the watercrafts were so close that Callie could see the drivers' faces. There were two boys and a girl. They whooped with joy as they turned their watercrafts sharply in the water, sending up huge waves and painting the sky with spray. Callie gasped as she was hit in the face by salty waves. Every time she called out, she got a mouthful of water, and each time she lifted an arm to wave for attention, she began sinking beneath the waves. But she wasn't worried about herself. She was worried about Spinner.

Callie found herself at the bottom of the ladder on *Belle*, and she climbed aboard.

"Hey!" she shouted. "Stop, please!"

She was sure the watercrafts must have seen her, but they continued to carve up the sea. They were tourists, Callie decided. A Payocos islander wouldn't dream of coming so close to the precious reef with its delicate coral and wildlife. The watercrafts were dangerously near.

They raced and stopped, again and again. The waves rocked *Belle* from side to side, and Callie was thrown back and forth across the deck. She had to do something quickly—she didn't know how much time Spinner had left.

A Clever Plan

The watercrafts started to race around the boats, rocking them violently. At first, Callie was afraid that *Belle* might capsize. Then she was just plain angry.

The tourists must know how close to the reef they were. It was impossible to ignore the change in sea color, from deep blue to brilliant turquoise. Callie wished she was back there, in the safety of the shallow water. But she had to save Spinner. If she didn't.... She couldn't bear to think about it.

But first, she had to stop the tourists from ruining the rescue.

Callie staggered into the cabin and gripped the boat's wheel to steady herself. She looked at the basic controls. If she could find a phone or radio, she might be able to get a signal to someone on Payocos. They could send help right away.

"Come on, come on!" she said to herself, looking around desperately. "There's got to be something here."

But there was no radio. What was she going to do?

"Think, Callie!" she said. "What would a vet do?"

Animals can't tell humans what's wrong, so vets have to think fast and make decisions using whatever information they have. That's how Callie saw this situation. She had to make do with what she had. And what she had was a fishing boat with little on board other than a tub of smelly fish bait.

Just then, the girl on the watercraft zoomed close, unaware of the creatures she was putting in danger. Callie would have loved to throw that bucket of stinky fish guts all over her!

A-ha!

Callie dragged the bucket to the edge of the boat. She had a plan. And if it worked, she would be back with Spinner very soon.

As the three watercrafts roared closer, Callie took a handful of fish bait—old

guts and tails and skin and scales—
and threw it. And then another. And
another. Callie was only trying to get
their attention, but the fish bait landed
with a splat on their faces, necks, and
shoulders. In horror, they came to a
sudden stop. They stared at her.

"What did you do that for?" the girl asked.

Callie thought quickly. Use what you know! These people were probably tourists, and Sandy's words came to her…. *Tourists are always afraid of sharks.* That's it!

"I'm sorry. I had to get you to stop! I wanted to warn you—there's a huge school of sharks down there. Vicious bull sharks. If you fall off…." Callie didn't finish the sentence. She thought it was better if they figured it out for themselves, now that they were covered in shark bait.

"Let's get out of here!" one of the boys shouted.

And they did. They revved their engines and shot back out to sea, away from the reef for good, Callie hoped.

Now there was no time to lose. Callie leaped into the water. Immediately, she could see the pod was gone. The annoying watercrafts had scared them away. What about Spinner? She peered around, trying to make out his shape in the deep. But the place where he had been was now a void—an area of nothing.

Then she heard it—a squeal. It sounded so thin and weak— it was as though Spinner had nothing left. Callie realized he had been washed farther out to sea.

"Oh, Spinner!"

Callie had been so brave. She had conquered the triangle of open sea between the reef, the boats, and the place where Spinner had first gotten tangled. It was just a few swimming strokes to each point. But now he had drifted far out of her comfort zone, and she knew she had to be braver than ever before.

"I'm coming, Spinner!" she said.

Before Callie could think about being alone in the deep without anything to hold on to, she swam. She swam as fast as she could.

A Daring Rescue

It was just Callie, the deep blue water, and somewhere, a baby dolphin who was in real trouble.

"Spinner, it's me. Where are you?" Callie shouted into the water. She knew he would recognize her voice. She waited. "Spinner! Talk to me!"

Then, finally, a squeal pierced the silence, followed by another! Callie swam toward the sound and called for Spinner again. This time, Spinner answered with a click and a whistle. She was getting closer. Spinner's replies were getting louder. But his cries were short and sharp. He was scared.

"I'm close now," Callie said, trying to reassure him. "I'm really close. Hang on in there!"

Callie peered down into the blue from the surface so she could bob up for air easily. She needed to save her energy for when she found Spinner. She didn't know how she would release the baby dolphin from the net, but she would do it. She was determined.

"Any moment now, I'll see you. You're not alone," she said.

Squeals came from up ahead, and Callie could make out a pale shape. She could see the frayed edges of a large fishing net, drifting like sea jelly tentacles. Yes! She'd found him! But Spinner wasn't alone.

A dark shape was circling him. At first Callie thought it was a member of his pod. But as she swam closer, she realized that this wasn't a dolphin shape.

It was flatter, leaner. It moved effortlessly through the water. It had stripes, but not like any dolphin she'd seen. Its tail was a different shape, too. It cut upright through the water, like a boat rudder. It was designed to swish from side to side, not to flick up and down like a dolphin.

By the time Callie realized what it was, the tiger shark had seen her. It approached slowly, and she saw its blank stare pass across her body. It was

small, maybe only a baby, but Callie
was chilled to the bone. She was too
terrified even to scream. She was going
to be a shark's dinner. This was it—
Payocos's first ever shark attack....

But the shark slid by and went back
toward Spinner. A dying baby dolphin
would be an easier target. Rage bubbled
up inside her.

"No, you don't!" Callie screamed, her voice crackling through the water.

She started to swim toward the shark. What was she doing? She was scared of deep water, sharks, and drowning. And what could she possibly do? She was slow and not used to the watery world. But something was driving her. She had promised Spinner. What would he think if she retreated now, leaving him with a shark, scared and alone?

As she got closer to Spinner and the shark, the dolphin started nodding frantically and thrashing from side to side. Callie knew why.

Don't worry about me! I'm staying. The only thing that's going to run away is that shark, Callie thought.

Hoping the young shark was only

being curious, she swam toward it and
pushed her hands gently against its
rough skin, guiding it away. It didn't
mind, but it didn't leave either. She was
going to have to be more forceful.

Callie stretched out her arms and legs
to make herself look as big as possible.
She pushed the shark's body again. This
time it flipped around to face her. Callie
continued to wave her arms and legs,
trying to look threatening. Then the
shark came too close. Callie flailed her
arms, trying to propel herself backward.
In the flurry, her seashell pendant
knocked against the creature's eye. The
shark's eyelid automatically slid shut
for protection, but it was annoyed. It
slithered back toward Spinner.

Scaredy-cat, Callie thought, although

her heart was beating fast. Then the
shark turned and came for her, building
up speed as its tail swished from side to
side.

Bop it on the nose! Sandy's words
popped into her mind.

Callie got her fists ready. The shark
zoomed toward her, and she bopped
it—bam! bam!—on the nose. And
again—bam! bam! The young shark
looked stunned.

It turned and snaked off into the deep.
This time, it didn't come back.

Callie was dizzy, and her lungs were screaming for air. She swam up to the surface and breathed in deeply until her head stopped spinning. Then she went down again. This time, she would rescue Spinner. The poor dolphin was now tilting to one side, as a single air bubble escaped from his blowhole.

"Spinner!" she shrieked.

Callie tried to yank the net upward, but it was too big and awkward. It was no good. Spinner had to be cut free. She needed something sharp. Maybe there was a knife on the boat. But if she went to look for one, would she get back in time?

It didn't look as though she had a choice. She cradled Spinner's head and rubbed his nose. *I'll be as quick as I can*, she thought, hoping that Spinner would understand that she wasn't abandoning him.

Then Spinner began biting at her necklace. *He doesn't want me to go!* she thought.

Callie pulled the shell from his mouth, but Spinner bit at it again. Callie was worried that he would break the beautiful shell. Then she had a memory of a sudden pain in her foot. A sharp cut. A razor edge.

Yes, Spinner, you clever dolphin!

Callie held the shell steady as Spinner bit down on it with the last of his strength, snapping it in two. Then she used the sharp edge to saw at the net until it started to fray. Spinner twisted to increase the pressure on the thinning strings. One by one they snapped, until finally the remaining net broke away into little pieces. It wouldn't be hurting any more animals now.

Callie's lungs burned as her oxygen ran out, but she had to hold on … just a little bit longer … for Spinner. He was now motionless and exhausted. He had been without air for 10 or 15 minutes. Too long for a little dolphin. Callie gritted her teeth and dived underneath him. She dropped the broken shell, placed her palms on Spinner's tummy, and pushed upward, moving him toward the surface.

Sensing freedom, Spinner shot forward, using his very last drop of energy. He broke through the surface, spat out the old air from his blowhole, and breathed again.

Callie bobbed up beside him, panting and gasping, clutching her chest. It burned with pain. She needed to rest, but she was in the middle of nowhere. Her muscles were drained, and she was too tired even to tread water. She was sinking back down. She was going to drown.... Then Spinner was right by her side.

He tilted his body toward her, brushing his thick dorsal fin against her arm. She took hold of it with both hands and allowed him to tow her toward the reef.

9

How to Celebrate with a Dolphin

Callie dragged herself onto a rock and sat on the very edge of the reef, between the light and dark blues of Payocos's incredible waters. Spinner was saying thank you with a very special display. He disappeared into the blue and then leaped out of the water, spinning in the air many times before landing with a splash.

"Bravo, Spinner!" Callie clapped as

she counted three full spins. "You're a gold medal gymnast!"

Callie was exhausted, and her arms and legs felt like jelly. But she couldn't have been happier as she sat in paradise, being entertained by Spinner, a baby dolphin that could have died but was now free. It was thanks to her vet's oath—the promise she made to care for animals in danger. She didn't think that many vets had to fight off sharks doing their job, so she was even a little bit proud of herself.

"What are you doing, Spinner?"

The dolphin was balancing upright on his tail, nodding at her. He disappeared under the water and then surfaced right next to her. He balanced on his tail again and nodded.

"Oh, you want me to come in for a
swim?"

Callie was tired, but would she ever
get the chance to see a baby dolphin
in the wild again? Or play with one?
If she stayed close to the reef, she'd be
okay, she decided. She could climb up
and rest when she needed to. She pulled
the mask onto her face and leaped

over Spinner's head into the water just beyond. Spinner spun with glee and then circled her.

Underwater, Callie and Spinner met face to face. His dark almond eyes peered into her mask and held eye contact. It was as if the little dolphin was taking time out from his fun to say something. *Thank you.*

You're welcome, Spinner, Callie thought. *And thank you, too.* She felt like the luckiest girl alive.

Spinner then released a huge bubble from his blowhole. It spread out in a huge, perfect circle toward her.

Is that for me? Callie wondered. She swam forward, using her dolphin kick to push herself through the bubble ring. "Ta-da!" she burbled in the water.

Spinner opened his mouth and made a clicking sound. A laugh? Then he blew another hoop and another—a whole string of bubble rings—and Callie swam through them all. Spinner seemed to love it. Callie stopped and nodded. *Your turn.*

Spinner understood. He swam right through it, just as she had. Wow! This was so much fun! Callie rose to the surface and danced in the water with happiness, waving her arms. Spinner copied, rocking his body from side to side.

"Let's play follow the leader!" said Callie.

She dived down, and Spinner followed. She rolled onto her back. Spinner swam upside down. She clapped three times. Spinner clicked three times. Then they both came up for air, laughing.

Callie never wanted the game to end, but she was very tired now. She needed to get out of the water and allow her skin to dry. Her fingertips were as wrinkly as prunes! First, she called to Spinner, and he came to her.

"Spinner, I've had the best time. I

never imagined I'd be friends with a dolphin! But I'm a land animal, and I need to rest. I also need to find my way home, and so do you! You're too little to be away from your pod. You need your mother's milk. You should go." Callie held out her hand, and Spinner brushed it with his fin. "High-five, Spinner! We make a great team."

Callie swam to the reef and climbed onto the rock. The beach in the distance looked inviting. Her tummy rumbled. Some coconut chips and a glass of fruit juice at Izad's shack was exactly what she needed. But Spinner didn't agree. He was still next to the reef, popping out of the water every now and then to look at her.

"No more games now, Spinner. We

both need to get home."

But Spinner wouldn't go, and Callie started to worry. Dolphins lived in pods— they weren't supposed to be alone. Especially not a baby one. She remembered the tiger shark. There would be bigger ones out there….

"You can't hang around here. You have to go and find your family," Callie told him.

Spinner had started somersaulting in the air and tail-walking backward and forward to get her attention. Callie shook her head and crossed her arms, trying to look serious. Spinner didn't understand. He only seemed to understand having fun and playing games.

Callie had an idea. It was crazy, and she was dangerously tired, but she couldn't walk away until she knew he was safe.

"Another game of follow the leader, then," Callie called. She jumped back into the water, and Spinner circled her with joy—his playmate was back!

Callie ignored his bubble rings and tail walks and swam out to sea. She tried not to think of sharks and the deep water below her. She kept her mind on her mission— reuniting Spinner with his pod. Spinner followed, nudging her to roll over or play a game, but she had another game in mind. They were two pool lengths out past the reef when Callie stopped. She started to tread water to get her breath and then dived under.

What she saw made her heart skip a beat and her head explode with wonder.

10

Reunited

Callie had been quietly frightened of what she would see when she went into the deep again. She had feared seeing the smooth, sleek shape of a larger sea creature. But this was something else!

As big as a bus, the shark cruised below her. Its skin was dusky gray and covered in white spots, like confetti. A wide mouth gaped as it looked for food, but it wasn't interested in Callie or Spinner. It only ate plankton and small fish. It was perfectly harmless.

Callie had always dreamed of seeing a whale shark. She'd seen one on a television program and envied the camera people who had swum alongside it. This was her chance!

Come on, Spinner! Callie beckoned.

Callie and Spinner dolphin-kicked alongside the magnificent beast, avoiding its big mouth. She didn't want to get sucked inside by accident! She took in as much as she could—the colors, the patterns, and the texture of its skin—so she would never forget it. If only she could swim with it forever.... In fact, how long *had* she been swimming with it?

Callie surfaced and looked around. She was a long, long way from the Blue Halo reef now—its bright blue water visible as just a sliver in the distance. Her heart started to pound. *Stay calm*, she told herself. *Panicking won't do you any good.* It wouldn't help Spinner find his family, either. Where *was* he, anyway?

"Spinner?" she shouted. "Spinner!"

Oh, no! Had he become annoyed with her for showing the whale shark so much attention? Had he been scared away by something more deadly? Suddenly, Callie felt alone and vulnerable. She was treading very deep water with little energy and no idea of what was below her. Just when she thought she might cry, a little dolphin shot out of the water and arced through the air above her! Callie held back tears of joy.

"You're like a kid who's had too much candy!" she scolded. "Playtime is definitely over. It's time to call your family. Ready?"

Callie dived down and squeaked like a mouse. Spinner copied. She did it for longer. Spinner did it for longer, too. Then, after they had both surfaced for more air, Callie tapped her mask. *Tap-tap-tap.*

Spinner peered into it, making her laugh. But it wasn't what Callie was after. She tapped it again, and she clicked her tongue. Spinner backed away. He understood, and he started to copy her.

Spinner's clicks were so loud that Callie felt them vibrating through her body. His squeals were so piercing that she had to put her fingers in her ears. But he was doing it! He thought he was playing follow the leader, but in fact he was making his voice heard.

"That's right. Do it again!" Callie tapped her mask and squeaked like a mouse.

The dolphin was so excited to

impress her that he made noises Callie knew would reach far out to sea. She only hoped that his pod hadn't given up hope and left the area.

"Keep going. We have to keep going." She tapped and squeaked and Spinner did the same, and then … dorsal fins appeared in the distance, slicing through the water. Twenty or thirty of them. A pod of dolphins!

"We did it, Spinner! They've come!" Callie cried.

Spinner nodded, then placed his fin under her hand. It was as if he knew she needed a rest before the swim back to the reef. "Thank you," Callie panted, grabbing hold of it tightly. "I just need to catch my breath."

She was confident that the pod would do

her no harm. But as they torpedoed through the water toward Spinner, they knocked her sideways, and she lost her grip on his fin. They began circling him in celebration, creating a whirlpool, and Callie felt the water pressure pushing her under. The collision had knocked the breath out of her. She needed air. But the busy dolphins were above and around her, and there was no way through.

"Spinner!" Callie used her last air to shout his name. She had nothing left. She kept her mouth shut tight. Her vision began to blur—it was turning dark as she drifted downward....

Something soft touched her stomach. Had she reached the seabed at the bottom of the ocean?

A Special Gift

Something rushed at her. It was sudden and fast. Callie shut her eyes tightly to protect them from the blast of water that pushed at her face. She felt around her with one hand. She could feel bodies, and thick dolphin skin. There were dolphins all around her! They were swimming, and she was moving alongside them. Then she realized the water wasn't rushing at her—she was rushing through it!

Within seconds, Callie was at the
surface. She was dizzy and gasping for air,
and she blinked against the sunlight and
seawater in her eyes. She had been saved!
She was alive! She was ... *sitting on a
dolphin!*

It hadn't been the seabed against her
tummy at all. A large dolphin had swum
beneath her and scooped her up. She was
now sitting on it like a
horse. She was
riding a
dolphin! She
had rescued
their little
calf, and
they had
rescued
her!

A tide of relief washed over Callie, and she lay across the dolphin's back.

"Stay here with me, Mr. Dolphin," she whispered. "Please don't go back under!"

If he dropped her back in, she'd fall straight to the bottom like a stone. But the dolphin was as sturdy as a boat, and he was swimming slowly, still on the surface, toward land.

"Are you taking me back?" Callie cried with joy. "Oh, you are! Thank you, thank you."

The entire pod flipped and flapped around her as they made their way toward the bright blue water in the distance. For a moment, Callie imagined she was part of this dolphin pod. They smiled at her, nudged her, and took care of her. They were like friends. And where was her best friend, Spinner? She couldn't see him. Maybe he was feeding after such a long time away from his mother. It was hard to see, though, as all of the dolphins wanted to play! They leaped around her, chirping and clicking.

"Woo-hoo!" Callie shouted as they spun and somersaulted over her head. "You're such show-offs!" she called. "But I love you all!"

Something swelled in Callie's heart. It was a feeling she couldn't describe. It was as if happiness had reached every part of her body, from her head to her toes.

The turquoise band of shallow water became bigger as they got closer, and Callie felt a jumble of emotions. She needed dry land—she needed to lie down, to walk, and feel human again. But it meant saying good-bye to the beautiful spinning dolphins. Tears welled up in her eyes. It wasn't until she brushed them away that she noticed the bright waters didn't belong to the reef at all. During her adventure with the whale shark and the dolphins, she'd gone off course, drifting farther out. This was a little island connected to Payocos by a thin strip of sand. Coral Point! The turquoise waters weren't reef, but the shallow sandy edges of the sea.

The dolphins took her as far as they could without stranding themselves on the beach. It had been so long since she stood upright that Callie's legs buckled as she touched the ground, and she fell with a plop backward into the water. The dolphins cackled.

"I'd like to see you try to walk on
land!" she said.

Callie sat on the beach, watching as
her friends played in front of her. She
still couldn't see Spinner. She searched
the dorsal fins and faces that bobbed
above the water. Except for some of
the bigger dolphins, who had scars

and scrapes from a life at sea, they all
had the same markings, the same sleek
bodies, and long noses. Still, she knew
she'd recognize Spinner in an instant.
But he wasn't there. Maybe the poor
little thing was exhausted, too.

The dolphins started to move away
from the beach. Callie watched them
go, straining to look at every last detail.
She wanted to remember it all. Even
when they entered the darker waters,
she kept her eyes on their shiny backs
that dipped in and out of the water,
like gentle rolling waves. She waved and
shouted, "Good-bye!" long after they
had disappeared from sight.

Then she was alone. The beach on Coral
Point was beautiful, with soft white sands,
swaying palm trees, and bright green

vegetation. There were banana trees and coconut trees…. Callie's tummy rumbled. She gorged on ripe bananas, and she cracked a hole in a coconut with a sharp rock and drank the warm water inside. Then she watched the sun go down, wondering why she was still in paradise. She had saved a dolphin and returned him home. If she had been put here for a reason, that was surely it!

Just then, in the fading light, she saw a baby turtle scuttle past her toward the water. "Hey, little one, where are you going?"

From behind her, hundreds of the little flat-footed creatures were staggering from their sandy nests farther up the beach, heading for the ocean. It was an incredible sight.

"Good luck!" called Callie.

When the last baby turtle had flopped into the water, Callie stood up and looked around. The water was turning silvery, the turquoise disappearing with the light.

"I get it!" she exclaimed. "Shells wash up on the beach, but tides return them to the sea. Turtles lay their eggs on land, but the hatchlings always go back to the water. Maybe I'm the same!"

She had come here by being in water, so maybe that's how she had to return. And now that the dolphins were gone, it was a sign that her time on the white sands of Payocos was up.

Callie took off her reef slippers and mask and placed them on the beach. She stepped carefully into the water, feeling for sharp shells with her toes. She went in

up to her shoulders and stood still for a
moment, taking a last look at the tropical
island that Emma would go nuts for.
Then something knocked against her leg.
Callie stepped backward in fright.

It was Spinner!

The little dolphin's face appeared
above the water. Callie shrieked and
held out her arms.

"Spinner, you've come to say good-
bye!" She cuddled his neck and rubbed

his back. The
dolphin had
something
in its
mouth.
"Is that
a gift for
me?"

Spinner nodded. Callie took the shell from his mouth. It was a huge, pearly, multicolored abalone shell, just like the one she'd lost. Only this one was bigger and brighter and even more beautiful.

When she looked up, the dolphin was gone. "'Bye, Spinner. Thanks for everything."

It was time. Callie looked at the shell in her hands. Should she let go of it? Not this time. She didn't take it from the beach, after all—it was given to her. *A gift from the sea to me*, she smiled, *and it's a good reason to come back to Payocos one day*.

Then she stepped farther into the ocean, and the water closed over her head.

Home Again

For a moment, Callie thought she had ended up back at the reef. Colorful coral and shoals of bright fish surrounded her. But they weren't swaying or swimming with the underwater currents. They were perfectly still. Callie reached out to touch them to be sure, and her fingers met the swimming pool wall.

She surfaced, held on to the side of the pool, and wiped the water from her eyes.

"You dropped your goggles." Denny was

at her side.

"Thanks, Denny." Callie blinked.

"They fell to the bottom right in the middle of the pool. I know it can be scary being out of your depth, so I got them for you."

Callie might have found being out of her depth scary before. But now? She had proved that she could tread water, swim above and below water, dive deep, and kick fast. She had proved that she was brave. What would Denny do if he found himself face-to-face with a tiger shark, she wondered....

"Denny, what would you do if you were swimming in the ocean and—"

Mr. Luck's whistle shrilled loudly. Callie would have to find out the answer another time.

111

"Make your way to the shallow end, please," Mr. Luck called. As it was only Callie and Denny at the deep end, everyone turned to look at them. Callie tapped Denny on the shoulder.

"Dolphin-kick race?"

"Yeah, all right," he grinned.

With their feet on the back wall, they counted to three and pushed off. Deep down, right on the bottom, they rolled and kicked the entire length of the pool. They surfaced at the shallow end to the sound of cheering.

"Well, there's no question—you two are definitely going to be on the new under-12 team," Mr. Luck said, clapping his hands. "Great control. Callie, you've improved in leaps and bounds!"

"She's a fast learner," Denny said, high-fiving Callie.

Everyone started to get out of the water, but Mr. Luck blew his whistle again.

"Before we finish the lesson, we need some team names. Have you thought of any?"

"How about The Inflatables?" Emma called, still sitting in the doughnut.

"That makes us sound as if we could be easily popped!" Mr. Luck laughed. "Anyone else?"

"The Cannonballs!" Ben shouted.

"That suggests sinking to the bottom.... How about something more physical and lively."

"The Spinners," Callie said. Everyone looked at her. "Like spinner dolphins. They're super-fast but can also do a lot of tricks."

"I think we have a winner!" Mr. Luck said.

"When does she get the tickets to a tropical island?" Emma said quickly. "I'm her best friend, so I'll be going, too, obviously."

Callie shook her head and laughed at her funny friend.

"The prize is…."

"A submarine!" Kevin shouted.

"I bet it's an extra swimming lesson," Maya groaned.

"If you'll let me finish," Mr. Luck said. "The prize is something very special. At every swim meet from now on, we'll be collecting money to donate to a charity of our choice. Callie, would you like to choose the charity?"

Callie didn't need even a second to think. "A charity that rescues dolphins."

"How about International Dolphin Rescue?" suggested Denny. "I love dolphins," he added.

"Me, too," Callie said. She wondered if one day she'd tell Denny about her experience. But would he ever believe it?

"What's that?" Emma tugged at the hem of Callie's bathing suit. Tucked inside the leg was a large, flat object. Emma yanked it out and held it in the air. "A shell! Where did you get that?"

Callie blushed. "The reef down at the deep end," she said. It was pretty much the truth! "It's an abalone shell."

"Mr. Luck, Mr. Luck, come and see what Callie has!"

She handed it to the teacher.

"What a remarkable specimen," said Mr. Luck.

"You didn't buy it from a shop, did you?" said Denny, leaning over to look. "I heard you shouldn't buy shells because they're stolen from the sea."

"No, I found it, and one day I'll return it," Callie said. "I know how important it is to protect our coral reefs."

"Is it a big oyster shell?" Mr. Luck said, handing it back. "Where did you get it?"

Where did she get it? What should she say?!

Thanks to Emma, she didn't have to say anything.

"Mr. Luck, it's not an oyster. It's a baloney. Anyone can see that," Emma said, matter-of-fact. "Baloneys are very special."

"I hope you meant *abalone*," Callie said, giggling.

"What's a baloney, then?"

"A type of sandwich meat."

Emma shrieked and covered her mouth. Then she ran off to tell everyone else her hilarious mistake as they walked to the changing rooms.

Callie was the last to go. She stood by the pool and looked down at the coral reef mural. She already missed the beautiful sea plants and pretty fish. She even missed the bigger creatures in the deep blue beyond. But most of all, she missed the playful little dolphin.

"I'll think about you every day," she said under her breath.

She began to walk away when there was a plopping sound in the pool. She turned back quickly. A large, silvery bubble ring rose up through the water from the bottom of the pool and burst on the surface, splashing Callie.

"Ha ha, Spinner. Very funny. And that reminds me—it's time I paid Emma back!"

Callie scooped up some water and headed toward the changing rooms to splash Emma, feeling as playful as Spinner, and wearing a smile just as mischievous.

ABOUT THE AUTHOR

Rachel Delahaye was born in Australia but
has lived in the UK since she was six years old.
She studied linguistics and worked as a magazine
writer and editor before becoming a children's author.
She loves words and animals; when she can combine
the two, she is very happy indeed! At home, Rachel
loves to read, write, and watch wildlife documentaries.
She loves to go walking in the woods. She also follows
news about animal rights and the environment and
hopes that one day the world will be a better home for
all species, not just humans!

Rachel lives in the beautiful city of Bath, England,
with her two lively children and a dog named Rocket.